# FISH-FISHING TECHNOLOGY

# FISH-FISHING TECHNOLOGY

*By*

**Manju Yadav**

*Lecturer*
*Department of Zoology*
*M.M.H. College*
*Ghaziabad (U.P.)*
*(India)*

**DISCOVERY PUBLISHING HOUSE PVT. LTD.**
**NEW DELHI-110 002**

*Published by:*
**Tilak Wasan**
**DISCOVERY PUBLISHING HOUSE PVT. LTD.**
4383/4B, Ansari Road, Darya Ganj
New Delhi-110 002 (India)
*Phone* : +91-11-23279245, 43596064-65
*Fax* : +91-11-23253475
*E-mail* : discoverypublishinghouse@gmail.com
namitwasan9@gmail.com
sales@discoverypublishinggroup.com
*web* : www.discoverypublishinggroup.com

***Reprinted:* 2019**

***First Edition:* 2013**

**ISBN: 978-93-5056-268-0**

**Fish-Fishing Technology**



*Printed at:*
Infinity Imaging Systems
Delhi

# Preface

Fishing techniques are methods for catching fish. The term may also be applied to methods for catching other aquatic animals such as molluscs (shellfish, squid, octopus) and edible marine invertebrates.

Fishing techniques include hand gathering, spear-fishing, netting, angling and trapping. Recreational, commercial and artisanal fishers use different techniques, and also, sometimes, the same techniques. Recreational fishers fish for pleasure or sport, while commercial fishers fish for profit. Artisanal fishers use traditional, low-tech methods, for survival in third-world countries, and as a cultural heritage in other countries. Mostly, recreational fishers use angling methods and commercial fishers use netting methods.

There is an intricate link between various fishing techniques and knowledge about the fish and their behaviour including migration, foraging and habitat. The effective use of fishing techniques often depends on this additional knowledge. Which techniques are appropriate is dictated mainly by the target species and by its habitat.

It is possible to fish and gather many sea foods with minimal equipment by using the hands. Gathering seafood by hand can be as easily as picking shellfish or kelp up off the beach, or doing some digging for clams or crabs. The earliest evidence for shellfish gathering dates back to a 300,000 year old site in France called 'Terra Amata'. This is a hominid site as modern Homo sapiens did not appear until around 50,000 years ago.

Generally, a fishery is an entity engaged in raising and/or harvesting fish, which is determined by some authority to be a fishery. According to the FAO, a fishery is typically defined in terms of the "people involved, species or type of fish, area of water or seabed, method of fishing, class of boats, purpose of the activities or a combination of the foregoing features". The definition often includes a combination of fish and fishers in a region, the latter fishing for similar species with similar gear types.

A fishery may involve the capture of wild fish or raising fish through fish farming or aquaculture. Directly or indirectly, the livelihood of over 500 million people in developing countries depends on fisheries and aquaculture. Overfishing, including the taking of fish beyond sustainable levels, is reducing fish stocks and employment in many world regions. Close to 90 per cent of the world's fishery catches come from oceans and seas, as opposed to inland waters. These marine catches have remained relatively stable since the mid-nineties (between 80 and 86 million tonnes). Most marine fisheries are based near the coast. This is not only because harvesting from relatively shallow waters is easier than in the open ocean, but also because fish are much more abundant near the coastal shelf, due to coastal upwelling and the abundance of nutrients available there. However, productive wild fisheries also exist in open oceans, particularly by seamounts, and inland in lakes and rivers.

Most fisheries are wild fisheries, but increasingly fisheries are farmed. Farming can occur in coastal areas, such as with oyster farms, but more typically occur inland, in lakes, ponds, tanks and other enclosures.

There is an increasing demand for fish and fish protein, which has resulted in widespread overfishing in wild fisheries. Fish farming offers fish marketers another source. However, farming carnivorous fish, such as salmon, does not necessarily reduce pressure on wild fisheries, since carnivorous farmed fish are usually fed fishmeal and fish oil extracted from wild forage fish. In this way, the salmon can consume in weight more wild fish than they weigh themselves.

**—Author**

# Contents

# 1

# Introduction

Fishing techniques are methods for catching fish. The term may also be applied to methods for catching other aquatic animals such as molluscs (shellfish, squid, octopus) and edible marine invertebrates.

Fishing techniques include hand gathering, spear-fishing, netting, angling and trapping. Recreational, commercial and artisanal fishers use different techniques, and also, sometimes, the same techniques. Recreational fishers fish for pleasure or sport, while commercial fishers fish for profit. Artisanal fishers use traditional, low-tech methods, for survival in third-world countries, and as a cultural heritage in other countries. Mostly, recreational fishers use angling methods and commercial fishers use netting methods.

There is an intricate link between various fishing techniques and knowledge about the fish and their behaviour including migration, foraging and habitat. The effective use of fishing techniques often depends on this additional knowledge. Which techniques are appropriate is dictated mainly by the target species and by its habitat.

It is possible to fish and gather many sea foods with minimal equipment by using the hands. Gathering seafood by hand can be as easily as picking shellfish or kelp up off the beach, or doing some digging for clams or crabs. The earliest evidence for shellfish gathering dates back to a 300,000 year old site in France called 'Terra Amata'. This is a hominid site as modern Homo sapiens did not appear until around 50,000 years ago.

***Flounder Tramping***

Every August, the small Scottish village of Palnackie hosts the world flounder tramping championships where flounder are captured by stepping on them.

***Noodling***

Noodling is practiced in the United States. The noodler places his hand inside a catfish hole. If all goes as planned, the catfish swims forward and latches onto the noodler's hand, and can then be dragged out of the hole.

Pearl Divers traditionally harvested oysters by free-diving to depths of thirty metres. Today, free-diving recreational fishers catch lobster and abalone by hand.

***Trout Binning***

It is another method of taking trout. Rocks in a rocky stream are struck with a sledgehammer. The force of the blow stuns the fish.

***Trout Tickling***

In the British Isles, the practice of catching trout by hand is known as trout tickling; it is an art mentioned several times in the plays of Shakespeare.

Spearfishing is an ancient method of fishing conducted with an ordinary spear or a specialised variant such as a harpoon, trident, arrow or eel spear. Some fishing spears use slings (or rubber loops) to propel the spear.

***Bowfishing***

It uses a bow and arrow to kill fish in shallow water from above.

***Gigging***

It uses small trident type spears with long handles for gigging bullfrogs with a bright light at night, or for gigging suckers and other rough fish in shallow water. Gigging is popular in the American South and Midwest.

*Hawaiian Slings*

Hawaiian slings have a sling separate from the spear, in the manner of an underwater bow and arrow.

*Harpoons*

Spearfishing with barbed poles was widespread in palaeolithic times. Cosquer cave in Southern France contains cave art over 16,000 years old, including drawings of seals which appear to have been harpooned.

*Polespears*

Polespears have a sling attached to the spear.

*Modern Spearguns*

Traditional spearfishing is restricted to shallow waters, but the development of the speargun has made the method much more efficient. With practice, divers are able to hold their breath for up to four minutes and sometimes longer. Of course, a diver with underwater breathing equipment can dive for much longer periods.

*Tridents*

Tridents are three-pronged spears. They are also called leisters or gigs. They are used for spear fishing and were formerly also a military weapon. They feature widely in early mythology and history.

Fishing nets are meshes usually formed by knotting a relatively thin thread. About AD 180 the Greek author Oppian wrote the *Halieutica*, a didactic poem about fishing. He described various means of fishing including the use of nets cast from boats, scoop nets held open by a hoop, and various traps "which work while their masters sleep".

Netting is the principal method of commercial fishing, though longlining, trolling, dredging and traps are also used.

**Artisanal Techniques**

*Chinese Fishing Nets*

These nets are shore operated lift nets. Huge mechanical contrivances hold out horizontal nets with diameters of twenty metres or more. The nets are dipped into the water and raised again, but otherwise cannot be moved.

***Lampuki Nets***

Lampuki nets are an example of a traditional artisanal use of nets. Since Roman times, Maltese fishers have cut the larger, lower fronds from palm trees which they then weave into large flat rafts. The rafts are pulled out to sea by a *luzzu*, a small traditional fishing boat. In the middle of the day, lampuki fish (the Maltese name for *mahi-mahi*) school underneath the rafts, seeking the shade, and are caught by the fishers using large mesh nets.

***Cast Nets***

Cast nets are round nets with small weights distributed around the edge. They are also called *throw nets*. The net is caste or thrown by hand in such a manner that it spreads out on the water and sinks. Fish are caught as the net is hauled back in. This simple device has been in use, with various modifications, for thousands of years.

***Drift Net***

Drift net are nets which are not anchored. They are usually gillnets, and are commonly used in the coastal waters of many countries. Their use on the high seas is prohibited, but still occurs.

***Ghost Nets***

Ghost nets are nets that have been lost at sea. They can be a menace to marine life for many years.

***Gillnets***

Gillnets catch fish which try to pass through by snagging on the gill covers. Trapped, the fish can neither advance through the net nor retreat.

***Hand Nets***

Hand nets are small nets held open by a hoop. They have been used since antiquity. They are also called scoop nets, and are used for scooping up fish near the surface of the water. They may or may not have a handle–if they have a long handle they are called *dip nets*. When used by anglers to help land fish they are called *landing nets*. Because hand netting is not destructive to fish, hand nets are used for tag and release, or capturing aquarium fish.

### *Seine Nets*

Seine nets are large fishing nets that can be arranged in different ways. In purse seining fishing the net hangs vertically in the water by attaching weights along the bottom edge and floats along the top. Danish seining is a method which has some similarities with trawling. A simple and commonly used fishing technique is beach seining, where the seine net is operated from the shore.

### *Trawl Nets*

*Trawl nets* are large nets, conical in shape, designed to be towed in the sea or along the sea bottom. The trawl is pulled through the water by one or more boats, called trawlers. The activity of pulling the trawl through the water is called trawling.

## Angling

Angling is a method of fishing by means of an "angle" (hook). The hook is usually attached to a line, and is sometimes weighed down by a sinker so it sinks in the water. This is the classic "hook, line and sinker" arrangement, used in angling since prehistoric times. The hook is usually baited with lures or bait fish.

Additional arrangements include the use of a fishing rod, which can be fitted with a reel, and functions as a delivery mechanism for casting the line. Other delivery methods for projecting the line include fishing kites and cannons, kontiki rafts and remote controlled devices. Floats can can also be used to help set the line or function as bite indicators. The hook can be dressed with lures or bait. Angling is the principal method of sport fishing, but commercial fisheries also use angling methods involving multiple hooks, such as longlining or commercial trolling.

## Line Fishing

Line fishing is fishing with a fishing line. A fishing line is any cord made for fishing. Important parameters of a fishing line are its length, material, and weight (thicker, sturdier lines are more visible to fish). Factors that may determine what line an angler chooses for a given fishing environment include breaking strength, knot strength, UV resistance, castability, limpness, stretch, abrasion resistance, and visibility.

Modern fishing lines are usually made from artificial substances. The most common type is *monofilament*, made of a single strand. There are also *braided fishing lines* and thermally fused *superlines*.

## Droplining

A dropline consists of a long fishing line set vertically down into the water, with a series of baited hooks Droplines have a weight at the bottom and a float at the top. They are not usually as long as longlines and have fewer hooks.

### *Handlining*

Handlining is fishing with a single fishing line, baited with lures or bait fish, which is held in the hands. Handlining can be done from boats or from the shore. It is used mainly to catch groundfish and squid, but smaller pelagic fish can also be caught.

### *Longlining*

Longlining is a commercial technique that uses a long heavy fishing line with a series of hundreds or even thousands of baited hooks hanging from the main line by means of branch lines called "snoods". Longlines are usually operated from specialised boats called longliners. They use a special winch to haul in the line, and can operate in deeper waters targeting pelagic species such as swordfish, tuna, halibut and sable.

### *Slabbing*

Slabbing involves repetitively lifting and dropping a flat lure, usually made of 1 to 2.5 oz of lead painted to look like a baitfish, through a school of actively feeding fish that the angler has located on a fish finder. Used on white and striped bass in the reservoirs of the southern USA.

***Trolling***

Trolling is fishing with one or more baited lines which are drawn through the water. This may be done by pulling the line behind a slow moving boat, or by slowly winding the line in when fishing from the land. Trolling is used to catch pelagic fish such as mackerel and kingfish.

***Trotlining***

Trotlining a trotline is like a dropline, except that a dropline has a series of hooks suspended vertically in the water, while a trotline has a series of hooks suspended horizontally in the water. Trotlines can be physically set in many ways, such as tying each end to something fixed, and adjusting the set of the rest of the line with weights and floats. They are used for catching crabs or fish, such as catfish, particularly across rivers.

Fishing rods give more control of the fishing line. The rod is usually fitted with a fishing reel which functions as a mechanism for storing, retrieving and paying out the line. Floats may also be used, and can function as bite indicators. The hook can be dressed with lures or bait.

***Bank Fishing***

Fishing from river banks and similar shorelines. Bank fishing is usually performed with a rod and reel, although nets, traps, and spears can also be used. People who fish from a boat can sometimes access more areas in prime locations with greater ease than bank fishermen. However many people don't own boats and find fishing from the bank has its own advantages. Bank fishing has its own requirements, and many things come into play for success, such as local knowledge, water depth, bank structure, location, time of day, and the type of bait and lures.

***Casting***

Casting the act of throwing the fishing line out over the water using a flexible fishing rod. The usual technique is for the angler to quickly flick the rod from behind toward the water. Casting is also a sport adjunct to fishing, much as shooting is to hunting. The sport is supervised by the International Casting Sport Federation, which sponsors tournaments and recognizes world records for accuracy and distance.

***Float Tubes***

Float tubes small doughnut-shaped boats with an underwater seat in the "hole". Float tubes are used for fly fishing and enable the angler to reach deeper water without splashing and disturbing stillwater fish.

***Fly Fishing***

Fly fishing the use of artificial flies as lures. These are cast with specially constructed fly rods and fly lines. The fly line (today, almost always coated with plastic) is heavy enough cast in order to send the fly to the target. Artificial flies vary dramatically in size, weight and colour. Fly fishing is a distinct and ancient angling method, most renowned as a method for catching trout and salmon, but employed today for a wide variety of species including pike, bass, panfish, and carp, as well as marine species, such as redfish, snook, tarpon, bonefish and striped bass. There is a growing population of anglers whose aim is to catch as many different species as possible with the fly.

***Rock Fishing***

Fishing from rocky outcrops into the sea. It is a popular pastime in Australia and New Zealand. It can be a dangerous pastime and claims many lives each year.

***Surfcasting***

Fishing from a shoreline using a rod to cast into the surf. With few exceptions, surf fishing is done in saltwater, often from a beach. The basic idea of most surfcasting is to cast a bait or lure as far out into the water as is necessary to reach the target fish from the shore. This may or may not require long casting distances and muscular techniques. Basic surf fishing can be done with a surfcasting rod between seven and twelve feet long, with an extended butt section, equipped with an appropriate spinning or conventional casting reel. Dedicated surfcasters usually possess an array of terminal and other tackle, with rods and reels of different lengths and actions, and lures and baits of different weights and capabilities. Depending on fishing conditions and the fish they are targeting, such surfcasters tailor bait and terminal tackle to rod and reel and the size and species of the fish. Reels and other equipment need to be constructed so they resist the corrosive and abrasive effects of salt and sand.

### *Bottom Fishing*

Fishing the bottom of a body of water. In the United Kingdom it is called "legering". A common rig for fishing on the bottom is a weight tied to the end of the line, with a hook about an inch up line from the weight. The method can be used both with hand lines and rods. There are fishing rods specialized for bottom fishing, called "donkas". The weight is used to cast or throw the line an appropriate distance. Bottom fishing can be done both from boats and from the land. It targets groundfish such as sucker fish, bream, catfish, and crappie.

### *Ice Fishing*

It is the practice of catching fish with lines and hooks through an opening in the ice on a frozen body of water. It is practised by hunter-gatherers such as the Inuit and by anglers in other cold or continental climates.

### *Kayak Fishing*

Kayak fishing has a long history, and has gained popularity in recent times. Many of the techniques used are the same as those used on other fishing boats, apart from difference is in the set-up, how each piece of equipment is fitted to the kayak, and how each activity is carried out on such a small craft.

### *Kite Fishing*

Kite fishing is said to have been invented in China. It was, and still is, used by the people of New Guinea and other Pacific Islands - either by cultural diffusion from China or independent invention. Kites can provide the boatless fishermen access to waters that would otherwise be available only to boats. Similarly, for boat owners, kites provide a way to fish in areas where it is not safe to navigate such as shallows or coral reefs where fish may be plentiful. Kites can also be used for trolling a lure through the water. Suitable kites may be of very simple construction. Those of Tobi Island are a large leaf stiffened by the ribs of the fronds of the coconut palm. The fishing line may be made from coconut fibre and the lure made from spiders webs. Modern kitefishing is popular in New Zealand, where large delta kites of synthetic materials are used to fish from beaches, taking a line and hooks far out past the breakers. Kite fishing is also emerging in Melbourne where sled kites are becoming popular, both off beaches and off boats and in freshwater areas. The disabled community are increasingly using the kites for fishing as they allow mobility impaired people to cast the bait further out than they would otherwise be able to.

***Boat Anglers***

Fishing is usually done either from a boat or from a shoreline or river bank. When fishing from a boat, pretty much any fishing technique can be used, from nets to fish traps, but some form of angling is by far the most common. Compared to fishing from the land, fishing from a boat allows more access to different fishing grounds and different species of fish. Some tackle is specialised for boat anglers, such as sea rods.

***Remote Control Fishing***

Fishing can also be done using a remote controlled boat. This type of fishing is commonly referred to as *RC fishing*. The boat is usually one to three feet long and runs on a small DC battery. A radio transmitter controls the boat. The fisherman connects the fishing line/bait to the boat; drives it; navigating the water by manipulating the remote controller. The technique is growing in popularity. People have used home-made adaptations to remote control boats for this purpose, and recently commercial versions have appeared. There are also patented devices to adapt a regular RC boat into an RC fishing boat. There is debate about whether RC fishing should be legal. Most states will allow it if the line disconnects when a fish is hooked to the boat, and the fisherman reels in the fish with a fishing pole. When the RC boat is used to pull in the fish, it may be illegal unless on private property.

***Traps***

Traps are culturally almost universal and seem to have been independently invented many times. There are essentially two types of trap, a permanent or semi-permanent structure placed in a river or tidal area and pot-traps that are baited to attract prey and periodically lifted.

## Artisanal Techniques

***Dam Fishing***

An artisanal technique called dam fishing is used by the Baka pygmies. This involves the construction of a temporary dam resulting in a drop in the water levels downstream — allowing fish to be easily collected.

***Basket Weir Fish Traps***

Basket weir fish traps were widely used in ancient times. They are shown in medieval illustrations and surviving examples have been found. Basket weirs are about 2 m long and comprise two wicker cones, one inside the other—easy to get into and hard to get out.

***Fishing Weir***

In medieval Europe, large fishing weir structures were constructed from wood posts and wattle fences. 'V' shaped structures in rivers could be as long as 60 metres and worked by directing fish towards fish traps or nets. Such fish traps were evidently controversial in medieval England. The Magna Carta includes a clause requiring that they be removed: "All fish-weirs shall be removed from the Thames, the Medway, and throughout the whole of England, except on the sea coast".

### *Fish Wheels*

Fish wheels operate alongside streams, much as a water-powered mill wheel. A wheel complete with baskets and paddles is attached to a floating dock. The wheel rotates due to the current of the stream. The baskets on the wheel capture fish travelling upstream and transfer them into a holding tank. When the holding tank is full, the fish are removed.

### *Lobster Traps*

Lobster traps also called lobster pots, are traps used to catch lobsters. They resemble fish traps, yet are usually smaller and consist of several sections. Lobster traps are also used to catch other crustaceans, such as crabs and crayfish. They can be constructed in various shapes, but the design strategy is to make the entry into the trap much easier than exit. The pots are baited and lowered into the water and checked frequently. Historically lobster pots were constructed with wood or metal. Today most traps are made from checkered wire and mesh. It is common for the trap to be weighted down with bricks. A bait bag is hung in the middle of the trap. In theory the lobster walks up the mesh and then falls into the wire trap. Bait varies from captain to captain but it is common to use herring. In commercial lobstering five to ten of these traps will be connected with line. A buoy marks each end of the string of pots. Two buoys are important to make retrieval easier and so captains don't set their traps over each other. Each buoy is painted differently so the various captains can identify their traps.

Cooperative human-dolphin fisheries date back to the ancient Roman author and natural philosopher Pliny the Elder. A modern human-dolphin fishery still takes place in Laguna, Santa Catarina, Brazil. Here, dolphins drive fish towards fishermen waiting along the shore and give them a signal when they can cast their nets. The dolphins then feed off the fish that manage to escape the nets.

### *Cormorant Fishing*

In China and Japan, the practice of cormorant fishing is thought to date back some 1300 years. Fishermen use the natural fish-hunting instincts of the cormorants to catch fish, but a metal ring placed round the bird's neck prevents large, valuable fish from being swallowed. The fish are instead collected by the fisherman.

***Frigatebirds Fishing***

The people of Nauru used trained frigatebirds to fish on reefs.

***Portuguese Water Dogs***

Dating from the 16th century in Portugal, Portuguese Water Dogs were used by fishermen to send messages between boats, to retrieve fish and articles from the water, and to guard the fishing boats. Labrador Retrievers have been used by fishermen to assist in bringing nets to shore; the dog would grab the floating corks on the ends of the nets and pull them to shore.

***Remora Fishing***

The practice of tethering a remora, a sucking fish, to a fishing line and using the remora to capture sea turtles probably originated in the Indian Ocean. The earliest surviving records of the practice are Peter Martyr d'Anghera's 1511 accounts of the second voyage of Columbus to the New World (1494). However, these accounts are probably apocryphal, and based on earlier, no longer extant accounts from the Indian Ocean region.

Scientists carrying out a population and species survey using electrofishing equipment.

***Electrofishing***

It is another recently developed technique, primarily used in freshwater by fisheries scientists. Electrofishing uses electricity to stun fish so they can be caught. It is commonly used in scientific surveys, sampling fish populations for abundance, density, and species composition. When performed correctly, electrofishing results in no permanent harm to fish, which return to their natural state a few minutes after being stunned.

***Fish Aggregating Devices***

Fish aggregating devices are man-made objects used to attract pelagic fish such as marlin, tuna and mahi-mahi (dolphin fish). They usually consist of buoys or floats tethered to the ocean floor with concrete blocks.

***Dredging***

There are types of dredges used for collecting scallops, oysters or sea cucumbers from the seabed. They have the form of a scoop made of chain mesh and they are towed by a fishing boat. Dredging can be destructive to the seabed, because the marine life is unable to survive the weight of the dredge. It is extremely detrimental to coral beds since they take centuries to rebuild themselves. Unmonitored dredging can be compared to unmonitored forest clearing, where it can wipe out ecosystems. Nowadays, this method of fishing is often replaced by mariculture or by scuba diving.

***Fish Finders***

Fish finders are electronic sonar devices which indicate the presence of fish and fish schools. They are widely used by recreational fishermen. Commercially, they are used with other electronic locating and positioning devices.

***Fishing Light Attractors***

Fishing light attractors use lights attached (above or underwater) to some structure to attract fish and bait fish. Fishing light attractor are operated every night. After a while, fish discover the increased concentration of bait surrounding the light. Once located, the fish return regularly, and can be harvested.

***Harvesting Machines***

Harvesting machines have recently been developed for commercial fishing. Harvesting machines use pumps to pump fish out of the sea. Dredges have also been mechanized so that they directly transfer mollusks to the surface as are dredged.

***Payaos***

It is a type of fish aggregating device used in Southeast Asia, particularly in the Philippines. Payaos were traditionally bamboo rafts for handline fishing before World War II, but modern steel payaos use fish lights and fish location sonar to increase yields. While payaos fishing is sustainable on a small scale, the large scale, modern applications have been linked to adverse impacts on fish stocks.

*Shrimp Baiting*

It is a method used by recreational fisherman for of catching shrimp. It uses a cast net, bait and long poles. The poles are used to mark a specific location and then bait is thrown in the water near the pole. After several minutes the cast net is thrown as close to the bait as possible and shrimp are caught in the net. In the 1980s the sport became popular in the south eastern coastal states of the USA.

**Destructive Techniques**

Destructive fishing practices are practices that easily result in irreversible damage to aquatic habitats and ecosystems. Many fishing techniques can be destructive if used inappropriately, but some practices are particularly likely to result in irreversible damage. These practices are mostly, though not always, illegal. Where they are illegal, they are often inadequately enforced. Some examples are:

*Explosives*

Dynamite or blast fishing, is done easily and cheaply with dynamite or homemade bombs made from locally available materials. Fish are killed by the shock from the blast and are then skimmed from the surface or collected from the bottom. The explosions indiscriminately kill large numbers of fish and other marine organisms in the vicinity and can damage or destroy the physical environment. Explosions are particularly harmful to coral reefs. Blast fishing is also illegal in many waterways around the world.

*Cyanide Fishing*

Cyanides are used to capture live fish near coral reefs for the aquarium and seafood market. This illegal fishing occurs mainly in or near the Philippines, Indonesia, and the

Caribbean to supply the two million marine aquarium owners in the world. Many fish caught in this fashion die either immediately or in shipping. Those that survive often die from shock or from massive digestive damage. The high concentrations of cyanide on reefs harvested in this fashion damages the coral polyps and has also resulted in cases of cyanide poisoning among local fishermen and their families.

*Muroami*

It is a destructive artisan fishing method employed on coral reefs in Southeast Asia. An encircling net is used with pounding devices, such as large stones fitted on ropes that are pounded onto the coral reefs. They can also consist of large heavy blocks of cement suspended above the sea by a crane fitted to the vessel. The pounding devices are repeatedly lowered into the area encircled by the net, smashing the coral into small fragments in order to scare the fish out of their coral refuges. The "crushing" effect on the coral heads has been described as having longlasting and practically totally destructive effects.

Ancient remains of spears, hooks and fishnet have been found in ruins of the Stone Age. The people of the early civilization drew pictures of nets and fishing lines in their arts. Early hooks were made from the upper bills of eagles and from bones, shells, horns and plant thorns. Spears were tipped with the same materials, or sometimes with flints. Lines and nets were made from leaves, plant stalk and cocoon silk. Ancient fishing nets were rough in design and material but they were amazingly, as if some now use. Literature on the indigenous fishing practices is very scanty. Use of the herbal fish poisons in catching fishes from fresh water and sea documented from New Caledonia. Researcher documented fishing techniques and overall life style of the Mukkuvar fishing Community of Kanyakumari district of Tamil Nadu, India. Tribal people using various plants for medicinal and various purposes extends the use notion for herbal fish stupefying plants. Use of the fish poisons is very old practice in the history of human kind. In 1212, King Frederick II prohibited the use of certain plant piscicides, and by the 15th century similar laws had been decreed in other European countries as well. All over the globe, indigenous people use various fish poisons to kill the fishes, documented in America and among Tarahumara Indian.

# 2

# Fishery and Fish Farming

Generally, a fishery is an entity engaged in raising and/or harvesting fish, which is determined by some authority to be a fishery. According to the FAO, a fishery is typically defined in terms of the "people involved, species or type of fish, area of water or seabed, method of fishing, class of boats, purpose of the activities or a combination of the foregoing features". The definition often includes a combination of fish and fishers in a region, the latter fishing for similar species with similar gear types.

A fishery may involve the capture of wild fish or raising fish through fish farming or aquaculture. Directly or indirectly, the livelihood of over 500 million people in developing countries depends on fisheries and aquaculture. Overfishing, including the taking of fish beyond sustainable levels, is reducing fish stocks and employment in many world regions.

In biology – the term *fish* is most strictly used to describe any animal with a backbone that has gills throughout life and has limbs, if any, in the shape of fins. Many types of aquatic animals commonly referred to as *fish* are not fish in this strict sense; examples include shellfish, cuttlefish, starfish, crayfish and jellyfish. In earlier times, even biologists did not make a distinction - sixteenth century natural historians classified also seals, whales, amphibians, crocodiles, even hippopotamuses, as well as a host of aquatic invertebrates, as fish.

In fisheries – the term *fish* is used as a collective term, and includes mollusks, crustaceans and any aquatic animal which is harvested The strict biological definition of a fish, above, is sometimes called a *true fish*. True fish are also referred to as *finfish* or *fin fish* to distinguish them from other aquatic life harvested in fisheries or aquaculture.

Fisheries are harvested for their value (commercial, recreational or subsistence). They can be saltwater or freshwater, wild or farmed. Examples are the salmon fishery of Alaska, the cod fishery off the Lofoten islands, the tuna fishery of the Eastern Pacific, or the shrimp farm fisheries in China. Capture fisheries can be broadly classified as industrial scale, small-scale or artisanal, and recreational.

Close to 90 per cent of the world's fishery catches come from oceans and seas, as opposed to inland waters. These marine catches have remained relatively stable since the mid-nineties (between 80 and 86 million tonnes). Most marine fisheries are based near the coast. This is not only because harvesting from relatively shallow waters is easier than in the open ocean, but also because fish are much more abundant near the coastal shelf, due to coastal upwelling and the abundance of nutrients available there. However, productive wild fisheries also exist in open oceans, particularly by seamounts, and inland in lakes and rivers.

Most fisheries are wild fisheries, but increasingly fisheries are farmed. Farming can occur in coastal areas, such as with oyster farms, but more typically occur inland, in lakes, ponds, tanks and other enclosures.

There are species fisheries worldwide for finfish, mollusks, crustaceans and echinoderms, and by extension, aquatic plants such as kelp. However, a very small number of species support the majority of the world's fisheries. Some of these species are herring, cod, anchovy, tuna, flounder, mullet, squid, shrimp, salmon, crab, lobster, oyster and scallops. All except these last four provided a worldwide catch of well over a million tonnes in 1999, with herring and sardines together providing a harvest of over 22 million metric tons in 1999. Many other species are harvested in smaller numbers.

### Fish Farming

Fish farming is the principal form of aquaculture, while other methods may fall under mariculture. Fish farming involves raising fish commercially in tanks or enclosures, usually for food. A facility that releases young (juvenile) fish into the wild for recreational fishing or to supplement a species' natural numbers is generally referred to as a fish hatchery. The most common fish species raised by fish farms are salmon, carp, tilapia, European seabass, catfish and cod.

There is an increasing demand for fish and fish protein, which has resulted in widespread overfishing in wild fisheries. Fish farming offers fish marketers another source. However, farming carnivorous fish, such as salmon, does not necessarily reduce pressure on wild fisheries, since carnivorous farmed fish are usually fed fishmeal and fish oil extracted from wild forage fish. In this way, the salmon can consume in weight more wild fish than they weigh themselves. The global returns for fish farming recorded by the FAO in 2008 totalled 33.8 million tonnes worth about $US 60 billion.

Limiting for growth here is the available food supply by natural sources, commonly zooplankton feeding on pelagic algae or benthic animals, such as crustaceans and mollusks. Tilapia species filter feed directly on phytoplankton, which makes higher production possible. The photosynthetic production can be increased by fertilizing the pond water with artificial fertilizer mixtures, such as potash, phosphorus, nitrogen and micro-elements. Because most fish are carnivorous, they occupy a higher place in the trophic chain and therefore only a tiny fraction of primary photosynthetic production (typically 1%) will be converted into harvest-able fish. As a result, without additional feeding the fish harvest will not exceed 200 kilograms of fish per hectare per year, equivalent to 1 per cent of the gross photosynthetic production.

A second point of concern is the risk of algal blooms. When temperatures, nutrient supply and available sunlight are optimal for algal growth, algae multiply their biomass at an exponential rate, eventually leading to an exhaustion of available nutrients and a subsequent die-off. The decaying algal biomass will deplete the oxygen in the pond water because it blocks out the sun and pollutes it with organic and inorganic solutes (such as ammonium ions), which can (and frequently do) lead to massive loss of fish.

Another option is to use a wetland system such as that of Veta La Palma.

In order to tap all available food sources in the pond, the aquaculturist will choose fish species which occupy different places in the pond ecosystem, e.g., a filter algae feeder such as tilapia, a benthic feeder such as carp or catfish and a zooplankton feeder (various carps) or submerged weeds feeder such as grass carp.

Despite these limitations significant fish farming industries use these methods. In the Czech Republic thousands of natural and semi-natural ponds are harvested each year for trout and carp. The large ponds around Trebon were built from around 1650 and are still in use.

In these kinds of systems fish production per unit of surface can be increased at will, as long as sufficient oxygen, fresh water and food are provided. Because of the requirement of sufficient fresh water, a massive water purification system must be integrated in the fish farm.

A clever way to achieve this is the combination of hydroponic horticulture and water treatment, see below. The exception to this rule are cages which are placed in a river or sea, which supplements the fish crop with sufficient oxygenated water. Some environmentalists object to this practice.

The cost of inputs per unit of fish weight is higher than in extensive farming, especially because of the high cost of fish feed, which must contain a much higher level of protein (up to 60%) than cattle food and a balanced amino acid composition as well.

However, these higher protein level requirements are a consequence of the higher food conversion efficiency (FCR—kg of feed per kg of animal produced) of aquatic animals. Fish like salmon have FCR's in the range of 1.1 kg of feed per kg of salmon whereas chickens are in the 2.5 kg of feed per kg of chicken range. Fish don't have to stand up or keep warm and this eliminates a lot of carbohydrates and fats in the diet, required to provide this energy. This frequently is offset by the lower land costs and the higher productions which can be obtained due to the high level of input control.

Essential here is aeration of the water, as fish need a sufficient oxygen level for growth. This is achieved by bubbling, cascade flow or aqueous oxygen.

Catfish, Clarias spp. can breathe atmospheric air and can tolerate much higher levels of pollutants than trout or salmon, which makes aeration and water purification less necessary and makes *Clarias* species especially suited for intensive fish production. In some *Clarias* farms about 10 per cent of the water volume can consist of fish biomass.

The risk of infections by parasites like fish lice, fungi (*Saprolegnia* spp.), intestinal worms (such as nematodes or trematodes), bacteria (e.g., *Yersinia* spp., *Pseudomonas* spp.), and protozoa (such as Dinoflagellates) is similar to animal husbandry, especially at high population densities.

However, animal husbandry is a larger and more technologically mature area of human agriculture and better solutions to pathogen problem exist. Intensive aquaculture does have to provide adequate water quality (oxygen, ammonia, nitrite, etc.) levels to minimize stress, which makes the pathogen problem more difficult. This means, intensive aquaculture requires tight monitoring and a high level of expertise of the fish farmer.

Very high intensity recycle aquaculture systems (RAS), where there is control over all the production parameters, are being used for high value species. By recycling the water, very little water is used per unit of production. However, the process does have high capital and operating costs. The higher cost structures mean that RAS is only economical for high value products like broodstock for egg production, fingerlings for net pen aquaculture operations, sturgeon production, research animals and some special niche markets like live fish.

Raising ornamental cold water fish (goldfish or koi), although theoretically much more profitable due to the higher income per weight of fish produced, has never been successfully carried out until very recently. The increased incidences of dangerous viral diseases of koi carp, together with the high value of the fish has led to initiatives in closed system koi breeding and growing in a number of countries. Today there are a few commercially successful intensive koi growing facilities in the U.K., Germany and Israel.

One of the largest problems with freshwater aquaculture is that it can use a million gallons of water per acre (about 1 $m^3$ of water per $m^2$) each year. Extended water purification systems allow for the reuse (recycling) of local water.

The largest-scale pure fish farms use a system derived (admittedly much refined) from the New Alchemy Institute in the 1970s. Basically, large plastic fish tanks are placed in a greenhouse. A hydroponic bed is placed near, above or between them. When tilapia are raised in the tanks, they are able to eat algae, which naturally grows in the tanks when the tanks are properly fertilized.

The tank water is slowly circulated to the hydroponic beds where the tilapia waste feeds commercial plant crops. Carefully cultured microorganisms in the hydroponic bed convert ammonia to nitrates, and the plants are fertilized by the nitrates and phosphates. Other wastes are strained out by the hydroponic media, which doubles as an aerated pebble-bed filter.

This system, properly tuned, produces more edible protein per unit area than any other. A wide variety of plants can grow well in the hydroponic beds. Most growers concentrate on herbs (e.g. parsley and basil), which command premium prices in small quantities all year long. The most common customers are restaurant wholesalers.

Since the system lives in a greenhouse, it adapts to almost all temperate climates, and may also adapt to tropical climates. The main environmental impact is discharge of water that must be salted to maintain the fishes' electrolyte balance. Current growers use a variety of proprietary tricks to keep fish healthy, reducing their expenses for salt and waste water discharge permits. Some veterinary authorities speculate that ultraviolet ozone disinfectant systems (widely used for ornamental fish) may play a prominent part in keeping the Tilapia healthy with recirculated water.

### Irrigation Ditch or Pond Systems

These use irrigation ditches or farm ponds to raise fish. The basic requirement is to have a ditch or pond that retains water, possibly with an above-ground irrigation system (many irrigation systems use buried pipes with headers.) Using this method, one can store one's water allotment in ponds or ditches, usually lined with bentonite clay. In small systems the fish are often fed commercial fish food, and their waste products can help fertilize the fields. In larger ponds, the pond grows water plants and algae as fish food. Some of the most successful ponds grow introduced strains of plants, as well as introduced strains of fish.

Control of water quality is crucial. Fertilizing, clarifying and pH control of the water can increase yields substantially, as long as eutrophication is prevented and oxygen levels stay high. Yields can be low if the fish grow ill from electrolyte stress.

### Composite Fish Culture

The composite fish culture system is a technology developed in India by the Indian Council of Agricultural

Research in the 1970s. In this system both local and imported fish species, a combination of five or six fish species is used in a single fish pond. These species are selected so that they do not compete for food among them having different types of food habitats. As a result the food available in all the parts of the pond is used. Fish used in this system include catla and silver carp which are surface feeders, rohu a column feeder and mrigal and common carp which are bottom feeders. Other fish will also feed on the excreta of the common carp and this helps contribute to the efficiency of the system which in optimal conditions will produce 3000-6000 kg of fish per hectare per year.

### Cage System

Fish cages are placed in lakes, bayous, ponds, rivers or oceans to contain and protect fish until they can be harvested. They can be constructed of a wide variety of components. Fish are stocked in cages, artificially fed, and harvested when they reach market size. A few advantages of fish farming with cages are that many types of waters can be used (rivers, lakes, filled quarries, etc.), many types of fish can be raised, and fish farming can co-exist with sport fishing and other water uses. Cage farming of fishes in open seas is also gaining popularity. Concerns of disease, poaching, poor water quality, etc., lead some to believe that in general, pond systems are easier to manage and simpler to start. Also, past occurrences of cage-failures leading to escapes, have raised concern regarding the culture of non-native fish species in open-water cages. Even though the cage-industry has made numerous technological advances in cage construction in recent years, the concern for escapes remains valid.

### Classic Fry Farming

Trout and other sport fish are often raised from eggs to fry or fingerlings and then trucked to streams and released. Normally, the fry are raised in long, shallow concrete tanks, fed with fresh stream water. The fry receive commercial fish food in pellets. While not as efficient as the New Alchemists' method, it is also far simpler, and has been used for many years to stock streams with sport fish. European eel (*Anguilla anguilla*) aquaculturalists procure a limited supply of glass eels, juvenile stages of the European eel which swim north from the Sargasso Sea breeding grounds, for their farms. The European eel is threatened with extinction because of the excessive catch of glass eels by Spanish fishermen and overfishing of adult eels in, *e.g.*, the Dutch IJsselmeer, Netherlands. As per 2005, no one has managed to breed the European eel in captivity. The issue of feeds in fish farming has been a controversial one. Many cultured fishes (tilapia, carp, catfish, many others) require no meat or fish products in their diets. Top-level carnivores (most salmon species) depend on fish feed of which a portion is usually derived from wild caught fish (anchovies, menhaden, etc.). Vegetable-derived proteins have successfully replaced fish meal in feeds for carnivorous fishes, but vegetable-derived oils have not successfully been incorporated into the diets of carnivores.

Secondly, farmed fish are kept in concentrations never seen in the wild [*e.g.* 50,000 fish in a 2-acre (8,100 $m^2$) area.] with each fish occupying less room than the average bathtub. This can cause several forms of pollution. Packed tightly, fish rub against each other and the sides of their cages, damaging their fins and tails and becoming sickened with various diseases and infections. This also causes stress.

However, fish tend also to be animals that aggregate into large schools at high density. Most successful aquaculture species are schooling species, which do not have social problems at high density. Aquaculturists tend to feel that operating a rearing system above its design capacity or above the social density limit of the fish will result in decreased growth rate and increased FCR (food conversion ratio - kg dry feed/kg of fish produced), which will result in increased cost and risk of health problems along with a decrease in profits.

Stressing the animals is not desirable, but the concept of and measurement of stress must be viewed from the perspective of the animal using the scientific method.

Sea lice, particularly *Lepeophtheirus salmonis* and various *Caligus* species, including *Caligus clemensi* and *Caligus rogercresseyi*, can cause deadly infestations of both farm-grown and wild salmon. Sea lice are ectoparasites which feed on mucous, blood, and skin, and migrate and latch onto the skin of wild salmon during free-swimming, planktonic *nauplii* and *copepodid* larval stages, which can persist for several days.

Large numbers of highly populated, open-net salmon farms can create exceptionally large concentrations of sea lice; when exposed in river estuaries containing large numbers of open-net farms, many young wild salmon are infected, and do not survive as a result. Adult salmon may survive otherwise critical numbers of sea lice, but small, thin-skinned juvenile salmon migrating to sea are highly vulnerable. On the Pacific coast of Canada, the louse-induced mortality of pink salmon in some regions is commonly over 80 per cent.

A 2008 meta-analysis of available data show that salmon farming reduces the survival of associated wild salmon populations. This relationship has been shown to hold for Atlantic, steelhead, pink, chum, and coho salmon. The decrease in survival or abundance often exceeds 50 per cent.

Diseases and parasites are the most commonly cited reasons for such decreases. Some species of sea lice have been noted to target farmed coho and Atlantic salmon. Such parasites have been shown to have an effect on nearby wild fish. One place that has garnered international media attention is British Columbia's Broughton Archipelago. There, juvenile wild salmon must "run a gauntlet" of large fish farms located off-shore near river outlets before making their way to sea.

It is alleged that the farms cause such severe sea lice infestations that one study predicted a 99 per cent collapse in the wild salmon population in another four years. This claim, however, has been criticized by numerous scientists who question the correlation between increased fish farming and increases in sea lice infestation among wild salmon.

Because of parasite problems, some aquaculture operators frequently use strong antibiotic drugs to keep the fish alive (but many fish still die prematurely at rates of up to 30 per cent). In some cases, these drugs have entered the environment. Additionally, the residual presence of these drugs in human food products has become controversial.

Use of antibiotics in food production is thought to increase the prevalence of antibiotic resistance in human diseases. At some facilities, the use of antibiotic drugs in aquaculture has decreased considerably due to vaccinations and other techniques. However, most fish farming operations still use antibiotics, many of which escape into the surrounding environment.The lice and pathogen problems of the 1990s facilitated the development of current treatment methods for sea lice and pathogens. These developments reduced the stress from parasite/pathogen problems. However, being in an ocean environment, the transfer of disease organisms from the wild fish to the aquaculture fish is an ever-present risk.

The very large number of fish kept long-term in a single location contributes to habitat destruction of the nearby areas. The high concentrations of fish produce a significant amount of condensed faeces, often contaminated with drugs, which again affect local waterways. However, these effects are very local to the actual fish farm site and are minimal to non-measurable in high current sites.

Concern remains that resultant bacterial growth strips the water of oxygen, reducing or killing off the local marine life. Once an area has been so contaminated, the fish farms are moved to new, uncontaminated areas. This practice has angered nearby fishermen.

Other potential problems faced by aquaculturists are the obtaining of various permits and water-use rights, profitability, concerns about invasive species and genetic engineering depending on what species are involved, and interaction with the United Nations Convention on the Law of the Sea.

In regards to genetically modified farmed salmon, concern has been raised over their proven reproductive advantage and how it could potentially decimate local fish populations, if released into the wild. Biologist Rick Howard did a controlled laboratory study where wild fish and GMO fish were allowed to breed.

The GMO fish crowded out the wild fish in spawning beds, but the offspring were less likely to survive. The Center for Food Safety criticized the FDA's analysis as misguided and dangerous. Federal tests were "insufficient in determining the long-term, unforeseen consequences" of genetic engineering, said Wenonah Hauter, director of Food & Water Watch. The FDA's tests (historically used to determine if a non-GM food was safe) were created before GM products became a reality and are insufficient in determining the long-term, unforeseen consequences of the GM salmon in question.

These dated tests cannot determine the salmon's full allergenicity and toxicity. The FDA is reviewing data submitted by AquaBounty, the company that spliced a growth hormone gene into Atlantic salmon, forcing it to grow up to five times faster, and reach market size in about 18 months instead of 3 years. According to the evidence, their salmon might have higher levels of a cancer promoting hormone IGF-1, more antibiotics, and more of a potentially life-threatening allergen(s).

In 2005, Alaska passed legislation requiring that any genetically altered fish sold in the state be labeled. In 2006, a Consumer Reports investigation revealed that farm-raised salmon is frequently sold as wild.

In 2008, the US National Organic Standards Board allowed farmed fish to be labeled as organic provided less than 25 per cent of their feed came from wild fish. This decision was criticized by the advocacy group Food & Water Watch as "bending the rules" about organic labelling. In the European Union, fish labelling as to species, method of production and origin, has been required since 2002.

Concerns continue over the labelling of salmon as farmed or wild caught, as well as about the humane treatment of farmed fish. The Marine Stewardship Council has established an Eco label to distinguish between farmed and wild caught salmon, while the RSPCA has established the Freedom Food label to indicate humane treatment of farmed salmon as well as other food products.

### Indoor Fish Farming

An alternative to outdoor open ocean cage aquaculture, one in which the risk of environmental damage is high, is through the use of a recirculation aquaculture system (RAS). A RAS is a series of culture tanks and filters where water is continuously recycled and monitored to keep optimal conditions year round. To prevent the deterioration of water quality, the water is treated mechanically through the removal of particulate matter and biologically through the conversion of harmful accumulated chemicals into nontoxic ones.

In 2005, Alaska passed legislation requiring that any genetically altered fish sold in the state be labelled. In 2006, a Consumer Reports investigation revealed that farm-raised salmon is frequently sold as wild.

In 2008, the US National Organic Standards Board allowed farmed fish to be labelled as organic provided less than 25 per cent of their feed came from wild fish. This decision was criticized by the advocacy group Food and Water Watch as "bending the rules" about organic labelling. In the European Union, fish labelling as to species, method of production and origin, has been required since 2002.

Concerns continue over the labelling of salmon as farmed or wild caught, as well as about the humane treatment of farmed fish. The Marine Stewardship Council has established an Eco label to distinguish between farmed and wild caught salmon, while the RSPCA has established the Freedom Food label to indicate humane treatment of farmed salmon as well as other food products. Because of its high capital and operating costs, RAS has generally been restricted to practices such as broodstock maturation, larval rearing, fingerling production, research animal production, SPF (specific pathogen free) animal production, and caviar and ornamental fish production. Although the use of RAS for other species is considered by many aquaculturalists to be impractical, there has been some limited successful implementation of this with high value product such as barramundi, sturgeon and live tilapia in the US.

# 3

# Fishing

Fishing is the activity of trying to catch fish. Fish are normally caught in the wild. Techniques for catching fish include hand gathering, spearing, netting, angling and trapping.

The term, fishing, may be applied to catching other aquatic animals such as molluscs, cephalopods, crustaceans, and echinoderms. The term is not normally applied to catching aquatic mammals, such as whales, where the term whaling is more appropriate, or to farmed fish.

According to FAO statistics, the total number of commercial fishermen and fish farmers is estimated to be 38 million. Fisheries and aquaculture provide direct and indirect employment to over 500 million people. In 2005, the worldwide per capita consumption of fish captured from wild fisheries was 14.4 kilograms, with an additional 7.4 kilograms harvested from fish farms. In addition to providing food, modern fishing is also a recreational pastime.

Fishing is an ancient practice that dates back to, at least, the beginning of the Paleolithic period about 40,000 years ago. Isotopic analysis of the skeletal remains of Tianyuan man, a 40,000-year old modern human from eastern Asia, has shown that he regularly consumed freshwater fish. Archaeology features such as shell middens, discarded fish bones and cave paintings show that sea foods were important for survival and consumed in significant quantities. During this period, most people lived a hunter-gatherer lifestyle and were, of necessity, constantly on the move. However, where there are early examples of permanent settlements (though not necessarily permanently occupied) such as those at Lepenski Vir, they are almost always associated with fishing as a major source of food.

The ancient river Nile was full of fish; fresh and dried fish were a staple food for much of the population. The Egyptians had implements and methods for fishing and these are illustrated in tomb scenes, drawings, and papyrus documents. Some representations hint at fishing being pursued as a pastime. In India, the Pandyas, a classical Dravidian Tamil kingdom, were known for the pearl fishery as early as the 1st century BC. Their seaport Tuticorin was known for deep sea pearl fishing. The paravas, a Tamil caste centred in Tuticorin, developed a rich community because of their pearl trade, navigation knowledge and fisheries. Fishing scenes are rarely represented in ancient Greek culture, a reflection of the low social status of fishing. However, Oppian of Corycus, a Greek author wrote a major treatise on sea fishing, the *Halieulica* or *Halieutika*, composed between 177 and 180. This is the earliest such work to have survived to the modern day. Pictorial evidence of Roman fishing comes from mosaics. The Greco-Roman sea god Neptune is depicted as wielding a fishing trident. The Moche people of ancient Peru depicted fisherman in their ceramics.

One of the world's longest trading histories is the trade of dry cod from the Lofoten area of Norway to the southern parts of Europe, Italy, Spain and Portugal. The trade in cod started during the Viking period or before, has been going on for more than 1,000 years and is still important.

There are many fishing techniques or methods for catching fish. The term can also be applied to methods for catching other aquatic animals such as molluscs (shellfish, squid, octopus) and edible marine invertebrates.

Fishing techniques include hand gathering, spearfishing, netting, angling and trapping. Recreational, commercial and artisanal fishers use different techniques, and also, sometimes, the same techniques. Recreational fishers fish for pleasure or sport, while commercial fishers fish for profit. Artisanal fishers use traditional, low-tech methods, for survival in third-world countries, and as a cultural heritage in other countries. Mostly, recreational fishers use angling methods and commercial fishers use netting methods.

There is an intricate link between various fishing techniques and knowledge about the fish and their behaviour including migration, foraging and habitat. The effective use of fishing techniques often depends on this additional knowledge.

Fishing tackle is a general term that refers to the equipment used by fishermen when fishing.

Almost any equipment or gear used for fishing can be called fishing tackle. Some examples are hooks, lines, sinkers, floats, rods, reels, baits, lures, spears, nets, gaffs, traps, waders and tackle boxes.

Tackle that is attached to the end of a fishing line is called terminal tackle. This includes hooks, sinkers, floats, leaders, swivels, split rings and wire, snaps, beads, spoons, blades, spinners and clevises to attach spinner blades to fishing lures.

Fishing tackle can be contrasted with fishing techniques. Fishing tackle refers to the physical equipment that is used when fishing, whereas fishing techniques refers to the ways the tackle is used when fishing.

Recreational and sport fishing describe fishing primarily for pleasure or competition. Recreational fishing has conventions, rules, licensing restrictions and laws that limit the way in which fish may be caught; typically, these prohibit the use of nets and the catching of fish with hooks not in the mouth. The most common form of recreational fishing is done with a rod, reel, line, hooks and any one of a wide range of baits or lures such as artificial flies. The practice of catching or attempting to catch fish with a hook is generally known as angling. In angling, it is sometimes expected or required that fish be returned to the water (catch and release). Recreational or sport fishermen may log their catches or participate in fishing competitions.

Big-game fishing describes fishing from boats to catch large open-water species such as tuna, sharks and marlin. Sport fishing (sometimes game fishing) describes recreational fishing where the primary reward is the challenge of finding and catching the fish rather than the culinary or financial value of the fish's flesh. Fish sought after include marlin, tuna, tarpon, sailfish, shark and mackerel although the list is endless.

The fishing industry includes any industry or activity concerned with taking, culturing, processing, preserving, storing, transporting, marketing or selling fish or fish products. It is defined by the FAO as including recreational, subsistence and commercial fishing, and the harvesting, processing, and marketing sectors. The commercial activity is aimed at the delivery of fish and other seafood products for human consumption or for use as raw material in other industrial processes.

There are three principal industry sectors:

1. The commercial sector comprises enterprises and individuals associated with wild-catch or aquaculture resources and the various transformations of those resources into products for sale. It is also referred to as the "seafood industry", although non-food items such as pearls are included among its products.
2. The traditional sector comprises enterprises and individuals associated with fisheries resources from which aboriginal people derive products in accordance with their traditions.
3. The recreational sector comprises enterprises and individuals associated for the purpose of recreation, sport

or sustenance with fisheries resources from which products are derived that are not for sale.

Commercial fishing is the capture of fish for commercial purposes. Those who practice it must often pursue fish far into the ocean under adverse conditions. Commercial fishermen harvest almost all aquatic species, from tuna, cod and salmon to shrimp, krill, lobster, clams, squid and crab, in various fisheries for these species. Commercial fishing methods have become very efficient using large nets and sea-going processing factories. Individual fishing quotas and international treaties seek to control the species and quantities caught.

A commercial fishing enterprise may vary from one man with a small boat with hand-casting nets or a few pot traps, to a huge fleet of trawlers processing tons of fish every day.

Commercial fishing gear includes weights, nets (*e.g.* purse seine), seine nets (*e.g.* beach seine), trawls (*e.g.* bottom trawl), dredges, hooks and line (*e.g.* long line and handline), lift nets, gillnets, entangling nets and traps.

According to the Food and Agriculture Organization of the United Nations, total world capture fisheries production in 2000 was 86 million tons. The top producing countries were, in order, the People's Republic of China (excluding Hong Kong and Taiwan), Peru, Japan, the United States, Chile, Indonesia, Russia, India, Thailand, Norway and Iceland. Those countries accounted for more than half of the world's production; China alone accounted for a third of the world's production. Of that production, over 90 per cent was marine and less than 10 per cent was inland.

A small number of species support the majority of the world's fisheries. Some of these species are herring, cod, anchovy, tuna, flounder, mullet, squid, shrimp, salmon, crab, lobster, oyster and scallops. All except these last four provided a worldwide catch of well over a million tonnes in 1999, with herring and sardines together providing a catch of over 22 million metric tons in 1999. Many other species as well are fished in smaller numbers.

Fish farming is the principal form of aquaculture, while other methods may fall under mariculture. It involves raising fish commercially in tanks or enclosures, usually for food. A facility that releases juvenile fish into the wild for recreational fishing or to supplement a species' natural numbers is generally referred to as a fish hatchery. Fish species raised by fish farms include Atlantic salmon, carp, tilapia, catfish, trout and others.

Increased demands on wild fisheries by commercial fishing has caused widespread overfishing. Fish farming offers an alternative solution to the increasing market demand for fish and fish protein.

### Fish Products

Fish and fish products are consumed as food all over the world. With other seafoods, it provides the world's prime source of high-quality protein: 14-16 per cent of the animal protein consumed worldwide. Over one billion people rely on fish as their primary source of animal protein.

Fish and other aquatic organisms are also processed into various food and non-food products, such as sharkskin leather, pigments made from the inky secretions of cuttlefish, isinglass used for the clarification of wine and beer, fish emulsion used as a fertilizer, fish glue, fish oil and fish meal.

A fishing vessel is a boat or ship used to catch fish in the sea, or on a lake or river. Many different kinds of vessels are used in commercial, artisanal and recreational fishing.

According to the FAO, there are currently (2004) four million commercial fishing vessels. About 1.3 million of these are decked vessels with enclosed areas. Nearly all of these decked vessels are mechanised, and 40,000 of them are over 100 tons. At the other extreme, two-thirds (1.8 million) of the undecked boats are traditional craft of various types, powered only by sail and oars. These boats are used by artisan fishers.

It is difficult to estimate how many recreational fishing boats there are, although the number is high. The term is fluid, since most recreational boats are also used for fishing from time to time. Unlike most commercial fishing vessels, recreational fishing boats are often not dedicated just to fishing. Just about anything that will stay afloat can be called a recreational fishing boat, so long as a fisher periodically climbs aboard with the intent to catch a fish. Fish are caught for recreational purposes from boats which range from dugout canoes, kayaks, rafts, pontoon boats and small dingies to runabouts, cabin cruisers and cruising yachts to large, hi-tech and luxurious big game rigs. Larger boats, purpose-built with recreational fishing in mind, usually have large, open cockpits at the stern, designed for convenient fishing.

Fisheries management draws on fisheries science in order to find ways to protect fishery resources so sustainable exploitation is possible. Modern fisheries management is often referred to as a governmental system of (hopefully appropriate) management rules based on defined objectives and a mix of management means to implement the rules, which are put in place by a system of monitoring control and surveillance.

Fisheries science is the academic discipline of managing and understanding fisheries. It is a multidisciplinary science, which draws on the disciplines of oceanography, marine biology, marine conservation, ecology, population dynamics, economics and management in an attempt to provide an integrated picture of fisheries. In some cases new disciplines have emerged, such as bioeconomics.

**Sustainability**

Issues involved in the long term sustainability of fishing include overfishing, by-catch, marine pollution, environmental effects of fishing, climate change and fish farming.

Conservation issues are part of marine conservation, and are addressed in fisheries science programs. There is a growing gap between how many fish are available to be caught and humanity's desire to catch them, a problem that gets worse as the world population grows.

Similar to other environmental issues, there can be conflict between the fishermen who depend on fishing for their livelihoods and fishery scientists who realise that if future fish populations are to be sustainable then some fisheries must limit fishing or cease operations. Fishing is the activity of catching fish. It is an ancient practice dating back at least 40,000 years. Since the 16th century fishing vessels have been able to cross oceans in pursuit of fish and since the 19th century it has been possible to use larger vessels and in some cases process the fish on board. Fish are normally caught in the wild. Techniques for catching fish include hand gathering, spearing, netting, angling and trapping.

The term fishing may be applied to catching other aquatic animals such as shellfish, cephalopods, crustaceans, and echinoderms. The term is not usually applied to catching aquatic mammals, such as whales, where the term whaling is more appropriate, or to farmed fish. In addition to providing food, modern fishing is also a recreational sport.

According to FAO statistics, the total number of fishermen and fish farmers is estimated to be 38 million. Fisheries and aquaculture provide direct and indirect employment to over 500 million people. In 2005, the worldwide per capita consumption of fish captured from wild fisheries was 14.4 kilograms, with an additional 7.4 kilograms harvested from fish farms.

Fishing is an ancient practice that dates back at least to the Upper Paleolithic period which began about 40,000 years ago. Isotopic analysis of the skeletal remains of Tianyuan man, a 40,000 year old modern human from eastern Asia, has shown that he regularly consumed freshwater fish. Archaeological features such as shell middens, discarded fish bones and cave paintings show that sea foods were important for survival and consumed in significant quantities. During this period, most people lived a hunter-gather lifestyle and were, of necessity, constantly on the move. However, where there are early examples of permanent settlements (though not necessarily permanently occupied) such as those at Lepenski Vir, they are almost always associated with fishing as a major source of food.

Spearfishing with barbed poles (harpoons) was widespread in palaeolithic times. Cosquer cave in Southern France contains cave art over 16,000 years old, including drawings of seals which appear to have been harpooned.

The Neolithic culture and technology spread worldwide between 4,000 and 8,000 years ago. With the new technologies of farming and pottery came basic forms of the main fishing methods that are still used today.

From 7500 to 3000 years ago, Native Americans of the California coast were known to engage in fishing with gorge hook and line tackle. In addition, some tribes are known to have used plant toxins to induce torpor in stream fish to enable their capture.

Copper harpoons were known to the seafaring Harappans well into antiquity. Early hunters in India include the Mincopie people, aboriginal inhabitants of India's Andaman and Nicobar islands, who have used harpoons with long cords for fishing since early times.

The ancient river Nile was full of fish; fresh and dried fish were a staple food for much of the population. The Egyptians invented various implements and methods for fishing and these are clearly illustrated in tomb scenes, drawings, and papyrus documents. Simple reed boats served for fishing. Woven nets, weir baskets made from willow branches, harpoons and hook and line (the hooks having a length of between eight millimetres and eighteen centimetres) were all being used. By the 12th dynasty, metal hooks with barbs were being used. As is fairly common today, the fish were clubbed to death after capture. Nile perch, catfish and eels were among the most important fish. Some representations hint at fishing being pursued as a pastime.

**External Images**

There are numerous references to fishing in ancient literature; in most cases, however, the descriptions of nets and fishing-gear do not go into detail, and the equipment is described in general terms.

Fishing scenes are rarely represented in ancient Greek culture, a reflection of the low social status of fishing. There is a wine cup, dating from c. 500 BC, that shows a boy crouched on a rock with a fishing-rod in his right hand and a basket in his left. In the water below there is a rounded object of the same material with an opening on the top. This has been identified as a fish-cage used for keeping live fish, or as a fish-trap. It is clearly not a net. This object is currently in the Museum of Fine Arts, Boston.

Oppian of Corycus, a Greek author wrote a major treatise on sea fishing, the *Halieulica* or *Halieutika*, composed between 177 and 180. This is the earliest such work to have survived intact to the modern day. Oppian describes various means of fishing including the use of nets cast from boats, scoop nets held open by a hoop, spears and tridents, and various traps "which work while their masters sleep". Oppian's description of fishing with a "motionless" net is also very interesting:

> The fishers set up very light nets of buoyant flax and wheel in a circle round about while they violently strike the surface of the sea with their oars and make a din with sweeping blow of poles. At the flashing of the swift oars and the noise the fish bound in terror and rush into the bosom of the net which stands at rest, thinking it to be a shelter: foolish fishes which, frightened by a noise, enter the gates of doom. Then the fishers on either side hasten with the ropes to draw the net ashore.

The Greek historian Polybius (*ca* 203 BC–120 BC), in his Histories, describes hunting for swordfish by using a harpoon with a barbed and detachable head.

Pictorial evidence of Roman fishing comes from mosaics which show fishing from boats with rod and line as well as nets. Various species such as conger, lobster, sea urchin, octopus and cuttlefish are illustrated. In a parody of fishing, a type of gladiator called retiarius was armed with a trident and a casting-net. He would fight against the murmillo, who carried a short sword and a helmet with the image of a fish on the front.

In India, the Pandyas, a classical Dravidian Tamil kingdom, were known for the pearl fishery as early as the 1st century BC. Their seaport Tuticorin was known for deep sea pearl fishing. The paravas, a Tamil caste centred in Tuticorin, developed a rich community because of their pearl trade, navigation knowledge and fisheries.

From ancient representations and literature it is clear that fishing boats were typically small, lacking a mast or sail, and were only used close to the shore.

In traditional Chinese history, history begins with three semi-mystical and legendary individuals who taught the Chinese the arts of civilization around 2800-2600 BC: of these Fu Hsi was reputed to be the inventor of writing, hunting, trapping, and fishing.

Gillnets existed in ancient times as archaeological evidence from the Middle East demonstrates. In North America, aboriginal fishermen used cedar canoes and natural fibre nets, e.g., made with nettels or the inner bark of cedar. They would attach stones to the bottom of the nets as weights, and pieces of wood to the top, to use as floats. This allowed the net to suspend straight up and down in the water. Each net would be suspended either from shore or between two boats. Native fishers in the Pacific Northwest, Canada, and Alaska still commonly use gillnets in their fisheries for salmon and steelhead.

Both drift gillnets and setnets also have been widely adapted in cultures around the world. The antiquity of gillnet technology is documented by a number of sources from many countries and cultures. Japanese records trace fisheries exploitation, including gillnetting, for over 3,000 years. Many relevant details are available concerning the Edo period (1603-1867). Fisheries in the Shetland Islands, which were settled by Norsemen during the Viking era, share cultural and technological similarities with Norwegian fisheries, including gillnet fisheries for herring. Many of the Norwegian immigrant fishermen who came to fish in the great Columbia River salmon fishery during the second half of the 19th century did so because they had experience in the gillnet fishery for cod in the waters surrounding the Lofoten Islands of northern Norway. Gillnets were used as part of the seasonal round by Swedish fishermen as well. Welsh and English fishermen gillnetted for Atlantic salmon in the rivers of Wales and England in coracles, using hand-made nets, for at least several centuries. These are but a few of the examples of historic gillnet fisheries around the world.

Gillnetting was an early fishing technology in Colonial America, used for example, in fisheries for Atlantic salmon and shad. Immigrant fishermen from northern Europe and the Mediterranean brought a number of different adaptations of the technology from their respective homelands with them to the rapidly expanding salmon fisheries of the Columbia River from the 1860s forward. The boats used by these fisherman were typically around 25 feet (8 m) long and powered by oars. Many of these boats also had small sails and were called "row-sail" boats. At the beginning of the 20th century, steam powered ships would haul these smaller boats to their fishing grounds and retrieve them at the end of each day. However, at this time gas powered boats were beginning to make their appearance, and by the 1930s, the row-sail boat had virtually disappeared, except in Bristol Bay, Alaska, where motors were prohibited in the gillnet fishery by territorial law until 1951.

In 1931, the first powered drum was created by Laurie Jarelainen. The drum is a circular device that is set to the side of the boat and draws in the nets. The powered drum allowed the nets to be drawn in much faster and along with the faster gas powered boats, fisherman were able to fish in areas they had previously been unable to go into, thereby revolutionizing the fishing industry.

During World War II, navigation and communication devices, as well as many other forms of maritime equipment (ex. depth-sounding and radar) were improved and made more compact. These devices became much more accessible to the average fisherman, thus making their range and mobility increasingly larger. It also served to make the industry much more competitive, as the fisherman were forced to invest more into their boats and equipment in order to stay up to date with the current technology.

The introduction of fine synthetic fibres such as nylon in the construction of fishing gear during the 1960s marked an expansion in the commercial use of gillnets. The new materials were cheaper and easier to handle, lasted longer and required less mainatenance than natural fibres. In addition, fibres such as nylon monofilaments become almost invisible in water, so nets made with synthetic twines generally caught greater numbers of fish than natural fibre nets used in comparable situations.

Nylon is highly resistant to abrasion, hence the netting has the potential to last for many years if it is not recovered. This ghost fishing is of environmental concern, however it is difficult to generalise about the longevity of ghost-fishing gillnets due to the varying environments in which they are used. Some researchers have found gill-nets to be still catching fish and crustaceans for over a year after loss , while others have found lost nets to be destroyed by wave action within one month or overgrown with seaweeds, increasing their visibility and reducing their catching potential to such an extent that they became a microhabitat used by small fishes.

This type of net was heavily used by many Japanese, South Korean, and Taiwanese fishing fleets on the high seas in the 1980s to target tunas. Although highly selective with respect to size class of animals captured, gill nets are associated with high numbers of incidental captures of cetaceans, (whales and dolphins). In the Sri Lankan gill net fishery, one dolphin is caught for every 1.7-4.0 tonnes of tuna landed . This compares poorly with the rate of one dolphin per 70 tonnes of tuna landed in the eastern Pacific purse seine tuna fishery. Gillnets were banned by the United Nations in 1993 in international waters, although their use is still permitted within 200 nautical miles (400 km) of a coast.

In the Middle Ages, Brixham was the largest fishing port in the South-West, and at one time it was the greatest in England. Brixham is also famous for being the town where the fishing trawler was invented in the 19th century. These elegant wooden boats were and all over the world, influencing fishing fleets everywhere. Their distinctive sails inspired the song Red Sails in the Sunset which was written aboard a Brixham sailing trawler called the *Torbay Lass*. Known as the "Mother of Deep-Sea Fisheries", its boats sailed all round the coasts and helped to establish the fishing industries of Hull, Grimsby and Lowestoft. In the 1890s there were about 300 trawling vessels here, each owned by one man who was often the skipper of his own boat.

The largest fishing port in Europe from the 1970s onwards has been Peterhead in the North-East corner of Scotland. In its prime in the 1980s Peterhead had over 500 trawlers staying at sea for a week each trip. Peterhead has seen a significant decline in the number of vessels and the value of fish landed has been reduced due to several decades of overfishing which in turn has reduced quotas.

One of the world's longest lasting trade histories is the trade of dry cod from the Lofoten area to the southern parts of Europe, Italy, Spain and Portugal. The trade in cod started during the Viking period or before, has been going on for more than 1000 years and is still important.

Cod has been an important economic commodity in an international market since the Viking period (around 800 AD). Norwegians used dried cod during their travels and soon a dried cod market developed in southern Europe. This market has lasted for more than 1000 years, passing through periods of Black Death, wars and other crises and still is an important Norwegian fish trade. The Portuguese have been fishing cod in the North Atlantic since the 15th century, and clipfish is widely eaten and appreciated in Portugal. The Basques also played an important role in the cod trade and are believed to have found the Canadian fishing banks in the 16th century.

The North American east coast developed in part due to the vast amount of cod, and many cities in the New England area spawned near cod fishing grounds.

Apart from the long history this particular trade also differs from most other trade of fish by the location of the fishing grounds, far from large populations and without any domestic market. The large cod fisheries along the coast of North Norway (and in particular close to the Lofoten islands) have been developed almost uniquely for export, depending on sea transport of stockfish over large distances. Since the introduction of salt, dried salt cod ('klippfisk' in Norwegian) has also been exported. The trade operations and the sea transport were by the end of the 14th century taken over by the Hanseatic League, Bergen being the most important port of trade.

William Pitt the Elder, criticizing the Treaty of Paris in Parliament, claimed that cod was "British gold"; and that it was folly to restore Newfoundland fishing rights to the French.

In the 17th and 18th centuries, the New World, especially in Massachusetts and Newfoundland, cod became a major commodity, forming trade networks and cross-cultural exchanges. In the 20th century, Iceland re-emerged as a fishing power and entered the Cod Wars to gain control over the north Atlantic seas. In the late 20th century and early 21st century, cod fishing off the coast of Europe and America severely depleted cod stocks there which has since become a major political issue as the necessity of restricting catches to allow fish populations to recover has run up against opposition from the fishing industry and politicians reluctant to approve any measures that will result in job losses. The 2006 Northwest Atlantic cod quota is set at 23,000 tons representing half the available stocks, while it is set to 473,000 tons for the Northeast Atlantic cod.

The Pacific Cod is currently enjoying a strong global demand. The 2006 TAC for the Gulf of Alaska and Berning Sea Aleutian Island was set at 574 million pounds.

### Trepanging

To supply the markets of Southern China, Muslim trepangers from Makassar, Indonesia traded with the Indigenous Australians of Arnhem Land from the early 18th century or before. This Macassan contact with Australia is the first recorded example of interaction between the inhabitants of the Australian continent and their Asian neighbours.

This contact had a major impact on the Indigenous Australians. The Macassans exchanged goods such as cloth, tobacco, knives, rice and alcohol for the right to trepang coastal waters and employ local labour. Macassan pidgin became a *lingua franca* along the north coast among different Indigenous Australian groups who were brought into greater contact with each other by the seafaring Macassan culture.

Remains of Macassan trepang processing plants from the 18th and 19th centuries can still be found at Australian locations such as Port Essington and Groote Eylandt, along with stands of tamarind trees (which are native to Madagascar and East Africa) introduced by the seafaring Muslims.

Countless experienced Chinese fishermen came from China's Pearl River Delta region to the California coast in the 1850s. They founded a fishing economy which grew exponentially, extending along the whole of the West Coast of the United States from Canada to Mexico by the 1880s. With entire fleets of small boats the Chinese fishermen caught herring, soles, smelts, cod, sturgeon, and shark in the sea. To catch the larger fish like the barracudas, they used Chinese junks, which were built in large numbers on the American west coast. Among the yield caught by the Chinese American fishermen also included crabs, clams, abalone, salmon, and seaweed – all of which, including shark, formed the staple of Chinese cuisine. The produce were then sold in the local markets or shipped salt-dried for East Asia and Hawaii.

Again this initial success was met with a hostile reaction. Since the late 1850s, European migrants – above all Greeks, Italians and Dalmatians – moved into fishing off the American west coast too, and they exerted pressure on the California legislature, which, finally, expelled the Chinese fishermen with a whole array of taxes, laws and regulations. They had to pay special taxes (Chinese Fisherman's Tax), and they were not allowed to fish with traditional Chinese nets nor with junks. The most disastrous effect occurred when the Scott Act, a federal US law adopted in 1888, established that the Chinese migrants, even when they had entered and were living the US legally, could not re-enter after having temporarily left US territory. The Chinese fishermen, in effect, could therefore not leave with their boats the 3-mile (4.8 km) zone of the west coast. Their work became unprofitable, and gradually they gave up fishing. The only area where the Chinese fishermen remained unchallenged was shark fishing, where they stood in no competition to the European-Americans. Many former fishermen found work in the salmon canneries which until the 1930s were major employers of Chinese migrants, because white workers were barely interested in engaging in such hard, seasonal and relatively unrewarding activities.

The earliest English essay on recreational fishing was published in 1496, shortly after the invention of the printing press. The authorship of this was attributed to Dame Juliana Berners, the prioress of the Benedictine Sopwell Nunnery. The essay was titled *Treatyse of Fysshynge wyth an Angle*, and was published in the second *Boke of St Albans*, a treatise on hawking, hunting and heraldry. These were major interests of the nobility, and the publisher, Wynkyn de Worde, was concerned that the book should be kept from those who were not gentlemen, since their immoderation in angling might "utterly destroye it".

During the 16th century the work was much read, and was reprinted many times. Treatyse includes detailed information on fishing waters, the construction of rods and lines, and the use of natural baits and artificial flies. It also includes modern concerns about conservation and angler etiquette.

Recreational fishing for sport or leisure took off during the 16th and 17th centuries, and coincides with the publication of Izaak Walton's *The Compleat Angler, or Contemplative Man's Recreation* in 1653. This book is the definitive work that champions the position of the angler who loves fishing for the sake of fishing.

More than 300 editions of *The Compleat Angler* have been published, which makes it one of the most frequently reprinted books in English literature. The pastoral discourse is enriched with country fishing folklore, songs and poems, recipes and anecdotes, moral meditations and quotes from classic literature. The central character, Piscator, champions the art of angling, but also tranquilly relishes the pleasures of friendship, verse and song, good food and drink.

Big-game fishing started as a sport after the invention of the motorized boat. In 1898, Dr. Charles Frederick Holder, a marine biologist and early conservationist, virtually invented this sport and went on to publish many articles and books on the subject noted for their combination of accurate scientific detail with exciting narratives.

In literary records, the earliest evidence of the fishing reel comes from a 4th century AD work entitled *Lives of Famous Immortals*. The earliest known depiction of a fishing reel comes from a Southern Song (1127-1279) painting done in 1195 by Ma Yuan (c. 1160-1225) called "Angler on a Wintry Lake," showing a man sitting on a small sampan boat while casting out his fishing line. Another fishing reel was featured in a painting by Wu Zhen (1280-1354). The book *Tianzhu lingqian* (Holy Lections from Indian Sources), printed sometime between 1208 and 1224, features two different woodblock print illustrations of fishing reels being used. An Armenian parchment Gospel of the 13th century shows a reel (though not as clearly depicted as the Chinese ones). The *Sancai Tuhui*, a Chinese encyclopedia published in 1609, features the next known picture of a fishing reel and vividly shows the windlass pulley of the device. These five pictures mentioned are the only ones which feature fishing reels before the year 1651 (when the first English illustration was made); after that year they became commonly depicted in world art.

Tenkara fishing is a type of recreational fly-fishing that originated in Japan at least as long as 430 years ago, when anglers discovered they could dress their flies with pieces of fabric and use those to fool the fish. The art became more refined as the samurai, who were forbidden to practice martial arts and sword fighting in the Edo period, found this type of fishing to be a good substitute for their training: the rod being a substitute to the sword, and walking on the rocks of a small stream good leg and balance training. "Only the samurai were permitted to do it [fish]. So, the samurai who enjoyed ayu fishing would take sewing needles and bend them themselves, and make their own flies by hand.". Nowadays, these rods along with fishing flies, are considered to be a traditional local craft of the Kaga region. The Meboso family in Kanazawa has been making these flies for as long as 400 years themselves, and are currently a 20-generation fly-tiers.

### United Kingdom

Modern western fly fishing is normally said to have originated on the fast, rocky rivers of Scotland and northern England. Other than a few fragmented references, however, little was written on fly fishing until *The Treatyse on Fysshynge with an Angle* was published (1496) within *The Boke of St. Albans* attributed to Dame Juliana Berners. The book contains, along with instructions on rod, line and hook making, dressings for different flies to use at different times of the year. The first detailed writing about the sport comes in two chapters of Izaak Walton's Compleat Angler, which were actually written by his friend Charles Cotton, and described the fishing in the Derbyshire Wye.

British fly-fishing continued to develop in the 19th Century, with the emergence of fly fishing clubs, along with the appearance of several books on the subject of fly tying and fly fishing techniques. In southern England, dry-fly fishing acquired an elitist reputation as the only acceptable method of fishing the slower, clearer rivers of the south such as the River Test and the other 'chalk streams' concentrated in Hampshire, Surrey, Dorset and Berkshire (see Southern England Chalk Formation for the geological specifics). The weeds found in these rivers tend to grow very close to the surface, and it was felt necessary to develop new techniques that would keep the fly and the line on the surface of the stream. These became the foundation of all later dry-fly developments. However, there was nothing to prevent the successful employment of wet flies on these chalk streams, as George E.M. Skues proved with his nymph and wet fly techniques. To the horror of dry-fly purists, Skues later wrote two books, *Minor Tactics of the Chalk Stream*, and *The Way of a Trout with the Fly*, which greatly influenced the development of wet fly fishing. In northern England and Scotland, many anglers also favored wet-fly fishing, where the technique was more popular and widely practised than in southern England. One of Scotland's leading proponents of the wet fly in the early-to-mid-19th century was W.C. Stewart, who published "The Practical Angler" in 1857.

**Scandinavia**

In Scandinavia and the United States, attitudes toward methods of fly fishing were not nearly as rigidly defined, and both dry- and wet-fly fishing were soon adapted to the conditions of those countries.

Lines made of silk replaced those of horse hair and were heavy enough to be cast in the modern style. Cotton and his predecessors fished their flies with long rods, and light lines allowing the wind to do most of the work of getting the fly to the fish. The introduction of new woods to the manufacture of fly rods, first greenheart and then bamboo, made it possible to cast flies into the wind on silk lines. These early fly lines proved troublesome as they had to be coated with various dressings to make them float and needed to be taken off the reel and dried every four hours or so to prevent them from becoming waterlogged.

## United States

American rod builders such as Hiram Leonard developed superior techniques for making bamboo rods: thin strips were cut from the cane, milled into shape, and then glued together to form light, strong, hexagonal rods with a solid core that were superior to anything that preceded them.

Fly reels were soon improved, as well. At first they were rather mechanically simple; more or less a storage place for the fly line and backing. In order to tire the fish, anglers simply applied hand pressure to the rim of the revolving spool, known as 'palming' the rim – see fishing reel. In fact, many superb modern reels still use this simple design.

In the United States, fly fishermen are thought to be the first anglers to have used artificial lures for bass fishing. After pressing into service the fly patterns and tackle designed for trout and salmon to catch largemouth and smallmouth bass, they began to adapt these patterns into specific bass flies. Fly fishermen seeking bass developed the spinner/fly lure and bass popper fly, which are still used today.

In the late 19th century, American anglers, such as Theodore Gordon, in the Catskill Mountains of New York began using fly tackle to fish the region's many brook trout-rich streams such as the Beaverkill and Willowemoc Creek. Many of these early American fly fishermen also developed new fly patterns and wrote extensively about their sport, increasing the popularity of fly fishing in the region and in the United States as a whole. The Junction Pool in Roscoe, where the Willowemoc flows into the Beaver Kill, is the center of an almost ritual pilgrimage every April 1, when the season begins. Albert Bigelow Paine, a New England author, wrote about fly fishing in *The Tent Dwellers*, a book about a three week trip he and a friend took to central Nova Scotia in 1908.

Participation in fly fishing peaked in the early 1920s in the eastern states of Maine and Vermont and in the Midwest in the spring creeks of Wisconsin. Along with deep sea fishing, Ernest Hemingway did much to popularize fly fishing through his works of fiction, including *The Sun Also Rises*. It was the development of inexpensive fiberglass rods, synthetic fly lines, and monofilament leaders, however, in the early 1950s, that revived the popularity of fly fishing, especially in the United States.

In the past years, interest in fly fishing has surged as baby boomers have discovered the sport. Movies such as Robert Redford's film *A River Runs Through It*, starring Brad Pitt, cable fishing shows, and the emergence of a competitive fly casting circuit have also added to the sport's visibility.

# 4

# Fishing Tackle

Fishing tackle, is a general term that refers to the equipment used by fishermen when fishing. Almost any equipment or gear used for fishing can be called fishing tackle. Some examples are hooks, lines, sinkers, floats, rods, reels, baits, lures, spears, nets, gaffs, traps, waders and tackle boxes.

Gear that is attached to the end of a fishing line is called terminal tackle. This includes hooks, leaders, swivels, sinkers, floats, split rings and wire, snaps, beads, spoons, blades, spinners and clevises to attach spinner blades to fishing lures.

Fishing tackle can be contrasted with fishing techniques. Fishing tackle refers to the physical equipment that is used when fishing, whereas fishing techniques refers to the manner in which the tackle is used when fishing.

The term *tackle*, with the meaning "apparatus for fishing", has been in use from 1398 CE. Fishing tackle is also called fishing gear. However the term fishing gear is more usually used in the context of commercial fishing, whereas fishing tackle is more often used in the context of recreational fishing. For this reason, this article covers equipment used by recreational fishermen.

The use of the hook in angling is descended, historically, from what would today be called a "gorge". The word "gorge", in this context, comes from an archaic word meaning "throat". Gorges were used by ancient peoples to capture fish. A gorge was a long, thin piece of bone or stone attached by its midpoint to a thin line. The gorge would be fixed with a bait so that it would rest parallel to the lay of the line. When a fish swallowed the bait, a tug on the line caused the gorge to orient itself at right angles to the line, thereby sticking in the fish's gullet.

A fish hook is a device for catching fish either by impaling them in the mouth or, more rarely, by snagging the body of the fish. Fish hooks have been employed for millennia by fishermen to catch fresh and saltwater fish. Early hooks were made from the upper bills of eagles and from bones, shells, horns and thorns of plants. In 2005, the fish hook was chosen by *Forbes* as one of the top twenty tools in the history of man. Fish hooks are normally attached to some form of line or lure device which connects the caught fish to the fisherman. There is an enormous variety of fish hooks. Sizes, designs, shapes, and materials are all variable depending on the intended purpose of the hook. They are manufactured for a range of purposes from general fishing to extremely limited and specialized applications. Fish hooks are designed to hold various types of artificial, processed, dead or live baits (bait fishing); to act as the foundation for artificial representations of fish prey (fly fishing); or to be attached to or integrated into other devices that represent fish prey.

A fishing line is a cord used or made for fishing. The earliest fishing lines were made from leaves or plant stalk. Later lines were constructed from horse hair or silk thread, with catgut leaders. From the 1850s, modern industrial machinery was employed to fashion fishing lines in quantity. Most of these lines were made from linen or silk, and more rarely cotton.

Modern lines are made from artificial substances, including nylon, polyethylene, dacron and dyneema. The most common type is monofilament made of a single strand. Fishermen often use monofilament because of its buoyant characteristics and its ability to stretch under load. Recently, other alternatives to standard nylon monofilament lines have been introduced made of copolymers or fluorocarbon, or a combination of the two materials. There are also braided fishing lines, *cofilament* and *thermally fused* lines, also known as 'superlines' for their small diameter, lack of stretch, and great strength relative to standard nylon monofilament lines.

Important parameters of a fishing line are its length, material, and weight (thicker, sturdier lines are more visible to fish). Factors that may determine what line an angler chooses for a given fishing environment include breaking strength, knot strength, UV resistance, castability, limpness, stretch, abrasion resistance, and visibility.

Fishing with a hook and line is called angling. In addition to the use of the hook and line used to catch a fish, a heavy fish may be landed by using a landing net or a hooked pole called a gaff. Trolling is a technique in which a fishing lure on a line is drawn through the water. Snagging is a technique where the object is to hook the fish in the body.

A sinker or plummet is a weight used when angling to force the lure or bait to sink more rapidly or to increase the distance that it may be cast. The ordinary plain sinker is traditionally made of lead. It can be practically any shape, and is often shaped round like a pipe-stem, with a swelling in the middle. However, the use of smaller lead based fishing sinkers has now been banned in the U.K., Canada and some states in the U.S.A., since lead can cause toxic lead poisoning if ingested. There are loops of brass wire on either end of the sinker to attach the line. Weights can range from a quarter of an ounce for trout fishing up to a couple of pounds or more for sea bass and menhaden.

The swivel sinker is similar to the plain one, except that instead of loops, there are swivels on each end to attach the line. This is a decided improvement, as it prevents the line from twisting and tangling. In trolling, swivel sinkers are indispensable. The slide sinker, for bottom fishing, is a leaden tube which allows the line to slip through it, when the fish bites. This is an excellent arrangement, as the fisherman can feel the smallest bite, whereas in the other case the fish must first move the sinker before the fisherman feels him.

A fishing rod is an additional tool used with the hook, line and sinker. A length of fishing line is attached to a long, flexible rod or pole: one end terminates with the hook for catching the fish. Early fishing rods are depicted on inscriptions in ancient Egypt, China, Greece and Rome. In Medieval England they were called *angles* (hence the term *angling*). As they evolved they were made from materials such as split Tonkin bamboo, Calcutta reed, or ash wood, which were light, tough, and pliable. The butts were frequently made of maple. Handles and grips were made of cork, wood, or wrapped cane. Guides were simple wire loops.

Modern rods are sophisticated casting tools fitted with line guides and a reel for line stowage. They are most commonly made of fibreglass, carbon fibre or, classically, bamboo. Fishing rods vary in action as well as length, and can be found in sizes between 24 inches and 20 feet. The longer the rod, the greater the mechanical advantage in casting. There are many different types of rods, such as fly rods, spin and bait casting rods, spinning rods, ice rods, surf rods, sea rods and trolling rods.

Fishing rods can be contrasted with fishing poles. A fishing pole is a simple pole or stick with a line which is fastened to the tip and suspended with a hooked lure or bait at the other end.

A fishing reel is a device used for the deployment and retrieval of a fishing line using a spool mounted on an axle. Fishing reels are traditionally used in angling. They are most often used in conjunction with a fishing rod, though some specialized reels are mounted on crossbows or to boat gunwales or transoms. The earliest known illustration of a fishing reel is from Chinese paintings and records beginning about A.D. 1195. Fishing reels first appeared in England around A.D. 1650 and by the 1760s, London tackle shops were advertising multiplying or gear-retrieved reels. Paris, Kentucky native George Snyder is generally given credit for inventing the first fishing reel in America around 1820, a bait casting design that quickly became popular with American anglers.

The natural bait angler usually uses a common prey species of the fish as an attractant. The natural bait used may be alive or dead. Common natural baits include bait fish, worms, leeches, minnows, frogs, salamanders, nightcrawlers and other insects. Natural baits are effective due to the lifelike texture, odour and colour of the bait presented.

The common earthworm is a universal bait for fresh water angling. In the quest for quality worms, some fishers culture their own worm compost or practice worm charming. Grubs and maggots are also considered excellent bait when trout fishing. Grasshoppers, bees and even ants are also used as bait for trout in their season, although many anglers believe that trout or salmon roe is superior to any other bait. Studies show that natural baits like croaker and shrimp are more recognized by the fish and are more readily accepted. A good bait for red drum is menhaden. Because of the risk of transmitting whirling disease, trout and salmon should not be used as bait.

Processed baits, such as groundbait and boilies, can work well with coarse fish, such as carp. For example, in lakes in southern climates such as Florida, fish such as bream will take bread bait. Bread bait is a small amount of bread, often moistened by saliva, balled up to a small size that is bite size to small fish.

Many people prefer to fish solely with lures, which are artificial baits designed to entice fish to strike. The artificial bait angler uses a man-made lure that may or may not represent prey. The lure may require a specialised presentation to impart an enticing action as, for example, in fly fishing. Recently, electronic lures have been developed to attract fish. Fishermen have also begun using plastic bait. A common way to fish a soft plastic worm is the Texas rig.

A bite indicator is a mechanical or electronic device which indicates to an angler that something is happening at the hook end of the fishing line. There are many types of bite indicators. Which ones work best depends on the type of fishing.

Other devices which are widely used as bite indicators are floats which float in the water, and dart about if a fish bites, and quiver tips which are mounted onto the tip of the fishing rod. Bite alarms are electronic devices which bleep when a fish tugs a fishing line. Whereas floats and quiver tips are used as visual bite detectors, bite alarms are audible bite detectors.

Spearfishing is an ancient method of fishing conducted with an ordinary spear or a specialised variant such as a harpoon, trident, arrow or eel spear.

Harpoons are spears which have a barb at the end. Their use was widespread in palaeolithic times. Cosquer cave in Southern France contains cave art over 16,000 years old, including drawings of seals which appear to have been harpooned. Tridents are spears which have three prongs at the business end. They are also called leisters or gigs. They feature widely in early mythology and history.

Modern spears can be used with a speargun. Some spearguns use slings (or rubber loops) to propel the spear. Polespears have a sling attached to the spear, Hawaiian slings have a sling separate from the spear, in the manner of an underwater bow and arrow.

Fishing nets are meshes usually formed by knotting a relatively thin thread. Between 177 and 180 the Greek author Oppian wrote the *Halieutica,* a didactic poem about fishing. He described various means of fishing including the use of nets cast from boats, scoop nets held open by a hoop, and various traps "which work while their masters sleep". Ancient fishing nets used threads made from leaves, plant stalk and cocoon silk. They could be rough in design and material but some designs were amazingly close to designs we use today. Modern nets are usually made of artificial polyamides like nylon, although nets of organic polyamides such as wool or silk thread were common until recently and are still used.

Hand nets are held open by a hoop, and maybe on the end of a long stiff handle. They have been known since antiquity and may be used for sweeping up fish near the water surface like muskellunge and northern pike. When such a net is used by an angler to help land a fish it is known as a *landing net*. In England, hand netting is the only legal way of catching eels and has been practised for thousands of years on the River Parrett and River Severn.

Cast nets are small round nets with weights on the edges which is thrown by the fisher. Sizes vary up to about four metres in diameter. The net is thrown by hand in such a manner that it spreads out on the water and sinks. Fish are caught as the net is hauled back in.

Fishing traps are culturally almost universal and seem to have been independently invented many times. There are essentially two types of trap, a permanent or semi-permanent structure placed in a river or tidal area and pot-traps that are baited to attract prey and periodically lifted. They might have the form of a fishing weir or a lobster trap. A typical trap can have a frame of thick steel wire in the shape of a heart, with chicken wire stretched around it. The mesh wraps around the frame and then tapers into the inside of the trap. When a fish swims inside through this opening, it cannot get out, as the chicken wire opening bends back into its original narrowness. In earlier times, traps were constructed of wood and fibre.

## Fly Fishing Tackle

Fly fishing tackle is equipment used by, and often specialised for use by fly anglers. Fly fishing tackle includes fly lines designed for easy casting, specialised fly reels designed to hold a fly line and supply drag if required for landing heavy or fast fish, specialised fly rods designed to cast fly lines and artificial flies, terminal tackle including artificial flies, and other accessories including fly boxes used to store and carry artificial flies.

Fishing tackle boxes have for many years been an essential part of the anglers equipment. Fishing tackle boxes were originally made of wood or wicker and eventually some metal fishing tackle boxes were manufactured. The first plastic fishing tackle boxes were manufactured by Plano in response to the need for a product that didn't rust. Early plastic fishing tackle boxes were similar to tool boxes but soon evolved into the hip roof cantilever tackle boxes with numerous small trays for a plethora of small tackle, these types of tackle boxes are still available today and still have the disadvantage of mixing up small tackle. Fishing tackle boxes have also been manufactured with drawers and a storage bin under a lid, some of these types of tackle box also have lids on the drawers which helps to stop small tackle from mixing, this turns each drawer into a container which is useful for carrying small tackle to a rod placed away from the main fishing area without having to pack up and fasten the whole tackle box. In response to the various catches, doors and lids that all have their own catches PDY Systems invented the Lift-n-Lok tackle box which fastens the tackle box automatically when picked up by the handle and also closes the clearance gaps at the same time which removes the need for lids on the drawers. The Plano and PDY Systems types of fishing tackle boxes both have their own advocates.

## Fish Hook

A fish hook is a device for catching fish either by impaling them in the mouth or, more rarely, by snagging the body of the fish. Fish hooks have been employed for centuries by fishermen to catch fresh and saltwater fish. In 2005, the fish hook was chosen by *Forbes* as one of the top twenty tools in the history of man. Fish hooks are normally attached to some form of line or lure device which connects the caught fish to the fisherman. There is an enormous variety of fish hooks in the world of fishing. Sizes, designs, shapes, and materials are all variable depending on the intended purpose of the fish hook. Fish hooks are manufactured for a range of purposes from general fishing to extremely limited and specialized applications. Fish hooks are designed to hold various types of artificial, processed, dead or live baits (bait fishing); to act as the foundation for artificial representations of fish prey (fly fishing); or to be attached to or integrated into other devices that represent fish prey (lure fishing).

The fish hook or similar device has probably been around man for many thousands of years. Examples of some of the earliest recorded fish hooks were from Palestine about 7000 BC. Man has crafted fish hooks from all sorts of materials to include wood, animal and human bone, horn, shells, stone, bronze, iron up to present day materials. In many cases, hooks were created from multiple materials to leverage the strength and positive characteristics of each material. Norwegians as late as the 1950s still used juniper wood to craft Burbot hooks. Quality steel hooks began to make their appearance in Europe in the 17th century and hook making became a task for professionals.

## Anatomy and Construction

Commonly referred to parts of a fish hook are: its *point* - the sharp end that penetrates the fish's mouth or flesh; the *barb* - the projection extending backwards from the point, that secures the fish from unhooking; the *eye* - the end of the hook that is connected to the fishing line or lure; the *bend* and *shank* - that portion of the hook that connects the point and the eye; and the *gap* - the distance between the shank and the point. In many cases, hooks are described by using these various parts of the hook.

Contemporary hooks are manufactured from either high-carbon steel, steel alloyed with Vanadium, or stainless steel, depending on application. Most quality fish hooks are covered with some form of corrosion-resistant surface coating. Corrosion resistance is required not only when hooks are used, especially in saltwater, but while they are stored. Additionally, coatings are applied to color and/or provide aesthetic value to the hook. At a minimum, hooks designed for freshwater use are coated with a clear lacquer, but hooks are also coated with gold, nickel, Teflon, tin and different colors. Mustad, for example, produces hooks in six colors, including black.

There are a large amount of different types of fish hooks. At the macro level, there are bait hooks, fly hooks and lure hooks. Within these broad categories there are wide varieties of hook types designed for different applications. Hook types differ in shape, materials, points and barbs, and eye type and ultimately in their intended application. When individual hook types are designed the specific characteristics of each of these hook components are optimized relative to the hook's intended purpose. For example, a delicate dry fly hook is made of thin wire with a tapered eye because weight is the overriding factor. Whereas Carlise or Aberdeen light wire bait hooks make use of thin wire to reduce injury to live bait but the eyes are not tapered because weight is not an issue. Many factors contribute to hook design, including corrosion resistance, weight, strength, hooking efficiency, and whether the hook is being used for specific types of bait, on different types of lures or for different styles of flies. For each hook type, there are ranges of acceptable sizes. For all types of hooks, sizes range from 32 (the smallest) to 20/0 (the largest).

### Shapes and Names

Hook shapes and names are as varied as fish themselves. In some cases hooks are identified by a traditional or historic name, e.g. Aberdeen, Limerick or O'Shaughnessy. In other cases, hooks are merely identified by their general purpose or have included in their name, one or more of their physical characteristics. Some manufacturers just give their hooks model numbers and describe their general purpose and characteristics. For example:

- *Eagle Claw:* 139 is a Snelled Baitholder, Offset, Down Eye, Two Slices, Medium Wire.
- *Lazer Sharp:* L2004EL is a Circle Sea, Wide Gap, Non-Offset, Ringed Eye, Light Wire.
- *Mustad Model:* 92155 is a Beak Baitholder hook.

- *Mustad Model:* 91715D is a O'Shaughnessy Jig Hook, 90 degree angle.
- *TMC Model 300:* Streamer D/E, 6XL, Heavy wire, Forged, Bronze.
- *TMC Model 200R*: Nymph & Dry Fly Straight eye, 3XL, Standard wire, Semidropped point, Forged, Bronze.

The shape of the hook shank can vary widely from merely straight to all sorts of curves, kinks, bends and offsets. These different shapes contribute in some cases to better hook penetration, fly imitations or bait holding ability. Many hooks intended to hold dead or artificial baits have sliced shanks which create barbs for better baiting holding ability. Jig hooks are designed to have lead weight molded onto the hook shank. Hook descriptions may also include shank length as standard, extra long, 2XL, short, etc. and wire size such as fine wire, extra heavy, 2X heavy, etc.

### Single, Double and Treble Hooks

Hooks are designed as either *single* hooks—a single eye, shank and point; *double* hooks—a single eye merged with two shanks and points; or *treble*—a single eye merged with three shanks and three evenly spaced points. Double hooks are formed from a single piece of wire and may or may not have their shanks brazed together for strength. Treble hooks are formed by adding a single eyeless hook to a double hook and brazing all three shanks together. Double hooks are used on some artificial lures and are a traditional fly hook for Atlantic Salmon flies, but are otherwise fairly uncommon. Treble hooks are used on all sorts of artificial lures as well as for a wide variety of bait applications.

### Bait Hook Shapes and Names

Bait hook shapes and names include the Salmon Egg, Beak, O'Shaughnessy, Baitholder, Shark Hook, Aberdeen, Carlisle, Carp Hook, Tuna Circle, Offset Worm, Circle Hook, suicide hook, Long Shank, Short Shank, J Hook, Octopus Hook and Big Game Jobu hooks.

### Fly Hook Shapes and Names

Fly hook shapes include Sproat, Sneck, Limerick, Kendal, Viking, Captain Hamilton, Barleet, Swimming Nymph, Bend Back, Model Perfect, Keel, and Kink-shank.

The hook point is probably the most important part of the hook. It is the point that must penetrate fish flesh and secure the fish. The profile of the hook point and its length influence how well the point penetrates. The barb influences how far the point penetrates, how much pressure is required to penetrate and ultimately the holding power of the hook. Hook points are mechanically (ground) or chemically sharpened. Some hooks are barbless. Historically, many ancient fish hooks were barbless, but today a barbless hook is used to make hook removal and fish release less stressful on the fish. Hook points are also described relative to their offset from the hook shank. A kirbed hook point is offset to the left, a straight point has no offset and a reversed point is offset to the right.

Care needs to be taken when handling hooks as they can 'hook' the user. If a hook goes in deep enough below the barb, pulling the hook out will tear the flesh. There are three methods to remove a hook. The first is by cutting the flesh to remove it. The second is to cut the eye of the hook off and then push the remainder of the hook through the flesh and the third is to place pressure on the shank towards the flesh which pulls the barb into the now oval hole the push the hook out the way it came in.

### Hook Point Types

Hook points are commonly referred to by these names: needle point, rolled-in, hollow, spear, beak, mini-barb, semi-dropped and knife edge. Some other hook point names are used for branding by manufacturers.

### Eyes

The eye of a hook, although some hooks are technically eyeless, is the point where the hook is connected to the line. Hook eye design is usually optimized for either strength, weight and/or presentation. There are different types of eyes to the hooks. Typical eye types include the ring or ball eye, a brazed eye-the eye is fully closed, a tapered eye to reduce weight, a looped eye—traditional on Atlantic Salmon flies, needle eyes, and spade end—no eye at all, but a flattened area to allow secure snelling of the leader to the hook. Hook eyes can also be positioned one of three ways on the shank—up turned, down turned or straight.

There are no internationally recognized standards for hooks and thus size is somewhat inconsistent between manufacturers. However, within a manufacturer's range of hooks, hook sizes are consistent.

Hook sizes generally are referred to by a numbering system that places the size 1 hook in the middle of the size range. Smaller hooks are referenced by larger whole numbers (e.g. 1, 2, 3...). Larger hooks are referenced by increasing whole numbers followed by a slash and a zero (e.g. 1/0 (one aught), 2/0, 3/0...) as their size increases. The numbers represent relative sizes, normally associated with the gap (the distance from the point tip to the shank). The smallest size available is 32 and largest 20/0.

**Fishing Line**

A fishing line is a cord used or made for angling. Important parameters of a fishing line are its length, material, and weight (thicker lines are more visible to fish). Factors that may determine what line an angler chooses for a given fishing environment include breaking strength, knot strength, UV resistance, castability, limpness, stretch, abrasion resistance, and visibility.

Fish are caught with a fishing line by encouraging a fish to bite on a fish hook. A fish hook will pierce the mouthparts of a fish and are normally barbed to make escape less likely. Another method is to use a gorge, which is buried in the bait such that it would be swallowed end first. The tightening of the line would fix it cross-wise in the quarry's stomach or gullet and so the capture would be assured.

Fishing with a hook and line is called angling. In addition to the use of the hook and line used to catch a fish, a heavy fish may be landed by using a landing net or a hooked pole called a gaff.

Trolling is a technique in which a fishing lure on a line is drawn through the water. Trolling from a moving boat is a technique of big-game fishing and is used when fishing from boats to catch large open-water species such as tuna and marlin. Trolling is also a freshwater angling technique most often used to catch trout. Trolling is also an effective way to catch northern pike in the great lakes. It's also good for muskellunge in deeper lake using large baits also known as crankbaits or other big baits using strong line. This technique allows anglers to cover a large body of water in a short time.

Long-line fishing is a commercial fishing technique that uses hundreds or even thousands of baited hooks hanging from a single line.

Snagging is a technique where the object is to hook the fish in the body. Generally, a large treble hook with a heavy sinker is cast into a river containing a large amount of fish, such as a Salmon, and is quickly jerked and reeled in. Due to the often illegal nature of this method some practitioners have added methods to disguise the practice, such as adding bait or reducing the jerking motion.

Modern fishing lines intended for spinning, spin cast, or bait casting reels are almost entirely made from artificial substances, including nylon, polyvinylidene fluoride (PVDF, and called fluorocarbon), polyethylene, Dacron and Dyneema (UHMWPE). The most common type is *monofilament*, made of a single strand. Fishermen often use monofilament because of its buoyant characteristics and its ability to stretch under load. Its ability to stretch has a huge advantage over the early developments as it prevents the rod from being ripped out of the user's hands when given a sudden pull. Recently, other alternatives to standard nylon monofilament lines have been introduced made of copolymers or fluorocarbon, or a combination of the two materials. Fluorocarbon fishing line is made of the fluoropolymer PVDF and it is valued for its refractive index, which is similar to that of water, making it less visible to fish. Fluorocarbon is also a more dense material, and therefore, is not nearly as buoyant as monofilament. Anglers often utilize fluorocarbon when they need their baits to stay closer to the bottom without the use of heavy sinkers. There are also braided fishing lines, *cofilament* and *thermally fused* lines, also known as 'superlines' for their small diameter, lack of stretch, and great strength relative to standard nylon monofilament lines. Both braided and thermally fused 'superlines' are now readily available.

## Specialty Lines

### *Fly Lines*

Fly lines consist of a tough braided or monofilament core, wrapped in a thick waterproof plastic sheath, often of polyvinyl chloride (PVC). In the case of floating fly lines, the PVC sheath is usually embedded with many 'micro-balloons' or air bubbles, and may also be impregnated with silicone or other lubricants to give buoyancy and reduce wear. In order to fill up the reel spool and ensure an adequate reserve in case of a run by a powerful fish, fly lines are usually attached to a secondary line at the butt section, called backing. Fly line backing is usually composed of braided dacron or gelspun monofilaments. All fly lines are equipped with a leader of monofilament or fluorocarbon fishing line, usually (but not always) tapered in diameter, and referred to by the 'X-size' (0X, 2X, 4X, etc.) of its final tip section, or tippet.

### *Tenkara Lines*

Tenkara lines are special lines used for the fixed-line fishing method of tenkara. Traditionally these are furled lines the same length as the tenkara rod. Although original to Japan, these lines are similar to the British tradition of furled leader. They consist of several strands being twisted together in decreasing numbers toward the tip of the line, thus creating a taper that allows the line to cast the fly. It serves the same purpose as the fly-line, to propel a fly forward. They may be tied of various materials, but most commonly are made of monofilament.

#### *Wire Lines*

Wire lines are frequently used as leaders to prevent the fishing line from being severed by toothy fish. Usually braided from several metal strands, wire lines may be made of stainless steel, titanium, or a combination of metal alloys.

### Fishing Sinker

A fishing sinker or plummet is a weight used in conjunction with a fishing lure or hook to increase its rate of sink, anchoring ability, and/or casting distance. Fishing sinkers may be as small as 1/32 of an ounce for applications in shallow water, and even smaller for fly fishing applications, or as large as several pounds or considerably more for deep sea fishing. They are formed into nearly innumerable shapes for diverse fishing applications. Environmental concerns surround the usage of lead and other materials in fishing sinkers.

A large variety of sinkers exist which are used depending on the fish being pursued, the environment, the current and personal preference.

#### *Pyramid Sinkers*

Pyramid sinkers are shaped like a pyramid and are used when it is desirable to anchor on the bottom of water bodies. They are attached to the terminal end of fishing line by loops of brass.

#### *Barrel or Egg Sinkers*

Barrel or egg sinkers are rounded and often bead-like with a narrow hole through which fishing line is threaded. These sinkers are desirable on rock or debris covered substrates.

### *Split-shot Sinkers*

Split-shot sinkers are small and round with a split cutting halfway through the sinker. The split can be placed on a piece of fishing line and then crimped closed. This feature makes adding and removing the weights easy and quick.

### *Bullet Sinkers*

Bullet sinkers are bullet-shaped and used widely in largemouth bass fishing for rigging plastic worms "Texas-style".

### *Dipsey*

Dipsey sinkers are ovate or egg-shaped and are attached to the fishing line with a loop of brass wire embedded in the sinker.

### *Bank Sinker*

Bank sinkers are long and ovate and have a small hole at the top for the fishing line to thread through.

## Materials

Today, an ideal material for a fishing sinker is environmentally nontoxic, cheap and dense. Density is desirable as weights must be as small as possible, in order to minimize visual cues which could drive fish away from a fishing operation.

In ancient times as well as sometimes today, fishing sinkers consisted of materials found ordinarily in the natural environment, such as stones, rocks, or bone. Later, lead became the material of choice for sinkers due to its low cost, ease of production and casting, chemical inertness (resistance to corrosion), and density. However, lead is known to cause lead poisoning and enter the environment as a result of the inevitable occasional loss of fishing sinkers during routine fishing. Thus, most lead-based fishing sinkers have been outlawed in the United Kingdom, Canada, and some states in the United States. Lead based fishing sinkers are banned in all of U.S. and Canadian National Parks. These bans have motivated the use of various other materials in sinkers.

Steel, brass, and bismuth sinkers have been marketed, but fishermen have not widely adopted them due to their lower density and higher cost compared to lead. Tungsten is now in use, especially among largemouth bass fishermen. Although several times costlier than lead, tungsten is just under twice as dense as lead and thus found desirable. The environmental effects of tungsten, however, are essentially unknown. Sandsinkers have also been developed, using sand as weight. However, sand has a comparably low density to that of lead and makes a poor replacement.

# 5

# Fishing Rod

A fishing rod or a fishing pole is a tool used to catch fish, usually in conjunction with the pastime of angling, and can also be used in competition casting. (Sustenance and commercial fishing usually involves nets). A length of fishing line is attached to a long, flexible rod or pole: one end terminates in a hook for catching the fish. A 'fishing pole' is a simple pole or stick for suspending a line (normally fastened to the tip), with a hooked lure or bait. They are most commonly made of fibreglass, carbon fibre, graphite or, classically, bamboo, and are the only fishing levers properly referred to as "poles". In contrast, 'fishing rod' refers to a more sophisticated casting tool fitted with line guides and a reel for line stowage. Fishing rods vary in action as well as length, and can be found in sizes between 24 inches and 20 feet. The longer the rod, the greater the mechanical advantage in casting.

### Carbon Fibre Rods

These high-tech rods are commonly used for coarse fishing in Europe, they are made using a variety of different qualities of carbon fibre. Varying in length from 3 feet through to the longest at about 18.5 feet, they allow very precise positioning of the bait, which in turn enables good catches of fish with accurate feeding, catches of carp on fisheries in the UK frequently reach 90 kg (200 pounds) in a 5 hour match, mostly made up of carp ranging in size from 250 grams (0.5 lb) to 1.3 kg (3 lb) in weight.

### Fly Rods

Fly rods, thin, flexible fishing rods designed to cast an artificial fly, usually consisting of a hook tied with fur, feathers, foam, or other lightweight material. More modern flies are also tied with synthetic materials. Originally made of yew, green hart, and later split bamboo (Tonkin cane), most modern fly rods are constructed from man-made composite materials, including fibreglass, carbon/graphite, or graphite/boron composites. Split bamboo rods are generally considered the most beautiful, the most "classic", and are also generally the most fragile of the styles, and they require a great deal of care to last well. Instead of a weighted lure, a fly rod uses the weight of the fly line for casting, and lightweight rods are capable of casting the very smallest and lightest fly. Typically, a monofilament segment called a "leader" is tied to the fly line on one end and the fly on the other.

Each rod is sized to the fish being sought, the wind and water conditions and also to a particular weight of line: larger and heavier line sizes will cast heavier, larger flies. Fly rods come in a wide variety of line sizes, from size #000 to #0 rods for the smallest freshwater trout and pan fish up to and including #16 rods for large saltwater game fish. Fly rods tend to have a single, large-diameter line guide (called a stripping guide), with a number of smaller looped guides (aka *snake* guides) spaced along the rod to help control the movement of the relatively thick fly line. To prevent interference with casting movements, most fly rods usually have little or no butt section (handle) extending below the fishing reel. However, the *Spey* rod, a fly rod with an elongated rear handle, is often used for fishing either large rivers for salmon and Steelhead or saltwater surf casting, using a two-handed casting technique.

Fly rods are, in modern manufacture, almost always built out of carbon graphite. The graphite fibres are laid down in increasingly sophisticated patterns to keep the rod from flattening when stressed (usually referred to as hoop strength). The rod tapers from one end to the other and the degree of taper determines how much of the rod flexes when stressed. The larger amount of the rod that flexes the 'slower' the rod. Slower rods are easier to cast, create lighter presentations but create a wider loop on the forward cast that reduces casting distance and is subject to the effects of wind. Fly Rods. Furthermore, the process of wrapping graphite fibre sheets to build a rod creates imperfections that result in rod twist during casting. Rod twist is minimized by orienting the rod guides along the side of the rod with the most 'give'. This is done by flexing the rod and feeling for the point of most give or by using computerized rod testing.

### Tenkara Rods

Tenkara rods are a type of fly rod used for tenkara fishing in Japan. A mixture of the rods in the other categories, they are carbon rods, fly rods and telescopic rods all in one. These are ultra-light and very portable telescopic rods. Their extended length normally ranges from 11-13 feet, and they have a very soft action. The action of tenkara rods has been standardized as a ratio of "how many parts are stiffer: how many tip parts bend more easily". The standard actions are 5:5, 6:4, 7:3, and 8:2, with 5:5 being a softer/slower rod, and 8:2 being a stiffer rod. Similar to western fly-rods tenkara rods also have cork, and sometimes even wooden handles, with wooden handles (such as red-pine, and phoenix-tree wood) being the more prized rods due to their increased sensitivity to fish bites and the heavier feel that helps balance the rods. Tenkara rods have no guides. Tenkara is a fixed-line fishing method, where no reel is used, but rather the line is tied directly to the tip of the rod. Like the carbon rods mentioned above this allows for "very precise positioning of the fly, which in turn enables huge catches of fish with accurate feeding". Tenkara fishing is very popular in Japan, where these rods can be found in every major tackle shop. In the US, tenkara is beginning to grow in popularity. IM6, IM7, etc. are trade names for particular graphite produced by the Hexcel Corporation. These numbers are not industry standards nor an indication of quality, especially since other companies use the designations to refer to graphite not made by Hexcel. At best, they allow you to compare the quality of the material used to build different rods by the same manufacturer: an IM7 rod would use better graphite than an IM6 rod if both are made by the same manufacturer. It's more difficult to say the same about rods from two different companies, since they could be made from material from completely different manufacturers.

Modulus refers to the stiffness of the graphite, not the amount of material used or the number of graphite fibres incorporated into the sheets. Buying a rod based solely on the modulus rating is a mistake because other factors must be considered, for example, if the fisherman does not want the stiffest rod for light line techniques or cranking. In addition, other qualities must be incorporated in the graphite itself and the rod must be designed correctly to ensure the best performance and durability of the rod. The other components that go into a quality rod can also add significantly to the cost.

As of both IM and modulus, the higher rating, the lighter and more sensitive the rod is, however such rods also become more brittle due to time and usage.

The most effective use in bass fishing are IM and Modulus rods when one is using lures like worms and jigs. When using faster lures, such as spinnerbaits, and crankbaits, the fisherman does not need to have the sensitivity needed when using the slow lures. The theoretical reason for a more sensitive rod when using a slower lure is that many of the strikes (or more gentle "pickups") will be harder to feel with a rod of a lower modulus rating.

## Spin and Bait Casting Rods

Spin casting rods are rods designed to hold a spin casting reel, which are normally mounted above the handle. Spin casting rods also have small eyes and, not infrequently, a forefinger grip trigger. They are very similar to bait casting rods, to the point where either type of reel may be used on a particular rod. While rods were at one time offered as specific "spin casting" or "bait casting" rods, this has become uncommon, as the rod design is suited to either fishing style, and today they are generally called simply "casting rods", and are usually offered with no distinction as to which style they are best suited for in use. Casting rods are typically viewed as somewhat more powerful than their spinning rod counterparts - they can use heavier line and can handle heavier cover.

## Spinning Rods

Spinning rods are made from graphite or fiberglass with a cork or PVC foam handle, and tend to be between 5 and 8.5 feet (1.5 - 2.6 m) in length. Typically, spinning rods have anywhere from 5-8 large-diameter guides arranged along the underside of the rod to help control the line. The eyes decrease in size from the handle to the tip, with the one nearest the handle usually much larger than the rest to allow less friction as the coiled line comes off the reel, and to gather the very large loops of line that come off the spinning reel's spool. Unlike bait casting and spin casting reels, the spinning reel hangs beneath the rod rather than sitting on top, and is held in place with a sliding or locking reel seat. The fisherman's second and third fingers straddle the "leg" of the reel where it is attached to the reel seat on the rod, and the weight of the reel hangs beneath the rod, which makes for a more comfortable way to fish for extended periods. This also allows the rod to be held in the fisherman's dominant hand (the handle on most modern spinning reels is reversible) which greatly increases control and nuance applied to the rod itself. Spinning rods and reels are widely used in fishing for popular

North American sport fish including bass, trout, pike and walleye. Popular targets for spinning in the UK and European continent are pike, perch, eel and zander (walleye). Longer spinning rods with elongated grip handles for two-handing casting are frequently employed for saltwater or steelhead and salmon fishing. Spinning rods are also widely used for trolling and still fishing with live bait.

### Ultra-light Rods

These rods are used to fish for smaller species, they provide more sport with larger fish, or to enable fishing with lighter line and smaller lures. Though the term is commonly used to refer to spinning or spin-cast rods and tackle, fly rods in smaller line weights have also long been utilized for ultra-light fishing, as well as to protect the thin-diameter, lightweight end section of leader, or tippet, used in this type of angling.

Ultra-light spinning and casting rods are generally shorter (4 - 5.5 feet is common) lighter, and more limber than normal rods. Tip actions vary from slow to fast, depending upon intended use. These rods usually carry 1 to 6 pound (4.5 to 27 N) test fishing line. Some ultra-light rods are capable of casting lures as light as 1/64th of an ounce - typically small spinners, wet flies, crappie jigs, tubes, or bait such as trout worms. Originally produced to bring more excitement to the sport, ultra-light spin fishing is now widely used for crappie, trout, bass, bluegill and other types of panfish.

### Ice Rods

Modern ice rods are typically very short spinning rods, varying between 24 and 36 inches in length. Classic ice rods - still widely used - are simply stiff rod-like pieces of wood, usually with a carved wooden handle, a couple of line guides, and two opposing hooks mounted ahead of the handle to hand-wind the line around. Ice rods are used to fish through holes in the cover ice of frozen lakes and ponds.

### Sea Rods

Sea rods are designed for use with huge fish from the ocean. They are long, (around 4 metres on average), extremely thick, and feature huge and heavy tips, eyes, and handles. The largest of sea rods are for use with sport fishing boats. Some of these are specialized rods, including shark rods, and marlin rods, and are for use with very heavy equipment.

### Surf Rods

The most common type of sea rods are for surf casting. Surf casting rods resemble oversized spinning or bait casting rods with long grip handles intended for two-handed casting techniques. Generally between 10 to 14 feet (3-4 m) in length, surf casting rods need to be longer in order for the user cast the lure or bait beyond the breaking surf where fish tend to congregate, and sturdy enough to cast heavy weighted lures or bait needed to hold the bottom in rough water. They are almost always used in shore fishing (sea fishing from the shoreline) from the beach, rocks or other shore feature. Some surfcasters use powerful rods to cast up to six ounces or more of lead weight, artificial lures, and/or bait over one hundred yards.

### Trolling Rods

Trolling is a fishing method of casting the lure or bait to the side of, or behind, a moving boat, and letting the motion of the boat pull the bait through the water. In theory, for light and medium freshwater gamefishing, any casting or spinning rod (with the possible exception of ultralight rods) can be used for trolling. In the last 30 years, most manufacturers have developed a complete line of generally long, heavily built rods sold as "Trolling Rods", and aimed generally at ocean anglers and Great Lakes salmon and steelhead fishermen. A rod effective for trolling should have relatively fast action, as a very "whippy" slow action rod is extremely frustrating to troll with, and a fast action (fairly stiff) rod is generally much easier to work with when fishing by this method. Perhaps the extreme in this philosophy was reached during the 1940s and early 1950s, when the now-defunct True Temper corporation - a maker of garden tools - marketed a line of trolling rods of 4.5 to 5 ft length made of tempered steel which were square in cross section. They acted as excellent trolling rods, though the action was much too stiff for sportsmanlike playing of fish once hooked. As Great Lakes sportfishing in particular becomes more popular with each passing year, all rod manufacturers continue to expand their lines of dedicated "trolling" rods, though as noted, for most inland lake and stream fishing, a good casting or spinning rod is perfectly adequate for trolling.

### Telescopic Rods

Telescopic fishing rods are designed to collapse down to a short length and open to a long rod. 20 or even 30 ft rods can close to as little as a foot and a half. This makes the rods very easy to transport to remote areas or travel on buses, compact cars, or public buses and subways. Telescopic fishing rods are made from the same materials as conventional one or two piece rods. Graphite and fibreglass or composites of these materials are designed to slip into each other so that they open and close. The eyes are generally but not always a special design to aid in making the end of each section stronger. Various grade eyes available in conventional rods are also available in telescopic fishing rods.

Care for telescopic fishing rods is much the same as other rods. The only difference being that one should not open the telescopic rod in manner that whips a closed rod into the open position rapidly. Whipping or flinging a telescopic fishing rod open may and likely will cause it to be difficult to close. When closing the rods make a slight twisting motion while pushing the sections together. Often the rods come with tip covers to protect the tip and guides.

Telescopic rods are popular among surf fishermen. Carrying around a 12 or 14 ft surf fishing rod, even in 2 pieces, is cumbersome. The shorter the sections the shorter they close, the more eyes they have, and the better the power curve is in them. More eyes means better weight and stress distribution throughout the parabolic arc. This translates to further casting, stronger fish fighting abilities, and less breaking of the rod.

Judging by stone inscriptions, fishing rods go back to ancient Egypt, China, Greece, Trinidad and Tobago, Rome and medieval England, where they were called "angles" (hence the term "angling" as a synonym for fishing). Prior to widespread availability of synthetic materials, such as fibreglass and graphite composites, fishing rods were typically made from split Tonkin bamboo, Calcutta reed, or ash wood, as it was necessary that they be made light, tough, and pliable. The butts were frequently made of maple, with bored bottom; this butt outlasted several tops. Handles and grips were generally of cork, wood, or wrapped cane. Guides were made of simple wire loops or, later, loops with ring-shaped agate inserts for better wear. Even today, Tonkin split-bamboo rods are still popular in fly fishing.

Rods for travellers were made with nickel-silver metal joints, or ferrules, that could be inserted into one another forming the rod. Some of them were made to be used as a walking cane until needed for sport. Since the 1980s, with the advent of flexible, yet stiff graphite ferrules, travel rod technology has greatly advanced, and multi-piece travel rods that can be transported in a suitcase or backpack constitute a large share of the market.

## Modern Design

In theory, an ideal rod should gradually taper from butt to tip, be tight in all its joints (if any), and have a smooth, progressive taper, without 'dead spots'. Modern design and fabrication techniques, along with advanced materials such as graphite, boron and fibreglass composites as well as stainless steel have allowed rod makers to tailor both the shape and action of fishing rods for greater casting distance, accuracy, and fish-fighting qualities. Today, fishing rods are identified by their weight (meaning the weight of line or lure required to flex a fully-loaded rod) and action (describing the location of the maximum flex along the length of the rod).

Modern fishing rods retain cork as a common material for grips. Cork is light, durable, keeps warm and tends to transmit rod vibrations better than synthetic materials, although EVA foam is also used. Reel seats are often of graphite-reinforced plastic, aluminium, or wood. Guides are available in steel and titanium with a wide variety of high-tech metal alloy inserts replacing the classic agate inserts of earlier rods.

Back- or butt-rests can also be used with modern fishing rods to make it easier to pull big fish off the water. These are fork-like supports that help keep the rod in position, providing leverage and counteracting tensions caused by a caught fish.

### Specifications

There are several specifications manufacturers use to delineate rod uses. These include power, action, line weight, lure weight, and number of pieces.

### Power

Also known as "power value" or "rod weight." Rods may be classified as Ultra-Light, Light, Medium-Light, Medium, Medium-Heavy, Heavy, Ultra-Heavy, or other similar combinations. Power is often an indicator of what types of fishing, species of fish, or size of fish a particular pole may be best used for. Ultra-light rods are suitable for catching small bait fish and also panfish, or situations where rod responsiveness is critical. Ultra-Heavy rods are used in deep sea fishing, surf fishing, or for heavy fish by weight. While manufacturers use various designations for a rod's power, there is no fixed standard, hence application of a particular power tag by a manufacturer is somewhat subjective. Any fish can theoretically be caught with any rod, of course, but catching panfish on a heavy rod offers no sport whatsoever, and successfully landing a large fish on an ultralight rod requires supreme rod handling skills at best, and more frequently ends in broken tackle and a lost fish. Rods are best suited to the type of fishing they are intended for.

### Action

"Action" refers to the responsiveness of the rod to bending force (bending curve), and the speed with which the rod returns to its neutral position. An action may be slow, medium, fast, or a combination (e.g. medium-fast.) Fast Action rods flex most in the tip section. Slow rods flex more towards the butt of the rod.

The construction material and construction method of a rod affects its action. Action, however, is also often a subjective description of a manufacturer; some manufacturers list the power value of the rod as its action. A "medium" action bamboo rod may have a faster action than a "fast" fibreglass rod. Action is also subjectively used by anglers, as an angler might compare a given rod as "faster" or "slower" than a different rod.

A rod's action and power may change when line weight is greater or lesser than the rod's specified range. When the line weight used greatly exceeds a rod's specifications a rod may break before the line parts. When the line weight is significantly less than the rod's recommended range the line may part prematurely, as the rod cannot fully flex to accommodate the pull of a given weight fish. In fly rods, exceeding weight ratings may warp the blank or have casting difficulties when rods are improperly loaded.

The action refers to how much a rod bends when a fisherman is casting or have a fish at the end of the line. An extra fast action rod bends just at the tip. A fast action bends in the last quarter of the rod. A moderate-fast action rod bends over the last third. A moderate action rod bends over the last half. A slow action rod bends all the way into the handle. Fast action rods allow the fisherman to make longer casts.

### Line Weight

A rod is usually also classified by the optimal weight of fishing line or in the case of fly rods, fly line the rod should handle. Fishing line weight is described in pounds of tensile force before the line parts. Line weight for a rod is expressed as a range that the rod is designed to support. Fly rod weights are typically expressed as a number from 1 to 12, written as "N"wt (e.g. 6wt.) and each weight represents a standard weight in grains for the first 30 feet of the fly line established by the American Fishing Tackle Manufacturing Association. For example, the first 30′ of a 6wt fly line should weigh between 152-168 grains, with the optimal weight being 160 grains. In casting and spinning rods, designations such as "8-15 lb. line" are typical.

### Lure Weight

A rod may also be described by the weight of lure or hook that the rod is designed to support. Lure weight is usually expressed in ounces or grams.

### Number of Pieces

Rods that are one piece from butt to tip are considered to have the most natural "feel", and are preferred by many, though the difficulty in transporting them safely becomes an increasing problem with increasing rod length. Two-piece rods, joined by a ferrule, are very common, and if well engineered (especially with tubular glass or carbon fibre rods), sacrifice very little in the way of natural feel. Some fishermen do feel a difference in sensitivity with two-piece rods, but most do not.

6

# Fishing Reel

A fishing reel is a device used for the deployment and retrieval of a fishing line using a spool mounted on an axle. Fishing reels are traditionally used in the recreational sport of angling. They are most often used in conjunction with a fishing rod, though some specialized reels are mounted directly to boat gunwales or transoms. The earliest known illustration of a fishing reel is from Chinese paintings and records beginning about AD 1195. Fishing reels first appeared in England around AD 1650 and by the 1760s, London tackle shops were advertising multiplying or gear-retrieved reels. Paris, Kentucky native George Snyder is generally given credit for inventing the first fishing reel in America around 1820, a bait casting design that quickly became popular with American anglers.

In literary records, the earliest evidence of the fishing reel comes from a 4th century AD work entitled *Lives of Famous Immortals*. The earliest known depiction of a fishing reel comes from a Southern Song (1127-1279) painting done in 1195 by Ma Yuan (c. 1160-1225) called "Angler on a Wintry Lake," showing a man sitting on a small sampan boat while casting out his fishing line. Another fishing reel was featured in a painting by Wu Zhen (1280-1354). The book *Tianzhu lingqian* (Holy Lections from Indian Sources), printed sometime between 1208 and 1224, features two different woodblock print illustrations of fishing reels being used. An Armenian parchment Gospel of the 13th century shows a reel (though not as clearly depicted as the Chinese ones). The *Sancai Tuhui*, a Chinese encyclopedia published in 1609, features the next known picture of a fishing reel and vividly shows the windlass pulley of the device. These five pictures mentioned are the only ones which feature fishing reels before the year 1651 (when the first English illustration was made); after that year they became commonly depicted in world art.

### Centrepin Reel

Mainly used for fly fishing. The fly reel or fly casting reel has traditionally been rather simple in terms of mechanical construction, little has changed from the design patented by Charles F. Orvis in 1874. However, in recent years improvements have been made with the development of better reels and drags for fighting larger fish. A fly reel is normally operated by stripping line off the reel with one hand, while casting the rod with the other hand. Early fly reels often had no drag at all, but merely a click/pawl mechanism intended to keep the reel from overrunning when line was pulled from the spool. To slow a fish, the angler simply applied hand pressure to the rim of the revolving spool (known as "palming the rim"). Later, these click/pawl mechanisms were modified to provide a limited adjustable drag. Although adequate for smaller fish, these did not possess a wide adjustment range or the power to slow larger fish.

Modern fly reels typically have more sophisticated disc-type drag systems made of composite materials that feature increased adjustment range, consistency, and resistance to high temperatures from drag friction. Most of these fly reels also feature large-arbor spools designed to reduce line memory, maintain consistent drag and assist the quick retrieval of slack line in the event a hooked fish makes a sudden run towards the angler.

At one time, multiplier fly reels were widely available. These reels had a geared line retrieve of 2:1 or 3:1 that allowed faster retrieval of the fly line. However, their additional weight, complexity and expense did not justify the advantage of faster line retrieval in the eyes of many anglers. As a result, today they are rarely used.

Automatic fly reels use a coiled spring mechanism that pulls the line into the reel with the flick of a lever. Automatic reels tend to be heavy for their size, and have limited line capacity. Automatic fly reels peaked in popularity during the 1960s, and since that time they have been outsold many times over by manual fly reels.

Saltwater fly reels are designed specifically for use in an ocean environment. Saltwater fly reels are normally much larger in diameter than most freshwater fly reels in order to provide a large line and backing capacity designed for the long runs of powerful ocean game fish. To prevent corrosion, saltwater fly reels often use aerospace aluminum frames and spools, electroplated and/or stainless steel components, with sealed and waterproof bearing and drive mechanisms.

### Fly Reel Operation

Fly reels are normally manual, single-action designs. Rotating a handle on the side of the reel rotates the spool which retrieves the line, usually at a 1:1 ratio (i.e., one complete revolution of the handle equals one revolution of the spool).

The centrepin reel is also used for coarse fishing, where one can use it to trot on a fast flowing river. Normally, the float would be pulled under because of the fast current, but the centrepin reel automatically releases line, thus making the float not go under.

### Other Centerpin Reels

Centerpin reels remain popular with anglers in Australia for all forms of fresh and saltwater fishing. Most common is the use of centerpin reels in Australia for surfcasting off the beach. A large diameter spool centerpin reel is attached in a low mount position on a 12-17 foot surfcasting pole by way of a bracket that allows the reel to be rotated 90° to the pole for casting and returned to a position to retrieve line. In the casting position the spool is perpendicular to the pole, opening the face of the reel allowing the line to run off the side of the spool when released in the cast. The surfcasting poles are specifically designed for use with these reels have the reel low mounted as the line is held and released during the cast by the lower hand on the rod, unlike fixed spool or multiplier surf reels, and the lowest ring is of large diameter and around halfway along the poles length.

### Bait Casting Reel

Bait casting reels are reels in which line is stored on a bearing supported revolving spool. The bait casting reel is mounted above the rod, hence its other (though rarely used) name, the *overhead reel*. The bait casting reel dates from at least the mid-17th century, but came into wide use by amateur anglers during the 1870s. Early bait casting reels were often constructed with brass or iron gears, with casings and spools made of brass, German silver, or hard rubber. Early reels were often operated by inverting the reel and using back winding to retrieve line. For this reason, the reel crank handle was positioned on the right side of the reel. As a result, the right-hand crank position for bait casting reels has become customary over the years, though models with left-hand retrieve are now gaining in popularity. Many of today's bait casting reels are constructed using aluminum, stainless steel, and/or synthetic composite materials. They typically include a level-wind mechanism to prevent the line from being trapped under itself on the spool during rewind and interfering with subsequent casts. Many are also fitted with anti-reverse handles and drags designed to slow runs by large and powerful game fish. Because the momentum of the forward cast must rotate the spool as well as propel the fishing lure, bait casting designs normally require heavier lures (>1/4 oz.) for proper operation than with other types of reels. The gear ratio in bait casting reels was initially about 3/1, later standardized at 4/1 in most reels, but recent developments have seen many bait casting reels with gear ratios as high as 5.5/1 or even 7.1/1. Higher gear ratios allow much faster retrieval of line, but sacrifice some amount of power in exchange.

Spool tension on most modern bait casting reels can be adjusted with adjustable spool tension, a centrifugal brake, or a magnetic "cast control." This reduces spool overrun during a cast and the resultant line snare, known as backlash, colloquially called a "bird's nest". Each time a lure of a different weight is attached, the cast control must be adjusted for the difference in weight. The bait casting reel design will operate well with a wide variety of fishing lines, ranging from braided multifilament and heat-fused "superlines" to copolymer, fluorocarbon, and nylon monofilaments. Most bait casting reels can also easily be palmed or thumbed to increase the drag, set the hook, or to accurately halt the lure at a given point in the cast.

A variation of the bait casting reel is the big game reel. These are very large and robust fishing reels, designed and built for heavy saltwater species such as tuna, marlin, sailfish and sharks. Big game reels are not designed for casting, but used for trolling or fishing set baits and lures on the open ocean.

Bait casting reels are sometimes referred to as *conventional reels* in the U.S. They are known as *multiplier reels* in Europe, on account of their geared line retrieve (one turn of the handle resulting in multiple turns of the spool).

**Bait Casting Reel Operation**

A bait casting reel and rod is cast by moving the rod backward, then snapping it forward. The rod is held with the handles of the reel facing upward. During the forward cast, the weight of the lure pulls the line off the reel. The thumb is used to halt the lure at the desired location and to prevent spool overrun. Though modern centrifigal braking systems help to control backlash, using a bait casting reel still requires practice, and a certain amount of finesse on the part of the fisherman for best results.

## Spinning (Fixed Spool) Reel

Reels utilizing a fixed spool were in use in North America as early as the 1870s. They were originally developed to allow the use of artificial flies, or other lures for trout or salmon, that were too light in weight to be easily cast by bait casting reels. Fixed spooled reels are normally mounted below the rod. Spinning reels also solved the problem of backlash, as they did not have a rotating spool to overrun and foul the line. The earliest fixed-spool reels turned the spool 90° in the body of the reel for retrieval, and then reversed it back into casting position. In casting position, line was drawn off in coils from the end of the fixed, non-rotating spool.

In 1948, the Mitchell Reel Company of Cluses, France introduced the Mitchell 300 with a design that oriented the face of the spool forward in a permanently fixed position below the fishing rod. A mechanical line pickup was used to retrieve the cast line (eventually developed into a wire bail design), and an anti-reverse lever prevented the crank handle from rotating while a fish was pulling line from the spool. Because the line did not have to pull against a rotating spool, much lighter lures could be cast than with a bait casting reel. Conversely, halting the cast and stopping the lure at the desired position requires practice in learning to feather the line with the forefinger as it uncoils from the spool. Most spinning reels operate best with fairly limp, flexible fishing lines.

Though spinning reels do not suffer from backlash, the line can be trapped underneath itself on the spool or even detach from the reel in loose loops of line. Various oscillating spool mechanisms have been introduced over the years in an effort to solve this problem. Spinning reels also tend to have more issues with twisting of the fishing line. Line twist in spinning reels can occur from the spin of an attached lure, the action of the wire bail against the line when engaged by the crank handle, or even retrieval of line that is under load (spinning reel users normally pump the rod up and down, then retrieve the slack line to avoid line twist and stress on internal components). Most anglers who use a spinning reel also manually reposition the bail after each cast in order to minimize line twist.

### Fixed Spool Reel Operation

Fixed spool reels are cast by opening the bail, grasping the line with the forefinger, and then using a backward snap of the rod followed by a forward cast while releasing the line with the forefinger at the same time. On the retrieve, the large rotating wire cage or bail (either manually or trigger-operated) serves as the line pickup, restoring the line to its original position on the spool.

### Spin Cast Reel

The first commercial spin cast reels were introduced by the Denison-Johnson Reel Company and the Zero Hour Bomb company in 1949. The spin cast reel is an attempt to solve the problem of backlash found in bait cast designs, while reducing line twist and snare complaints sometimes encountered with traditional spinning reel designs. Just as with the spinning reel, the line is thrown from a fixed spool and can therefore be used with relatively light lures and baits. However, the spin cast reel eliminates the large wire bail and line roller of the spinning reel in favor of one or two simple pickup pins and a metal cup to wind the line on the spool. Traditionally mounted above the rod, the spin cast reel is also fitted with an external nose cone that encloses and protects the fixed spool.

With a fixed spool, spin cast reels can cast lighter lures than bait cast reels, although friction of the nose cone against the unspooling line slightly reduces casting distance compared to spinning reels. Spin cast reels also generally have narrow spools with less line capacity than either bait casting or spinning reels of equivalent size. However, this tends to reduce line snare issues. Like other types of reels, spin cast reels are frequently fitted with both anti-reverse mechanisms and friction drags, and some also have level-wind (oscillating spool) mechanisms. Most spin cast reels operate best with limp monofilament lines, though at least one spin cast reel manufacturer installs a thermally fused "superline" into one of its models as standard equipment. During the 1950s and into the mid 1960's, they were widely used and very popular, though the spinning reel has since eclipsed them in popularity in North America. They remain a favorite fishing tool for beginners.

### Spin Cast Reel Operation

Pressing a button on the rear of the reel disengages the line pickup, and the button is then released during the forward cast to allow the line to fly off the spool. The button is pressed again to stop the lure at the position desired. Upon cranking the handle, the pickup pin immediately re-engages the line and spools it onto the reel.

### Underspin Reel

Underspin or Triggerspin reels are spin cast reels in which the reel is mounted underneath a standard spinning rod. With the reel's weight suspended beneath the rod, underspin reels are generally more comfortable to cast and hold for long periods, and the ability to use all standard spinning rods greatly increases its versatility compared to traditional spin cast reels.

### Underspin Reel Operation

A lever or trigger is grasped or rotated (usually by the forefinger) and this action suspends the line in place. During the forward cast, the lever/trigger is released, and the line flies off the fixed spool. When necessary, the lever can be activated once again to stop the lure at a given point in the cast.

### Direct-drive Reel

Direct-drive reels have the spool and handle directly coupled. When the handle moves forwards, the spool moves forwards, and *vice-versa*. With a fast-running fish, this may have consequences for the angler's knuckles. Traditional fly reels are direct-drive.

### Anti-reverse Reel

In anti-reverse reels, a mechanism allows line to pay out while the handle remains stationary. Depending on the drag setting, line may also pay out, as with a running fish, while the angler reels in. Bait casting reels and many modern saltwater fly reels are examples of this design. The mechanism works either with a 'dog' or 'pawl' design that engages into a cog wheel attached to the handle shaft. The latest design is Instant Anti-Reverse, or IAR. This system incorporates a one-way clutch bearing on the handle shaft to restrict handle movement to forward motion only.

### Drag Mechanisms

Drag is a mechanical means of applying variable pressure to the turning spool in order to act as a friction brake against it. It can be as simple as a flat spring pressing against the edge of the spool, or as sophisticated as a complicated arrangement of leather and Teflon discs. Properly set drag allows larger and more powerful fish to be safely brought to boat and landed, as the drag will "slip" below the breaking point of the line, but in combination with the angle of the rod, it puts relentless pressure on the fish, quickly tiring it. As a rough general rule, drag is nominally set at about one-half of the line's breaking strength. It can be adjusted up or down as needed by the fisherman while playing a fish, though it takes practice to do this without adding too much drag which frequently results in a broken line and a lost fish. With skillful use of the rod and drag mechanism, fish of greater weight than the line's breaking strength can be successfully played and landed, which gives the fish the most sporting chance, and the fisherman the greatest satisfaction in his skills properly applied.

# 7

# Fish Processing

The term fish processing refers to the processes associated with fish and fish products between the time fish are caught or harvested, and the time the final product is delivered to the customer. Although the term refers specifically to fish, in practice it is extended to cover any aquatic organisms harvested for commercial purposes, whether caught in wild fisheries or harvested from aquaculture or fish farming.

Larger fish processing companies often operate their own fishing fleets or farming operations. The products of the fish industry are usually sold to grocery chains or to intermediaries. Fish are highly perishable. A central concern of fish processing is to prevent fish from deteriorating, and this remains an underlying concern during other processing operations.

Fish processing can be subdivided into fish handling, which is the preliminary processing of raw fish, and the manufacture of fish products. Another natural subdivision is into primary processing involved in the filleting and freezing of fresh fish for onward distribution to fresh fish retail and catering outlets, and the secondary processing that produces chilled, frozen and canned products for the retail and catering trades.

There is evidence humans have been processing fish since the early Holocene. These days, fish processing is undertaken by artisan fishermen, on board fishing or fish processing vessels, and at fish processing plants.

Fish is a highly perishable food which needs proper handling and preservation if it is to have a long shelf life and retain a desirable quality and nutritional value. The central concern of fish processing is to prevent fish from deteriorating. The most obvious method for preserving the quality of fish is to keep them alive until they are ready for cooking and eating. For thousands of years, China achieved this through the aquaculture of carp. Other methods used to preserve fish and fish products include the control of temperature using ice, refrigeration or freezing the control of water activity by drying, salting, smoking or freeze-drying the physical control of microbial loads through microwave heating or ionizing irradiation the chemical control of microbial loads by adding acids oxygen deprivation, such as vacuum packing.

Usually more than one of these methods is used. When chilled or frozen fish or fish products are transported by road, rail, sea or air, the cold chain must be maintained. This requires insulated containers or transport vehicles and adequate refrigeration. Modern shipping containers can combine refrigeration with a controlled atmosphere.

Fish processing is also concerned with proper waste management and with adding value to fish products. There is an increasing demand for ready to eat fish products, or products that don't need much preparation.

When fish are captured or harvested for commercial purposes, they need some preprocessing so they can be delivered to the next part of the marketing chain in a fresh and undamaged condition. This means, for example, that fish caught by a fishing vessel need handling so they can be stored safely until the boat lands the fish on shore. Typical handling processes are transferring the catch from the fishing gear (such as a trawl, net or fishing line) to the fishing vessel holding the catch before further handling sorting and grading chilling storing the chilled fish unloading, or landing the fish when the fishing vessel returns to port.

The number and order in which these operations are undertaken varies with the fish species and the type of fishing gear used to catch it, as well as how large the fishing vessel is and how long it is at sea, and the nature of the market it is supplying. Catch processing operations can be manual or automated. The equipment and procedures in modern industrial fisheries are designed to reduce the rough handling of fish, heavy manual lifting and unsuitable working positions which might result in injuries.

An alternative, and obvious way of keeping fish fresh is to keep them alive until they are delivered to the buyer or ready to be eaten. This is a common practice worldwide. Typically, the fish are placed in a container with clean water, and dead, damaged or sick fish are removed. The water temperature is then lowered and the fish are starved to reduce their metabolic rate. This decreases fouling of water with metabolic products (ammonia, nitrite and carbon dioxide) that become toxic and make it difficult for the fish to extract oxygen.

Fish can be kept alive in floating cages, wells and fish ponds. In aquaculture, holding basins are used where the water is continuously filtered and its temperature and oxygen level are controlled. In China, floating cages are constructed in rivers out of palm woven baskets, while in South America simple fish yards are built in the backwaters of rivers. Live fish can be transported by methods which range from simple artisanal methods where fish are placed in plastic bags with an oxygenated atmosphere, to sophisticated systems which use trucks that filter and recycle the water, and add oxygen and regulate temperature.

### Preservation

Preservation techniques are needed to prevent fish spoilage and lengthen shelf life. They are designed to inhibit the activity of spoilage bacteria and the metabolic changes that result in the loss of fish quality. Spoilage bacteria are the specific bacteria that produce the unpleasant odours and flavours associated with spoiled fish. Fish normally host many bacteria that are not spoilage bacteria, and most of the bacteria present on spoiled fish played no role in the spoilage. To flourish, bacteria need the right temperature, sufficient water and oxygen, and surroundings that are not too acidic. Preservation techniques work by interrupting one or more of these needs. Preservation techniques can be classified as follows.

### Control of Temperature

If the temperature is decreased, the metabolic activity in the fish from microbial or autolytic processes can be reduced or stopped. This is achieved by refrigeration where the temperature is dropped to about 0 °C, or freezing where the temperature is dropped below -18°C. On fishing vessels, the fish are refrigerated mechanically by circulating cold air or by packing the fish in boxes with ice. Forage fish, which are often caught in large numbers, are usually chilled with refrigerated or chilled seawater. Once chilled or frozen, the fish need further cooling to maintain the low temperature. There are key issues with fish cold store design and management, such as how large and energy efficient they are, and the way they are insulated and palletized.

An effective method of preserving the freshness of fish is to chill with ice by distributing ice uniformly around the fish. It is a safe cooling method that keeps the fish moist and in an easily stored form suitable for transport. It has become widely used since the development of mechanical refrigeration, which makes ice easy and cheap to produce. Ice is produced in various shapes; crushed ice and ice flakes, plates, tubes and blocks are commonly used to cool fish. Particularly effective is slurry ice, made from micro crystals of ice formed and suspended within a solution of water and a freezing point depressant, such as common salt.

The water activity, ($a_w$), in a fish is defined as the ratio of the water vapour pressure in the flesh of the fish to the vapour pressure of pure water at the same temperature and pressure. It ranges between 0 and 1, and is a parameter that measures how available the water is in the flesh of the fish. Available water is necessary for the microbial and enzymatic reactions involved in spoilage. There are a number of techniques that have been or are used to tie up the available water or remove it by reducing the $a_w$. Traditionally, techniques such as drying, salting and smoking have been used, and have been used for thousands of years. These techniques can be very simple, for example, by using solar drying. In more recent times, freeze-drying, water binding humectants, and fully automated equipment with temperature and humidity control have been added. Often a combination of these techniques is used.

## Physical Control of Microbial Loads

Heat or ionizing irradiation can be used to kill the bacteria that cause decomposition. Heat is applied by cooking, blanching or microwave heating in a manner that pasteurizes or sterilizes fish products. Cooking or pasteurizing does not completely inactivate microorganisms and may need to be followed with refrigeration to preserve fish products and increase their shelf life. Sterilised products are stable at ambient temperatures up to 40°C, but to ensure they remain sterilized they need packaging in metal cans or retortable pouches before the heat treatment.

## Chemical Control of Microbial Loads

Microbial growth and proliferation can be inhibited by a technique called biopreservation. Biopreservation is achieved by adding antimicrobials or by increasing the acidity of the fish muscle. Most bacteria stop multiplying when the pH is less than 4.5. Acidity is increased by fermentation, marination or by directly adding acids (acetic, citric, lactic) to fish products. Lactic acid bacteria produce the antimicrobial nisin which further enhances preservation. Other preservatives include nitrites, sulphites, sorbates, benzoates and essential oils.

### Control of the Oxygen Reduction Potential

Spoilage bacteria and lipid oxidation usually need oxygen, so reducing the oxygen around fish can increase shelf life. This is done by controlling or modifying the atmosphere around the fish, or by vacuum packaging. Controlled or modified atmospheres have specific combinations of oxygen, carbon dioxide and nitrogen, and the method is often combined with refrigeration for more effective fish preservation.

### Combined Techniques

Two or more of these techniques are often combined. This can improve preservation and reduce unwanted side effects such as the denaturation of nutrients by severe heat treatments. Common combinations are salting/drying, salting/marinating, salting/smoking, drying/smoking, pasteurization/refrigeration and controlled atmosphere/refrigeration. Other process combinations are currently being developed along the multiple hurdle theory.

### Automated Processes

The search for higher productivity and the increase of labor cost has driven the development of computer vision technology, electronic scales and automatic skinning and filleting machines.

Waste produced during fish processing operations can be solid or liquid.

*Solid wastes:* include skin, viscera, fish heads and carcasses (fish bones). Solid waste can be recycled in fish meal plants or it can be treated as municipal waste.

*Liquid wastes:* include bloodwater and brine from drained storage tanks, and water discharges from washing and cleaning. This waste may need holding temporarily, and should be disposed of without damage to the environment. How liquid waste should be disposed from fish processing operations depends on the content levels in the waste of solid and organic matter, as well as nitrogen and phosphorous content, and oil and grease content.

It also depends on an assessment of parameters such acidity levels, temperature, odour, and biochemical oxygen demand and chemical oxygen demand. The magnitude of waste management issues depends on how much waste volume there is, the nature of the pollutants it carries, the rate at which it is discharged and the capacity of the receiving environment to assimilate the pollutants. Many countries dispose of such liquid wastes through their municipal sewage systems or directly into a waterway. The receiving waterbody should be able to degrade the organic and inorganic waste components in a way that does not damage the aquatic ecosystem.

Treatments can be primary and secondary:

- *Primary treatments:* use physical methods such as flotation, screening, and sedimentation to remove oil and grease and other suspended solids.
- *Secondary treatments:* use biological and physicochemical means.

Biological treatments use microorganisms to metabolise the organic polluting matter into energy and biomass. "These microorganisms can be aerobic or anaerobic. The most used aerobic processes are activated sludge system, aerated lagoons, trickling filters or bacterial beds and the rotating biological contractors. In anaerobic processes, the anaerobic microorganisms digest the organic matter in tanks to produce gases (mainly methane and $CO_2$) and biomass. Anaerobic digesters are sometimes heated, using part of the methane produced, to maintain a temperature of 30 to 35°C. In the physicochemical treatments, also called coagulation-flocculation, a chemical substance is added to the effluent to reduce the surface charges responsible for particle repulsions in a colloidal suspension, thus reducing the forces that keep its particles apart. This reduction in charge causes flocculation (agglomeration) and particles of larger sizes are settled and clarified effluent is obtained. The sludge produced by primary and secondary treatments is further processed in digesting tanks through anaerobic processes or sprayed over land as a fertilizer. In the latter case, care must be exercised to ensure that the sludge is freed of its pathogens."

## Transport

Fish is transported widely in ships, and by land and air, and much fish is traded internationally. It is traded live, fresh, frozen, cured and canned. Live, fresh and frozen fish need special care.

### *Live Fish*

When live fish are transported they need oxygen, and the carbon dioxide and ammonia that result from respiration must not be allowed to build up. Most fish transported live are placed in water supersaturated with oxygen (though catfish can breath air directly through their gills and body skin, and the climbing perch has special air breathing organs). The fish are often "conditioned" (starved) before they are transported to reduce their metabolism and increase packing density, and the water can be cooled to further reduce metabolism. Live crustaceans can be packed in wet sawdust to keep the air humid.

### *By Air*

Over five per cent of the global fish production is transported by air. Air transport needs special care in preparation and handling and careful scheduling. Airline transport hubs often require cargo transfers under their own tight schedules. This can influence when the product is delivered, and consequently the condition it is in when it is delivered. The air shipment of leaking seafood packages causes corrosion damage to aircraft, and each year, in the US, requires millions of dollars to repair the damage. Most airlines prefer fish that is packed in dry ice or gel, and not packed in ice.

### *By Land or Sea*

The most challenging aspect of fish transportation by sea or by road is the maintenance of the cold chain, for fresh, chilled and frozen products and the optimisation of the packing and stowage density. Maintaining the cold chain requires the use of insulated containers or transport vehicles and adequate quantities of coolants or mechanical refrigeration. Continuous temperature monitors are used to provide evidence that the cold chain has not been broken during transportation. Excellent development in food packaging and handling allow rapid and efficient loading, transport and unloading of fish and fishery products by road or by sea. Also, transport of fish by sea allows for the use of special containers that carry fish under vacuum, modified or controlled atmosphere, combined with refrigeration.

### Quality and Safety

the International Organization for Standardisation, (ISO), is the worldwide federation of national standards bodies. ISO defines *quality* as "the totality of features and characteristics of a product or service that bear on its ability to satisfy stated or implied needs." The quality of fish and fish products depends on safe and hygienic practices. Outbreaks of fish-borne illnesses are reduced if appropriate practices are followed when handling, manufacturing, refrigerating and transporting fish and fish products. Ensuring standards of quality and safety are high also minimizes the post-harvest losses.

The Hazard Analysis and Critical Control Points (HACCP) system of assuring food safety and quality has now gained worldwide recognition as the most cost-effective and reliable system available. It is based on the identification of risks, minimizing those risks through the design and layout of the physical environment in which high standards of hygiene can be assured, sets measurable standards and establishes monitoring systems. HACCP also establishes procedures for verifying that the system is working effectively. HACCP is a sufficiently flexible system to be successfully applied at all critical stages—from harvesting of fish to reaching the consumer. For such a system to work successfully, all stakeholders must cooperate which entails increasing the national capacity for introducing and maintaining HACCP measures. The system's control authority needs to design and implement the system, ensuring that monitoring and corrective measures are put in place.

The fishing industry must ensure that their fish handling, processing and transportation facilities meet requisite standards. Adequate training of both industry and control authority staff must be provided by support institutions, and channels for feedback from consumers established. Ensuring high standards for quality and safety is good economics, minimizing losses that result from spoilage, damage to trade and from illness among consumers.

Finfish are typically presented physically for marketing in one of the following forms:

- *whole fish:* the fish as it originally came from the water, with no physical processing;
- *drawn fish:* a whole fish which has been eviscerated, that is, had its internal organs removed;
- *dressed fish:* fish that has been scaled and eviscerated, and is ready to cook.
- *pan dressed fish:* a dressed fish which has had its head, tail, and fins removed, so it will fit in a pan.
- *filleted fish:* the "fleshy sides of the fish, cut lengthwise from the fish along the backbone. They are usually boneless, although in some fish small bones called "pins" may be present; skin may be present on one side, too. Butterfly fillets may be available. This refers to two fillets held together by the uncut flesh and skin of the belly".
- *fish steaks:* large dressed fish can be cut into cross section slices, usually half to one inch thick, and usually with a cross section of the backbone.
- *fish sticks:* are pieces of fish cut from blocks of frozen fillets into portions at least 3/8-inch thick. Sticks are available in fried form ready to heat or frozen raw, coated with batter and breaded, ready to be cooked.

- *fish cakes:* are prepared from flaked fish, potatoes, and seasonings, and shaped into cakes, coated with batter, breaded, and then packaged and frozen, ready-to-be-cooked.

In general value addition means "any additional activity that in one way or the other change the nature of a product thus adding to its value at the time of sale." Value addition is an expanding sector in the food processing industry, especially in export markets. Value is added to fish and fishery products depending on the requirement of different markets. Globally a transition period is taking place where cooked products are replacing traditional raw products in consumer preference. For example, there is a demand in urban centres for "ready to eat" and "ready to cook" convenience products in a frozen condition. There is also a need to divert low value fish to human consumption which can be facilitated by diversifying fishery products to value added products, such as minced meat from low priced fishes.

In addition to preservation, fish can be industrially processed into a wide array of products to increase their economic value and allow the fishing industry and exporting countries to reap the full benefits of their aquatic resources. In addition, value processes generate further employment and hard currency earnings. This is more important nowadays because of societal changes that have led to the development of outdoor catering, convenience products and food services requiring fish products ready to eat or requiring little preparation before serving.

However, despite the availability of technology, careful consideration should be given to the economic feasibility aspects, including distribution, marketing, quality assurance and trade barriers, before embarking on a value addition fish process.

***Surimi***

Surimi and surimi-based products are an example of value added products. Surimi is prepared from the mechanically deboned, washed (bleached) and stabilised flesh of fish. "It is an intermediate product used in the preparation of a variety of ready to eat seafood such as kamaboko, fish sausage, crab legs and imitation shrimp products. Surimi-based products are gaining more prominence worldwide, because of the emergence of Japanese restaurants and culinary traditions in North America, Europe and elsewhere. Ideally, surimi should be made from low-value, white fish with excellent gelling ability and which are abundant and available year-round. At present, Alaskan pollack accounts for a large proportion of the surimi supply. Other species, such as sardine, mackerel, barracuda, striped mullet have been successfully used for surimi production."

***Fishmeal and Fish Oil***

A significant proportion of the world catch (20%) is processed into fishmeal and fish oil. Fishmeal is a ground solid product that is obtained by removing most of the water and some or all of the oil from fish or fish waste. This industry was launched in the 19th century, based mainly on surplus catches of herring from seasonal coastal fisheries to produce oil for industrial uses in leather tanning and in the production of soap, glycerol and other non-food products. Presently, it uses small oily fish to produce fishmeal and oil. It is worthy to mention that, only where it is uneconomic or impracticable for human consumption, should the catch be reduced to fishmeal and oil. Indeed, cycling fish through poultry or pigs is a loss because there is a need for 3 kg of edible fish to produce approximately 1 kg of edible chicken or pork.

There is evidence humans have been processing fish since the early Holocene. For example, fishbones (c. 8140-7550 BP, uncalibrated) at Atlit-Yam, a submerged Neolithic site off Israel, have been analysed. What emerged was a picture of a pile of fish gutted and processed in a size-dependent manner, and then stored for future consumption or trade. This scenario suggests that technology for fish storage was already available, and that the Atlit-Yam inhabitants could enjoy the economic stability resulting from food storage and trade with mainland sites.

# 8

# Wild Fisheries

A fishery is an area with an associated fish or aquatic population which is harvested for its commercial value. Fisheries can be marine (saltwater) or freshwater. They can also be wild or farmed. This article is an overview of the habitats occupied by the worlds' wild fisheries, and the human impacts on those habitats.

Wild fisheries are sometimes called capture fisheries. The aquatic life they support is not controlled in any meaningful way and needs to be "captured" or fished. Wild fisheries exist primarily in the oceans, and particularly around coasts and continental shelves. They also exist in lakes and rivers. Issues with wild fisheries are overfishing and pollution. Significant wild fisheries have collapsed or are in danger of collapsing, due to overfishing and pollution. Overall, production from the world's wild fisheries has levelled out, and may be starting to decline.

As a contrast to wild fisheries, farmed fisheries can operate in sheltered coastal waters, in rivers, lakes and ponds, or in enclosed bodies of water such as tanks. Farmed fisheries are technological in nature, and revolve around developments in aquaculture. Farmed fisheries are expanding, and Chinese aquaculture in particular is making many advances. Nevertheless, the majority of fish consumed by humans continues to be sourced from wild fisheries. As of the early 21st century, fish is humanity's only significant wild food source.

According to the Food and Agriculture Organization (FAO), the world harvest by commercial fisheries in 2005 consisted of 93.2 million tonnes of aquatic animals captured in wild fisheries, plus another 1.3 million tons of aquatic plants (seaweed etc). This can be contrasted with 48.1 million tonnes harvested in fish farms and 14.8 million tons of aquatic plants produced by aquaculture.

The productivity of marine fisheries is largely determined by marine topography, including its interaction with ocean currents and the diminishment of sunlight with depth.

Marine topography is defined by various coastal and oceanic landforms, ranging from coastal estuaries and shorelines; to continental shelves and coral reefs; to underwater and deep sea features such as ocean rises and seamounts.

An ocean current is continuous, directed movement of ocean water. Ocean currents are rivers of relatively warm or cold water within the ocean. The currents are generated from the forces acting upon the water like the planet rotation, the wind, the temperature and salinity (hence isopycnal) differences and the gravitation of the moon. The depth contours, the shoreline and other currents influence the current's direction and strength.

Oceanic gyres are large-scale ocean currents caused by the Coriolis effect. Wind-driven surface currents interact with these gyres and the underwater topography, such as seamounts and the edge of continental shelves, to produce downwellings and upwellings. These can transport nutrients and provide feeding grounds for plankton eating forage fish. This in turn draws larger fish that predate on the forage fish, and can result in productive fishing grounds. Most upwellings are coastal, and many of them support some of the most productive fisheries in the world, such as small pelagics (sardines, anchovies, etc.). Regions of upwelling include coastal Peru, Chile, Arabian Sea, western South Africa, eastern New Zealand and the California coast.

Phytoplankton is usually the primary producer (the first level in the food chain or the first trophic level). Phytoplankton converts inorganic carbon into protoplasm. Phytoplankton is consumed by microscopic animals called zooplankton. These are the second level in the food chain, and include krill, the larva of fish, squid, lobsters and crabs–as well as the small crustaceans called copepods, and many other types. Zooplankton is consumed both by other, larger predatory zooplankters and by fish (the third level in the food chain). Fish that eat zooplankton could constitute the fourth trophic level, while seals consuming the fish are the fifth. Alternatively, for example, whales may consume zooplankton directly - leading to an environment with one less trophic level.

Aquatic habitats have been classified into marine and freshwater ecoregions by the Worldwide Fund for Nature (WWF). An ecoregion is defined as a "relatively large unit of land or water containing a characteristic set of natural communities that share a large majority of their species, dynamics, and environmental conditions.

Estuaries are often associated with high rates of biological productivity. They are small, in demand, impacted by events far upstream or out at sea, and concentrate materials such as pollutants and sediments.

Lagoons are bodies of comparatively shallow salt or brackish water separated from the deeper sea by a shallow or exposed sandbank, coral reef, or similar feature. *Lagoon* refers to both coastal lagoons formed by the build-up of sandbanks or reefs along shallow coastal waters, and the lagoons in atolls, formed by the growth of coral reefs on slowly sinking central islands. Lagoons that are fed by freshwater streams are estuaries.

The intertidal zone (foreshore) is the area that is exposed to the air at low tide and submerged at high tide, for example, the area between tide marks. This area can include many different types of habitats, including steep rocky cliffs, sandy beaches or vast mudflats. The area can be a narrow strip, as in Pacific islands that have only a narrow tidal range, or can include many meters of shoreline where shallow beach slope interacts with high tidal excursion.

Continental shelves are the extended perimeters of each continent and associated coastal plain, which is covered during interglacial periods such as the current epoch by relatively shallow seas (known as shelf seas) and gulfs.

The shelf usually ends at a point of decreasing slope (called the shelf break). The sea floor below the break is the continental slope. Below the slope is the continental rise, which finally merges into the deep ocean floor, the abyssal plain. The continental shelf and the slope are part of the continental margin.

Continental shelves are shallow (averaging 140 metres or 460 feet), and the sunlight available means they can teem with life. The shallowest parts of the continental shelf are called fishing banks. There the sunlight penetrates to the seafloor and the plankton, on which fish feed, thrive.

Fixed-net fishing on the littoral zone along the Suhua Highway on the East coast of Taiwan. The littoral zone is the part of the ocean closest to the shore. The word *littoral* comes from the Latin *litoralis*, which means *seashore*. The littoral zone extends from the high water mark to near shore areas that are permanently submerged, and includes the intertidal zone. Definitions vary. Encyclopaedia Britannica defines the littoral zone in a thoroughly vague way as the "marine ecological realm that experiences the effects of tidal and longshore currents and breaking waves to a depth of 5 to 10 metres (16 to 33 feet) below the low-tide level, depending on the intensity of storm waves". The US Navy defines it as extending "from the shoreline to 600 feet (183 meters) out into the water".

The sublittoral zone is the part of the ocean extending from the seaward edge of the littoral zone to the edge of the continental shelf. It is sometimes called the neritic zone. Websters defines the neritic zone as the region of shallow water adjoining the seacoast. The word *neritic* perhaps comes from the new Latin *nerita,* which refers to a genus of marine snails, 1891. The sublittoral zone is relatively shallow, extending to about 200 meters (100 fathoms), and generally has well-oxygenated water, low water pressure, and relatively stable temperature and salinity levels. These, combined with presence of light and the resulting photosynthetic life, such as phyoplankton and floating sargassum make the sublittoral zone the location of the majority of sea life. *Glossary of Coastal Terminology* Washington State Department of Ecology, publication Pollution is the introduction of contaminants into an environment. Wild fisheries flourish in oceans, lakes, and rivers, and the introduction of contaminants is an issue of concern, especially as regards plastics, pesticides, heavy metals, and other industrial and agricultural pollutants which do not disintegrate rapidly in the environment. Land run-off and industrial, agricultural, and domestic waste enter rivers and are discharged into the sea. Pollution from ships is also a problem.

**Plastic Waste**

Marine debris is human-created waste that ends up floating in the sea. Oceanic debris tends to accumulate at the centre of gyres and coastlines, frequently washing aground where it is known as beach litter. Eighty per cent of all known marine debris is plastic - a component that has been rapidly accumulating since the end of World War II. Plastics accumulate because they don't biodegrade as many other substances do; while they will photodegrade on exposure to the sun, they do so only under dry conditions, as water inhibits this process.

Discarded plastic bags, six pack rings and other forms of plastic waste which finish up in the ocean present dangers to wildlife and fisheries. Aquatic life can be threatened through entanglement, suffocation, and ingestion.

Nurdles, also known as mermaids' tears, are plastic pellets typically under five millimetres in diameter, and are a major contributor to marine debris. They are used as a raw material in plastics manufacturing, and are thought to enter the natural environment after accidental spillages. Nurdles are also created through the physical weathering of larger plastic debris. They strongly resemble fish eggs, only instead of finding a nutritious meal, any marine wildlife that ingests them will likely starve, be poisoned and die.

Many animals that live on or in the sea consume flotsam by mistake, as it often looks similar to their natural prey. Plastic debris, when bulky or tangled, is difficult to pass, and may become permanently lodged in the digestive tracts of these animals, blocking the passage of food and causing death through starvation or infection. Tiny floating particles also resemble zooplankton, which can lead filter feeders to consume them and cause them to enter the ocean food chain. In samples taken from the North Pacific Gyre in 1999 by the Algalita Marine Research Foundation, the mass of plastic exceeded that of zooplankton by a factor of six. More recently, reports have surfaced that there may now be 30 times more plastic than plankton, the most abundant form of life in the ocean.

Toxic additives used in the manufacture of plastic materials can leech out into their surroundings when exposed to water. Waterborne hydrophobic pollutants collect and magnify on the surface of plastic debris, thus making plastic far more deadly in the ocean than it would be on land. Hydrophobic contaminants are also known to bioaccumulate in fatty tissues, biomagnifying up the food chain and putting great pressure on apex predators. Some plastic additives are known to disrupt the endocrine system when consumed, others can suppress the immune system or decrease reproductive rates.

Apart from plastics, there are particular problems with other toxins which do not disintegrate rapidly in the marine environment. Heavy metals are metallic chemical elements that have a relatively high density and are toxic or poisonous at low concentrations. Examples are mercury, lead, nickel, arsenic and cadmium. Other persistent toxins are PCBs, DDT, pesticides, furans, dioxins and phenols.

Such toxins can accumulate in the tissues of many species of aquatic life in a process called bioaccumulation. They are also known to accumulate in benthic environments, such as estuaries and bay muds: a geological record of human activities of the last century.

Some specific examples are:

- Chinese and Russian industrial pollution such as phenols and heavy metals in the Amur River have devastated fish stocks and damaged its estuary soil.
- Wabamun Lake in Alberta, Canada, once the best whitefish lake in the area, now has unacceptable levels of heavy metals in its sediment and fish.
- Acute and chronic pollution events have been shown to impact southern California kelp forests, though the intensity of the impact seems to depend on both the nature of the contaminants and duration of exposure.

Due to their high position in the food chain and the subsequent accumulation of heavy metals from their diet, mercury levels can be high in larger species such as bluefin and albacore. As a result, in March 2004 the United States FDA issued guidelines recommending that pregnant women, nursing mothers and children limit their intake of tuna and other types of predatory fish.

Some shellfish and crabs can survive polluted environments, accumulating heavy metals or toxins in their tissues. For example, mitten crabs have a remarkable ability to survive in highly modified aquatic habitats, including polluted waters. The farming and harvesting of such species needs careful management if they are to be used as a food.

Mining has a poor environmental track record. For example, according to the United States Environmental Protection Agency, mining has contaminated portions of the headwaters of over 40 per cent of watersheds in the western continental US. Much of this pollution finishes up in the sea.

Heavy metals enter the environment through oil spills - such as the Prestige oil spill on the Galician coast - or from other natural or anthropogenic sources.

### Eutrophication

Eutrophication is an increase in chemical nutrients, typically compounds containing nitrogen or phosphorus, in an ecosystem. It can result in an increase in the ecosystem's primary productivity (excessive plant growth and decay), and further effects including lack of oxygen and severe reductions in water quality, fish, and other animal populations.

The biggest culprit are rivers that empty into the ocean, and with it the many chemicals used as fertilizers in agriculture as well as waste from livestock and humans. An excess of oxygen depleting chemicals in the water can lead to hypoxia and the creation of a dead zone.

Surveys have shown that 54 per cent of lakes in Asia are eutrophic; in Europe, 53 per cent; in North America, 48 per cent; in South America, 41 per cent; and in Africa, 28 per cent. Estuaries also tend to be naturally eutrophic because land-derived nutrients are concentrated where run-off enters the marine environment in a confined channel. The World Resources Institute has identified 375 hypoxic coastal zones around the world, concentrated in coastal areas in Western Europe, the Eastern and Southern coasts of the U.S., and East Asia, particularly in Japan. In the ocean, there are frequent red tide algae blooms that kill fish and marine mammals and cause respiratory problems in humans and some domestic animals when the blooms reach close to shore.

In addition to land runoff, atmospheric anthropogenic fixed nitrogen can enter the open ocean. A study in 2008 found that this could account for around one third of the ocean's external (non-recycled) nitrogen supply and up to three per cent of the annual new marine biological production. It has been suggested that accumulating reactive nitrogen in the environment may have consequences as serious as putting carbon dioxide in the atmosphere.

### Acidification

The oceans are normally a natural carbon sink, absorbing carbon dioxide from the atmosphere. Because the levels of atmospheric carbon dioxide are increasing, the oceans are becoming more acidic. The potential consequences of ocean acidification are not fully understood, but there are concerns that structures made of calcium carbonate may become vulnerable to dissolution, affecting corals and the ability of shellfish to form shells.

A report from NOAA scientists published in the journal Science in May 2008 found that large amounts of relatively acidified water are upwelling to within four miles of the Pacific continental shelf area of North America. This area is a critical zone where most local marine life lives or is born. While the paper dealt only with areas from Vancouver to northern California, other continental shelf areas may be experiencing similar effects.

### Habitat Destruction

Fishing nets that have been left or lost in the ocean by fishermen are called ghost nets, and can entangle fish, dolphins, sea turtles, sharks, dugongs, crocodiles, seabirds, crabs, and other creatures. Acting as designed, these nets restrict movement, causing starvation, laceration and infection, and—in those that need to return to the surface to breath—suffocation.

### Overfishing

On the east coast of the United States, the availability of bay scallops has been greatly diminished by the overfishing of sharks in the area. A variety of sharks have, until recently, fed on rays, which are a main predator of bay scallops. With the shark population reduced, in some places almost totally, the rays have been free to dine on scallops to the point of greatly decreasing their numbers.

Chesapeake Bay's once-flourishing oyster populations historically filtered the estuary's entire water volume of excess nutrients every three or four days. Today that process takes almost a year, and sediment, nutrients, and algae can cause problems in local waters. Oysters filter these pollutants, and either eat them or shape them into small packets that are deposited on the bottom where they are harmless.

The Australian government alleged in 2006 that Japan illegally overfished southern bluefin tuna by taking 12,000 to 20,000 tonnes per year instead of the their agreed 6,000 tonnes; the value of such overfishing would be as much as USD $2 billion. Such overfishing has resulted in severe damage to stocks. "Japan's huge appetite for tuna will take the most sought-after stocks to the brink of commercial extinction unless fisheries agree on more rigid quotas" stated the Japan disputes this figure, but acknowledges that some overfishing has occurred in the past.

### Loss of Biodiversity

Each species in an ecosystem is affected by the other species in that ecosystem. There are very few single prey-single predator relationships. Most prey are consumed by more than one predator, and most predators have more than one prey. Their relationships are also influenced by other environmental factors. In most cases, if one species is removed from an ecosystem, other species will most likely be affected, up to the point of extinction.

Species biodiversity is a major contributor to the stability of ecosystems. When an organism exploits a wide range of resources, a decrease in biodiversity is less likely to have an impact. However, for an organism which exploit only limited resources, a decrease in biodiversity is more likely to have a strong effect.

Reduction of habitat, hunting and fishing of some species to extinction or near extinction, and pollution tend to tip the balance of biodiversity. For a systematic treatment of biodiversity within a trophic level, see unified neutral theory of biodiversity.

## Threatened Species

The global standard for recording threatened marine species is the IUCN Red List of Threatened Species. This list is the foundation for marine conservation priorities worldwide. A species is listed in the threatened category if it is considered to be critically endangered, endangered, or vulnerable. Other categories are near threatened and data deficient.

## Marine

Many marine species are under increasing risk of extinction and marine biodiversity is undergoing potentially irreversible loss due to threats such as overfishing, bycatch, climate change, invasive species and coastal development.

By 2008, the IUCN had assessed about 3,000 marine species. This includes assessments of known species of shark, ray, chimaera, reef-building coral, grouper, marine turtle, seabird, and marine mammal. Almost one-quarter (22%) of these groups have been listed as threatened.

### *Sharks, Rays, and Chimaeras*

These are deep water pelagic species, which makes them difficult to study in the wild. Not a lot is known about their ecology and population status. Much of what is currently known is from their capture in nets from both targeted and accidental catch. Many of these slow growing species are not recovering from overfishing by shark fisheries around the world.

### *Groupers*

Major threats are overfishing, particularly the uncontrolled fishing of small juveniles and spawning adults.

*Coral Reefs*

The primary threats to corals are bleaching and disease which has been linked to an increase in sea temperatures. Other threats include coastal development, coral extraction, sedimentation and pollution. The coral triangle (Indo-Malay-Philippine archipelago) region has the highest number of reef-building coral species in threatened category as well as the highest coral species diversity. The loss of coral reef ecosystems will have devastating effects on many marine species, as well as on people that depend on reef resources for their livelihoods.

*Marine Mammals*

It include whales, dolphins, porpoises, seals, sea lions, walruses, sea otter, marine otter, manatees, dugong and the polar bear. Major threats include entanglement in ghost nets, targeted harvesting, noise pollution from military and seismic sonar, and boat strikes. Other threats are water pollution, habitat loss from coastal development, loss of food sources due to the collapse of fisheries, and climate change.

*Seabirds*

Major threats include longline fisheries and gillnets, oil spills, and predation by rodents and cats in their breeding grounds. Other threats are habitat loss and degradation from coastal development, logging and pollution.

*Marine Turtles*

Marine turtles lay their eggs on beaches, and are subject to threats such as coastal development, sand mining, and predators, including humans who collect their eggs for food in many parts of the world. At sea, marine turtles can be targeted by small scale subsistence fisheries, or become bycatch during longline and trawling activities, or become entangled in ghost nets or struck by boats.

An ambitious project, called the Global Marine Species Assessment, is under way to make IUCN Red List assessments for another 17,000 marine species by 2012. Groups targeted include the approximately 15,000 known marine fishes, and important habitat-forming primary producers such mangroves, seagrasses, certain seaweeds and the remaining corals; and important invertebrate groups including molluscs and echinoderms.

### Freshwater

Freshwater fisheries have a disproportionately high diversity of species compared to other ecosystems. Although freshwater habitats cover less than 1 per cent of the world's surface, they provide a home for over 25 per cent of known vertebrates, more than 126,000 known animal species, about 24,800 species of freshwater fish, molluscs, crabs and dragonflies, and about 2,600 macrophytes.

Continuing industrial and agricultural developments place huge strain on these freshwater systems. Waters are polluted or extracted at high levels, wetlands are drained, rivers channelled, forests deforestated leading to sedimentation, invasive species are introduced, and over-harvesting occurs.

In the 2008 IUCN Red List, about 6,000 or 22 per cent of the known freshwater species have been assessed at a global scale, leaving about 21,000 species still to be assessed. This makes clear that, worldwide, freshwater species are highly threatened, possibly more so than species in marine fisheries. However, a significant proportion of freshwater species are listed as data deficient, and more field surveys are needed.

### Fisheries Management

A recent paper published by the National Academy of Sciences of the USA warns that:

> "Synergistic effects of habitat destruction, overfishing, introduced species, warming, acidification, toxins, and massive runoff of nutrients are transforming once complex ecosystems like coral reefs and kelp forests into monotonous level bottoms, transforming clear and productive coastal seas into anoxic dead zones, and transforming complex food webs topped by big animals into simplified, microbially dominated ecosystems with boom and bust cycles of toxic dinoflagellate blooms, jellyfish, and disease".

# 9

# Population Dynamics of Fisheries

A fishery is an area with an associated fish or aquatic population which is harvested for its commercial or recreational value. Fisheries can be wild or farmed. Population dynamics describes the ways in which a given population grows and shrinks over time, as controlled by birth, death, and emigration or immigration. It is the basis for understanding changing fishery patterns and issues such as habitat destruction, predation and optimal harvesting rates. The population dynamics of fisheries is used by fisheries scientists to determine sustainable yields.

A fishery population is affected by three dynamic rate functions:

- *Birth rate or recruitment:* Recruitment means reaching a certain size or reproductive stage. With fisheries, recruitment usually refers to the age a fish can be caught and counted in nets.
- *Growth rate:* This measures the growth of individuals in size and length. This is important in fisheries where the population is often measured in terms of biomass.
- *Mortality:* This includes harvest mortality and natural mortality. Natural mortality includes non-human predation, disease and old age.

If these rates are measured over different time intervals, the harvestable surplus of a fishery can be determined. The harvestable surplus is the number of individuals that can be harvested from the population without affecting long term stability (average population size). The harvest within the harvestable surplus is called compensatory mortality, where the harvest deaths are substituting for the deaths that would otherwise occur naturally. Harvest beyond that is additive mortality, harvest in addition to all the animals that would have died naturally.

Care is needed when applying population dynamics to real world fisheries. Over-simplistic modelling of fisheries has resulted in the collapse of key stocks.

The first principle of population dynamics is widely regarded as the exponential law of Malthus, as modelled by the Malthusian growth model. The early period was dominated by demographic studies such as the work of Benjamin Gompertz and Pierre François Verhulst in the early 19th century, who refined and adjusted the Malthusian demographic model. A more general model formulation was proposed by F.J. Richards in 1959, by which the models of Gompertz, Verhulst and also Ludwig von Bertalanffy are covered as special cases of the general formulation.

**Population Size**

The effective population size ($N_e$) was defined by Sewall Wright, who wrote two landmark papers on it. He defined it as:

> "the number of breeding individuals in an idealized population that would show the same amount of dispersion of allele frequencies under random genetic drift or the same amount of inbreeding as the population under consideration".

It is a basic parameter in many models in population genetics. $N_e$ is usually less than $N$ (the absolute population size).

Small population size results in increased genetic drift. Population bottlenecks are when population size reduces for a short period of time.

Overpopulation may indicate any case in which the population of any species of animal may exceed the carrying capacity of its ecological niche.

## Virtual Population Analysis

Virtual population analysis (VPA) is a modelling technique commonly used in fisheries science for reconstructing historical fish numbers using information on death of individuals each year. This death is usually partitioned into catch by fisheries and natural mortality.

The VPA is the most commonly used term to refer to cohort reconstruction techniques used in fisheries. It is virtual in the sense that the population size is not observed or measured directly but is inferred or back-calculated to have been a certain size in the past in order to support the observed fish catches and an assumed death rate owing to non-fishery related causes.

## Minimum Viable Population

The minimum viable population (MVP) is a lower bound on the population of a species, such that it can survive in the wild. More specifically MVP is the smallest possible size at which a biological population can exist without facing extinction from natural disasters or demographic, environmental, or genetic stochasticity. The term "population" refers to the population of a species in the wild.

As a reference standard, MVP is usually given with a population survival probability of somewhere between ninety and ninety-five percent and calculated for between one hundred and one thousand years into the future.

The MVP can be calculated using computer simulations known as population viability analyses (PVA), where populations are modelled and future population dynamics are projected.

## Maximum Sustainable Yield

In population ecology and economics, the maximum sustainable yield or MSY is, theoretically, the largest catch that can be taken from a fishery stock over an indefinite period. Under the assumption of logistic growth, the MSY will be exactly at half the carrying capacity of a species, as this is the stage at when population growth is highest. The maximum sustainable yield is usually higher than the optimum sustainable yield.

This logistic model of growth is produced by a population introduced to a new habitat or with very poor numbers going through a lag phase of slow growth at first. Once it reaches a foothold population it will go through a rapid growth rate that will start to level off once the species approaches carrying capacity. The idea of maximum sustained yield is to decrease population density to the point of highest growth rate possible. This changes the number of the population, but the new number can be maintained indefinitely, ideally.

The MSY is extensively used for fisheries management. Unlike the logistic (Schaefer) model, MSY in most modern fisheries models occurs at around 30 per cent of the unexploited population size. This fraction differs among populations depending on the life history of the species and the age-specific selectivity of the fishing method.

However, the approach has been widely criticized as ignoring several key factors involved in fisheries management and has led to the devastating collapse of many fisheries. As a simple calculation, it ignores the size and age of the animal being taken, its reproductive status, and it focuses solely on the species in question, ignoring the damage to the ecosystem caused by the designated level of exploitation and the issue of bycatch. Among conservation biologists it is widely regarded as dangerous and misused.

## Recruitment

Recruitment is the number of new young fish that enter a population in a given year. The size of fish populations can fluctuate by orders of magnitude over time, and five to

10-fold variations in abundance are usual. This variability applies across time spans ranging from a year to hundreds of years. Year to year fluctuations in the abundance of short lived forage fish can be nearly as great as the fluctuations that occur over decades or centuries. This suggests that fluctuations in reproductive and recruitment success are prime factors behind fluctuations in abundance. Annual fluctuations often seem random, and recruitment success often has a poor relationship to adult stock levels and fishing effort. This makes prediction difficult.

The recruitment problem is the problem of predicting the number of fish larvae in one season that will survive and become juvenile fish in the next season. It has been called "the central problem of fish population dynamics" and "the major problem in fisheries science". Fish produce huge volumes of larvae, but the volumes are very variable and mortality is high. This makes good predictions difficult.

According to Daniel Pauly, the definitive study was made in 1999 by Ransom Myers. Myers solved the problem "by assembling a large base of stock data and developing a complex mathematical model to sort it out. Out of that came the conclusion that a female in general produced three to five recruits per year for most fish.

A current operational model used by some fisheries for predicting acceptable levels is the Harvest Control Rule (HCR). This formalizes and summarizes a management strategy which can actively adapt to subsequent feedback. The HCR is a variable over which the management has some direct control and describes how the harvest is intended to be controlled by management in relation to the state of some indicator of stock status. For example, a harvest control rule can describe the various values of fishing mortality which will be aimed at for various values of the stock abundance. Constant catch and constant fishing mortality are two types of simple harvest control rules.

Biological overfishing occurs when fishing mortality has reached a level where the stock biomass has negative marginal growth (slowing down biomass growth), as indicated by the red area in the figure. Fish are being taken out of the water so quickly that the replenishment of stock by breeding slows down. If the replenishment continues to slow down for long enough, replenishment will go into reverse and the population will decrease.

Economic or bioeconomic overfishing additionally considers the cost of fishing and defines overfishing as a situation of negative marginal growth of resource rent. Fish are being taken out of the water so quickly that the growth in the profitability of fishing slows down. If this continues for long enough, profitability will decrease.

### Metapopulation

A metapopulation is a group of spatially separated populations of the same species which interact at some level. The term was coined by Richard Levins in 1969. The idea has been most broadly applied to species in naturally or artificially fragmented habitats. In Levins' own words, it consists of "a population of populations".

A metapopulation generally consists of several distinct populations together with areas of suitable habitat which are currently unoccupied. Each population cycles in relative independence of the other populations and eventually goes extinct as a consequence of demographic stochasticity (fluctuations in population size due to random demographic events); the smaller the population, the more prone it is to extinction.

Although individual populations have finite life-spans, the population as a whole is often stable because immigrants from one population (which may, for example, be experiencing a population boom) are likely to re-colonize habitat which has been left open by the extinction of another population. They may also emigrate to a small population and rescue that population from extinction (called the *rescue effect*).

## Age Class Structure

Age can be determined by counting growth rings in fish scales, otoliths, cross-sections of fin spines for species with thick spines such as triggerfish, or teeth for a few species. Each method has its merits and drawbacks. Fish scales are easiest to obtain, but may be unreliable if scales have fallen off of the fish and new ones grown in their places. Fin spines may be unreliable for the same reason, and most fish do not have spines of sufficient thickness for clear rings to be visible. Otoliths will have stayed with the fish throughout its life history, but obtaining them requires killing the fish. Also, otoliths often require more preparation before ageing can occur.

An age class structure with gaps in it, for instance a regular bell curve for the population of 1-5 year-old fish, excepting a very low population for the 3-year-olds, implies a bad spawning year 3 years ago in that species.

Often fish in younger age class structures have very low numbers because they were small enough to slip through the sampling nets, and may in fact have a very healthy population.

## Population Cycle

A population cycle occurs where populations rise and fall over a predictable period of time. There are some species where population numbers have reasonably predictable patterns of change although the full reasons for population cycles is one of the major unsolved ecological problems. There are a number of factors which influence population change such as availability of food, predators, diseases and climate.

## Trophic Cascades

Trophic cascades occur when predators in a food chain suppress the abundance of their prey, thereby releasing the next lower trophic level from predation (or herbivory if the intermediate trophic level is an herbivore). For example, if the abundance of large piscivorous fish is increased in a lake, the abundance of their prey, zooplanktivorous fish, should decrease, large zooplankton abundance should increase, and phytoplankton biomass should decrease. This theory has stimulated new research in many areas of ecology. Trophic cascades may also be important for understanding the effects of removing top predators from food webs, as humans have done in many places through hunting and fishing activities.

### Classic Examples

In lakes, piscivorous fish can dramatically reduce populations of zooplanktivorous fish, zooplanktivorous fish can dramatically alter freshwater zooplankton communities, and zooplankton grazing can in turn have large impacts on phytoplankton communities. Removal of piscivorous fish can change lake water from clear to green by allowing phytoplankton to flourish.

In the Eel River, in Northern California, fish (steelhead and roach) consume fish larvae and predatory insects. These smaller predators prey on midge larvae, which feed on algae. Removal of the larger fish increases the abundance of algae.

In Pacific kelp forests, sea otters feed on sea urchins. In areas where sea otters have been hunted to extinction, sea urchins increase in abundance and decimate kelp.

A recent theory, the mesopredator release hypothesis, states that the decline of top predators in an ecosystem results in increased populations of medium-sized predators (mesopredators).

The classic predator-prey equations are a pair of first order, non-linear, differential equations used to describe the dynamics of biological systems in which two species interact, one a predator and one its prey. They were proposed independently by Alfred J. Lotka in 1925 and Vito Volterra in 1926.

An extension to these are the competitive Lotka-Volterra equations, which provide a simple model of the population dynamics of species competing for some common resource.

In the 1930s Alexander Nicholson and Victor Bailey developed a model to describe the population dynamics of a coupled predator-prey system. The model assumes that predators search for prey at random, and that both predators and prey are assumed to be distributed in a non-contiguous ("clumped") fashion in the environment.

# 10

# Fish — The Aquatic Vertebrate

A fish is any gill-bearing aquatic vertebrate (or craniate) animal that lacks limbs with digits. Included in this definition are the living hagfish, lampreys, and cartilaginous and bony fish, as well as various extinct related groups. Because the term is defined negatively, and excludes the tetrapods (i.e., the amphibians, reptiles, birds and mammals) which descend from within the same ancestry, it is paraphyletic. The traditional term pisces (also ichthyes) is considered a typological, but not a phylogenetic classification.

Most fish are "cold-blooded", or ectothermic, allowing their body temperatures to vary as ambient temperatures change. Fish are abundant in most bodies of water. They can be found in nearly all aquatic environments, from high mountain streams (e.g., char and gudgeon) to the abyssal and even hadal depths of the deepest oceans (e.g., gulpers and anglerfish). At 31,900 species, fish exhibit greater species diversity than any other class of vertebrates.

Fish, especially as food, are an important resource worldwide. Commercial and subsistence fishers hunt fish in wild fisheries (see fishing) or farm them in ponds or in cages in the ocean. They are also caught by recreational fishers, kept as pets, raised by fishkeepers, and exhibited in public aquaria. Fish have had a role in culture through the ages, serving as deities, religious symbols, and as the subjects of art, books and movies.

The term "fish" most precisely describes any non-tetrapod craniate (i.e. an animal with a skull and in most cases a backbone) that has gills throughout life and whose limbs, if any, are in the shape of fins. Unlike groupings such as birds or mammals, fish are not a single clade but a paraphyletic collection of taxa, including hagfishes, lampreys, sharks and rays, ray-finned fish, coelacanths, and lungfish. Indeed, lungfish and coelacanths are closer relatives of tetrapods (such as mammals, birds, amphibians, etc.) than of other fish such as ray-finned fish or sharks, so the last common ancestor of all fish is also an ancestor to tetrapods. As paraphyletic groups are no longer recognised in modern systematic biology, the use of the term "fish" as a biological group must be avoided.

Many types of aquatic animals commonly referred to as "fish" are not fish in the sense given above; examples include shellfish, cuttlefish, starfish, crayfish and jellyfish. In earlier times, even biologists did not make a distinction – sixteenth century natural historians classified also seals, whales, amphibians, crocodiles, even hippopotamuses, as well as a host of aquatic invertebrates, as fish. However, according the definition above, all mammals, including Cetaceans like Whales and Dolphins, are not fish. In some contexts, especially in aquaculture, the true fish are referred to as finfish (or fin fish) to distinguish them from these other animals.

A typical fish is ectothermic, has a streamlined body for rapid swimming, extracts oxygen from water using gills or uses an accessory breathing organ to breathe atmospheric oxygen, has two sets of paired fins, usually one or two (rarely three) dorsal fins, an anal fin, and a tail fin, has jaws, has skin that is usually covered with scales, and lays eggs.

Each criterion has exceptions. Tuna, swordfish, and some species of sharks show some warm-blooded adaptations—

they can heat their bodies significantly above ambient water temperature. Streamlining and swimming performance varies from fish such as tuna, salmon, and jacks that can cover 10-20 body-lengths per second to species such as eels and rays that swim no more than 0.5 body-lengths per second. Many groups of freshwater fish extract oxygen from the air as well as from the water using a variety of different structures. Lungfish have paired lungs similar to those of tetrapods, gouramis have a structure called the labyrinth organ that performs a similar function, while many catfish, such as *Corydoras* extract oxygen via the intestine or stomach. Body shape and the arrangement of the fins is highly variable, covering such seemingly un-fishlike forms as seahorses, pufferfish, anglerfish, and gulpers. Similarly, the surface of the skin may be naked (as in moray eels), or covered with scales of a variety of different types usually defined as placoid (typical of sharks and rays), cosmoid (fossil lungfish and coelacanths), ganoid (various fossil fish but also living gars and bichirs), cycloid, and ctenoid (these last two are found on most bony fish). There are even fish that live mostly on land. Mudskippers feed and interact with one another on mudflats and go underwater to hide in their burrows. The catfish *Phreatobius cisternarum* lives in underground, phreatic habitats, and a relative lives in waterlogged leaf litter.

Fish range in size from the huge 16-metre (52 ft) whale shark to the tiny 8-millimetre (0.3 in) stout infantfish.

### Taxonomy

Fish are a paraphyletic group: that is, any clade containing all fish also contains the tetrapods, which are not fish. For this reason, groups such as the "Class Pisces" seen in older reference works are no longer used in formal classifications.

Fish are classified into the following major groups:

| | |
|---|---|
| Class | Myxini (hagfish) |
| Class | Pteraspidomorphi (early jawless fish) |
| Class | Thelodonti |

| | |
|---|---|
| Class | Anaspida |
| Class | Petromyzontida or Hyperoartia |
| | Petromyzontidae (lampreys) |
| Class | Conodonta (conodonts) |
| Class | Cephalaspidomorphi early jawless fish) |
| (unranked) | Galeaspida |
| (unranked) | Pituriaspida |
| (unranked) | Osteostraci |
| Infraphylum | Gnathostomata (jawed vertebrates) |
| Class | Placodermi (armoured fish) |
| Class | Chondrichthyes (cartilaginous fish) |
| Class | Acanthodii (spiny sharks) |
| Superclass | Osteichthyes (bony fish) |
| Class | Actinopterygii (ray-finned fish) |
| Subclass | Chondrostei |
| | Order Acipenseriformes (Sturgeons and paddlefishes) |
| | Order Polypteriformes reedfishes and bichirs) |
| Subclass | Neopterygii |
| Infraclass | Holostei (gars and bowfins) |
| Infraclass | Teleostei (many orders of common fish) |
| Class | Sarcopterygii (lobe-finned fish) |
| Subclass | Coelacanthimorpha (coelacanths) |
| Subclass | Dipnoi ( lungfish) |

Some palaeontologists contend that because Conodonta are chordates, they are primitive fish.

The position of hagfish in the phylum chordata is not settled. Phylogenetic research in 1998 and 1999 supported the idea that the hagfish and the lampreys form a natural group, the Cyclostomata, that is a sister group of the Gnathostomata.

The various fish groups account for more than half of vertebrate species. There are almost 28,000 known extant species, of which almost 27,000 are bony fish, with 970 sharks, rays, and chimeras and about 108 hagfish and lampreys. third of these species fall within the nine largest families; from largest to smallest, these families are Cyprinidae, Gobiidae, Cichlidae, Characidae, Loricariidae, Balitoridae, Serranidae, Labridae, and Scorpaenidae. About 64 families are monotypic, containing only one species. The final total of extant species may grow to exceed 32,500.

Most fish exchange gases using gills on either side of the pharynx. Gills consist of threadlike structures called filaments. Each filament contains a capillary network that provides a large surface area for exchanging oxygen and carbon dioxide. Fish exchange gases by pulling oxygen-rich water through their mouths and pumping it over their gills. In some fish, capillary blood flows in the opposite direction to the water, causing counter current exchange. The gills push the oxygen-poor water out through openings in the sides of the pharynx. Some fish, like sharks and lampreys, possess multiple gill openings. However, most fish have a single gill opening on each side. This opening is hidden beneath a protective bony cover called an operculum.

Many fish can breathe air via a variety of mechanisms. The skin of anguillid eels may absorb oxygen. The buccal cavity of the electric eel may breathe air. Catfish of the families Loricariidae, Callichthyidae, and Scoloplacidae absorb air through their digestive tracts. Lungfish, with the exception of the Australian lungfish, and bichirs have paired lungs similar to those of tetrapods and must surface to gulp fresh air through the mouth and pass spent air out through the gills. Gar and bowfin have a vascularized swim bladder that functions in the same way. Loaches, trahiras, and many catfish breathe by passing air through the gut. Mudskippers breathe by absorbing oxygen across the skin (similar to frogs). A number of fish have evolved so-called accessory breathing organs that extract oxygen from the air. Labyrinth fish (such as gouramis and bettas) have a labyrinth organ above the gills that performs this function. A few other fish have structures resembling labyrinth organs in form and function, most notably snakeheads, pikeheads, and the Clariidae catfish family.

Breathing air is primarily of use to fish that inhabit shallow, seasonally variable waters where the water's oxygen concentration may seasonally decline. Fish dependent solely on dissolved oxygen, such as perch and cichlids, quickly suffocate, while air-breathers survive for much longer, in some cases in water that is little more than wet mud. At the most extreme, some air-breathing fish are able to survive in damp burrows for weeks without water, entering a state of aestivation (summertime hibernation) until water returns.

Tuna gills inside of the head. The fish head is oriented snout-downwards, with the view looking towards the mouth.

Fish can be divided into obligate air breathers and facultative air breathers. Obligate air breathers, such as the African lungfish, *must* breathe air periodically or they suffocate. Facultative air breathers, such as the catfish *Hypostomus plecostomus*, only breathe air if they need to and will otherwise rely on their gills for oxygen. Most air breathing fish are facultative air breathers that avoid the energetic cost of rising to the surface and the fitness cost of exposure to surface predators.

**Circulation**

Fish have a closed-loop circulatory system. The heart pumps the blood in a single loop throughout the body. In most fish, the heart consists of four parts, including two chambers and an entrance and exit. The first part is the sinus venosus, a thin-walled sac that collects blood from the fish's veins before allowing it to flow to the second part, the atrium, which is a large muscular chamber. The atrium serves as a one-way antechamber, sends blood to the third part, ventricle. The ventricle is another thick-walled, muscular chamber and it pumps the blood, first to the fourth part, bulbous arteriosus, a large tube, and then out of the heart. The bulbus arteriosus connects to the aorta, through which blood flows to the gills for oxygenation.

Jaws allow fish to eat a wide variety of food, including plants and other organisms. Fish ingest food through the mouth and break it down in the esophagus. In the stomach, food is further digested and, in many fish, processed in finger-shaped pouches called pyloric caeca, which secrete digestive enzymes and absorb nutrients. Organs such as the liver and pancreas add enzymes and various chemicals as the food moves through the digestive tract. The intestine completes the process of digestion and nutrient absorption.

**Excretion**

As with many aquatic animals, most fish release their nitrogenous wastes as ammonia. Some of the wastes diffuse through the gills. Blood wastes are filtered by the kidneys.

Saltwater fish tend to lose water because of osmosis. Their kidneys return water to the body. The reverse happens in freshwater fish: they tend to gain water osmotically. Their kidneys produce dilute urine for excretion. Some fish have specially adapted kidneys that vary in function, allowing them to move from freshwater to saltwater.

Fish typically have quite small brains relative to body size compared with other vertebrates, typically one-fifteenth the brain mass of a similarly sized bird or mammal. However, some fish have relatively large brains, most notably mormyrids and sharks, which have brains about as massive relative to body weight as birds and marsupials.

Fish brains are divided into several regions. At the front are the olfactory lobes, a pair of structures that receive and process signals from the nostrils via the two olfactory nerves. The olfactory lobes are very large in fish that hunt primarily by smell, such as hagfish, sharks, and catfish. Behind the olfactory lobes is the two-lobed telencephalon, the structural equivalent to the cerebrum in higher vertebrates. In fish the telencephalon is concerned mostly with olfaction. Together these structures form the forebrain.

Connecting the forebrain to the midbrain is the diencephalon (in the diagram, this structure is below the optic lobes and consequently not visible). The diencephalon performs functions associated with hormones and homeostasis. The pineal body lies just above the diencephalon. This structure detects light, maintains circadian rhythms, and controls color changes.

The midbrain or mesencephalon contains the two optic lobes. These are very large in species that hunt by sight, such as rainbow trout and cichlids.

The hindbrain or metencephalon is particularly involved in swimming and balance. The cerebellum is a single-lobed structure that is typically the biggest part of the brain. Hagfish and lampreys have relatively small cerebellae, while the mormyrid cerebellum is massive and apparently involved in their electrical sense.

The brain stem or myelencephalon is the brain's posterior. As well as controlling some muscles and body organs, in bony fish at least, the brain stem governs respiration and osmoregulation.

Most fish possess highly developed sense organs. Nearly all daylight fish have color vision that is at least as good as a human's. Many fish also have chemoreceptors that are responsible for extraordinary senses of taste and smell. Although they have ears, many fish may not hear very well. Most fish have sensitive receptors that form the lateral line system, which detects gentle currents and vibrations, and senses the motion of nearby fish and prey. Some fish, such as catfish and sharks, have organs that detect low-level electric current. Other fish, like the electric eel, can produce electric current.

Fish orient themselves using landmarks and may use mental maps based on multiple landmarks or symbols. Fish behavior in mazes reveals that they possess spatial memory and visual discrimination.

### Capacity for Pain

Experiments done by William Tavolga provide evidence that fish have pain and fear responses. For instance, in

Tavolga's experiments, toadfish grunted when electrically shocked and over time they came to grunt at the mere sight of an electrode.

In 2003, Scottish scientists at the University of Edinburgh and the Roslin Institute concluded that rainbow trout exhibit behaviors often associated with pain in other animals. Bee venom and acetic acid injected into the lips resulted in fish rocking their bodies and rubbing their lips along the sides and floors of their tanks, which the researchers concluded were attempts to relieve pain, similar to what mammals would do. Neurons fired in a pattern resembling human neuronal patterns.

Professor James D. Rose of the University of Wyoming claimed the study was flawed since it did not provide proof that fish possess "conscious awareness, particularly a kind of awareness that is meaningfully like ours". Rose argues that since fish brains are so different from human brains, fish are probably not conscious in the manner humans are, so that reactions similar to human reactions to pain instead have other causes. Rose had published a study a year earlier arguing that fish cannot feel pain because their brains lack a neocortex. However, animal behaviorist Temple Grandin argues that fish could still have consciousness without a neocortex because "different species can use different brain structures and systems to handle the same functions."

Animal welfare advocates raise concerns about the possible suffering of fish caused by angling. Some countries, such as Germany have banned specific types of fishing, and the British RSPCA now formally prosecutes individuals who are cruel to fish.

Most fish move by alternately contracting paired sets of muscles on either side of the backbone. These contractions form S-shaped curves that move down the body. As each curve reaches the back fin, backward force is applied to the water, and in conjunction with the fins, moves the fish forward. The fish's fins function like an airplane's flaps. Fins also increase the tail's surface area, increasing speed. The streamlined body of the fish decreases the amount of friction from the water. Since body tissue is denser than water, fish must compensate for the difference or they will sink. Many bony fish have an internal organ called a swim bladder that adjusts their buoyancy through manipulation of gases.

Although most fish are exclusively aquatic and ectothermic, there are exceptions to both cases.

Fish from multiple groups can live out of the water for extended time periods. Amphibious fish such as the mudskipper can live and move about on land for up to several days.

Certain species of fish maintain elevated body temperatures. Endothermic teleosts (bony fish) are all in the suborder Scombroidei and include the billfishes, tunas, and one species of "primitive" mackerel (*Gasterochisma melampus*). All sharks in the family Lamnidae – shortfin mako, long fin mako, white, porbeagle, and salmon shark – are endothermic, and evidence suggests the trait exists in family Alopiidae (thresher sharks). The degree of endothermy varies from the billfish, which warm only their eyes and brain, to bluefin tuna and porbeagle sharks who maintain body temperatures elevated in excess of 20°C above ambient water temperatures. Endothermy, though metabolically costly, is thought to provide advantages such as increased muscle strength, higher rates of central nervous system processing, and higher rates of digestion.

Fish reproductive organs include testes and ovaries. In most species, gonads are paired organs of similar size, which can be partially or totally fused. There may also be a range of secondary organs that increase reproductive fitness.

In terms of spermatogonia distribution, the structure of teleosts testes has two types: in the most common, spermatogonia occur all along the seminiferous tubules, while in Atherinomorph fish they are confined to the distal portion of these structures. Fish can present cystic or semi-cystic spermatogenesis in relation to the release phase of germ cells in cysts to the seminiferous tubules lumen.

Fish ovaries may be of three types: gymnovarian, secondary gymnovarian or cystovarian. In the first type, the oocytes are released directly into the coelomic cavity and then enter the ostium, then through the oviduct and are eliminated. Secondary gymnovarian ovaries shed ova into the coelom from which they go directly into the oviduct. In the third type, the oocytes are conveyed to the exterior through the oviduct. Gymnovaries are the primitive condition found in lungfish, sturgeon, and bowfin. Cystovaries characterize most teleosts, where the ovary lumen has continuity with the oviduct. Secondary gymnovaries are found in salmonids and a few other teleosts.

Oogonia development in teleosts fish varies according to the group, and the determination of oogenesis dynamics allows the understanding of maturation and fertilization processes. Changes in the nucleus, ooplasm, and the surrounding layers characterize the oocyte maturation process.

Postovulatory follicles are structures formed after oocyte release; they do not have endocrine function, present a wide irregular lumen, and are rapidly reabsorbed in a process involving the apoptosis of follicular cells. A degenerative process called follicular atresia reabsorbs vitellogenic oocytes not spawned. This process can also occur, but less frequently, in oocytes in other development stages.

Some fish are hermaphrodites, having both testes and ovaries either at different phases in their life cycle or, as in hamlets, have them simultaneously.

### Reproductive Method

Over 97 per cent of all known fish are oviparous, that is, the eggs develop outside the mother's body. Examples of oviparous fish include salmon, goldfish, cichlids, tuna, and eels. In the majority of these species, fertilisation takes place outside the mother's body, with the male and female fish shedding their gametes into the surrounding water. However, a few oviparous fish practice internal fertilization, with the male using some sort of intromittent organ to deliver sperm into the genital opening of the female, most notably the oviparous sharks, such as the horn shark, and oviparous rays, such as skates. In these cases, the male is equipped with a pair of modified pelvic fins known as claspers.

Marine fish can produce high numbers of eggs which are often released into the open water column. The eggs have an average diameter of 1 millimetre (0.039 in).

The newly hatched young of oviparous fish are called larvae. They are usually poorly formed, carry a large yolk sac (for nourishment) and are very different in appearance from juvenile and adult specimens. The larval period in oviparous fish is relatively short (usually only several weeks), and larvae rapidly grow and change appearance and structure (a process termed metamorphosis) to become juveniles. During this transition larvae must switch from their yolk sac to feeding on zooplankton prey, a process which depends on typically inadequate zooplankton density, starving many larvae.

In ovoviviparous fish the eggs develop inside the mother's body after internal fertilization but receive little or no nourishment directly from the mother, depending instead on the yolk. Each embryo develops in its own egg. Familiar examples of ovoviviparous fish include guppies, angel sharks, and coelacanths.

Some species of fish are viviparous. In such species the mother retains the eggs and nourishes the embryos. Typically, viviparous fish have a structure analogous to the placenta seen in mammals connecting the mother's blood supply with that of the embryo. Examples of viviparous fish include the surf-perches, splitfins, and lemon shark. Some viviparous fish exhibit oophagy, in which the developing embryos eat other eggs produced by the mother. This has been observed primarily among sharks, such as the shortfin mako and porbeagle, but is known for a few bony fish as well, such as the halfbeak *Nomorhamphus ebrardtii*. Intrauterine cannibalism is an even more unusual mode of vivipary, in which the largest embryos eat weaker and smaller siblings. This behavior is also most commonly found among sharks, such as the grey nurse shark, but has also been reported for *Nomorhamphus ebrardtii*.

**Immune System**

Immune organs vary by type of fish. In the jawless fish (lampreys and hagfish), true lymphoid organs are absent. These fish rely on regions of lymphoid tissue within other organs to produce immune cells. For example, erythrocytes, macrophages and plasma cells are produced in the anterior kidney (or pronephros) and some areas of the gut (where granulocytes mature.) They resemble primitive bone marrow in hagfish. Cartilaginous fish (sharks and rays) have a more advanced immune system. They have three specialized organs that are unique to chondrichthyes; the epigonal organs (lymphoid tissue similar to mammalian bone) that surround the gonads, the Leydig's organ within the walls of their esophagus, and a spiral valve in their intestine. These organs house typical immune cells (granulocytes, lymphocytes and plasma cells). They also possess an identifiable thymus and a well-developed spleen (their most important immune organ) where various lymphocytes, plasma cells and macrophages develop and are stored. Chondrostean fish (sturgeons, paddlefish and bichirs) possess a major site for the production of granulocytes within a mass that is associated with the meninges (membranes surrounding the central nervous system.) Their heart is frequently covered with tissue that contains lymphocytes, reticular cells and a small number of macrophages. The chondrostean kidney is an important hemopoietic organ; where erythrocytes, granulocytes, lymphocytes and macrophages develop.

Like chondrostean fish, the major immune tissues of bony fish (or teleostei) include the kidney (especially the anterior kidney), which houses many different immune cells. In addition, teleost fish possess a thymus, spleen and scattered immune areas within mucosal tissues (e.g. in the skin, gills, gut and gonads). Much like the mammalian immune system, teleost erythrocytes, neutrophils and granulocytes are believed to reside in the spleen whereas lymphocytes are the major cell type found in the thymus. In 2006, a lymphatic system similar to that in mammals was described in one species of teleost fish, the zebrafish. Although not confirmed as yet, this system presumably will be where naive (unstimulated) T cells accumulate while waiting to encounter an antigen.

## Diseases

Like other animals, fish suffer from diseases and parasites. To prevent disease they have a variety of defenses. *Non-specific* defenses include the skin and scales, as well as the mucus layer secreted by the epidermis that traps and inhibits the growth of microorganisms. If pathogens breach these defenses, fish can develop an inflammatory response that increases blood flow to the infected region and delivers white blood cells that attempt to destroy pathogens. Specific defenses respond to particular pathogens recognised by the fish's body, i.e., an immune response. In recent years, vaccines have become widely used in aquaculture and also with ornamental fish, for example furunculosis vaccines in farmed salmon and koi herpes virus in koi.

Some species use cleaner fish to remove external parasites. The best known of these are the Bluestreak cleaner wrasses of the genus *Labroides* found on coral reefs in the Indian and Pacific Oceans. These small fish maintain so-called "cleaning stations" where other fish congregate and perform specific movements to attract the attention of the cleaners. Cleaning behaviors have been observed in a number of fish groups, including an interesting case between two cichlids of the same genus, *Etroplus maculatus*, the cleaner, and the much larger *Etroplus suratensis*.

Fish do not represent a monophyletic group, and therefore the "evolution of fish" is not studied as a single event.

Proliferation of fish was apparently due to the hinged jaw, because jawless fish left very few descendants. Lampreys may approximate pre-jawed fish. The first jaws are found in Placodermi fossils. It is unclear if the advantage of a hinged jaw is greater biting force, improved respiration, or a combination of factors.

Fish may have evolved from a creature similar to a coral-like Sea squirt, whose larvae resemble primitive fish in important ways. The first ancestors of fish may have kept the larval form into adulthood (as some sea squirts do today), although perhaps the reverse is the case.

The 2006 IUCN Red List names 1,173 fish species that are threatened with extinction. Included are species such as Atlantic cod, Devil's Hole pupfish, coelacanths, and great white sharks. Because fish live underwater they are more difficult to study than terrestrial animals and plants, and information about fish populations is often lacking. However, freshwater fish seem particularly threatened because they often live in relatively small water bodies. For example, the Devil's Hole pupfish occupies only a single 3 by 6 metres (10 by 20 ft) pool.

Overfishing is a major threat to edible fish such as cod and tuna. Overfishing eventually causes population (known as stock) collapse because the survivors cannot produce enough young to replace those removed. Such commercial extinction does not mean that the species is extinct, merely that it can no longer sustain a fishery.

One well-studied example of fishery collapse is the Pacific sardine *Sadinops sagax caerulues* fishery off the California coast. From a 1937 peak of 790,000 long tons (800,000 t) the catch steadily declined to only 24,000 long tons (24,000 t) in 1968, after which the fishery was no longer economically viable.

The main tension between fisheries science and the fishing industry is that the two groups have different views on the resiliency of fisheries to intensive fishing. In places such as Scotland, Newfoundland, and Alaska the fishing industry is a major employer, so governments are predisposed to support it. On the other hand, scientists and conservationists push for stringent protection, warning that many stocks could be wiped out within fifty years.

A key stress on both freshwater and marine ecosystems is habitat degradation including water pollution, the building of dams, removal of water for use by humans, and the introduction of exotic species. An example of a fish that has become endangered because of habitat change is the pallid sturgeon, a North American freshwater fish that lives in rivers damaged by human activity.

**Exotic Species**

Introduction of non-native species has occurred in many habitats. One of the best studied examples is the introduction of Nile perch into Lake Victoria in the 1960s. Nile perch gradually exterminated the lake's 500 endemic cichlid species. Some of them survive now in captive breeding programmes, but others are probably extinct. Carp, snakeheads, tilapia, European perch, brown trout, rainbow trout, and sea lampreys are other examples of fish that have caused problems by being introduced into a lien environments.

In the Book of Jonah a "great fish" swallowed Jonah the Prophet. Legends of half-human, half-fish mermaids have featured in stories like those of Hans Christian Andersen and movies like *Splash*.

Among the deities said to take the form of a fish are Ika-Roa of the Polynesians, Dagon of various ancient Semitic peoples, the shark-gods of Hawai?i and Matsya of the Dravidas of India. The astrological symbol Pisces is based on a constellation of the same name, but there is also a second fish constellation in the night sky, Piscis Austrinus.

Fish have been used figuratively in many different ways, for example the ichthys used by early Christians to identify themselves, through to the fish as a symbol of fertility among Bengalis.

Fish feature prominently in art and literature, in movies such as *Finding Nemo* and books such as *The Old Man and the Sea*. Large fish, particularly sharks, have frequently been the subject of horror movies and thrillers, most notably the novel

*Jaws*, which spawned a series of films of the same name that in turn inspired similar films or parodies such as *Shark Tale*, *Snakehead Terror*, and *Piranha*.

In the semiotic of *Ashtamangala* (Buddhist symbolism) the golden fish (Sanskrit: *Matsya*), represents the state of fearless suspension in samsara, perceived as the harmless ocean, referred to as 'buddha-eyes' or 'rigpa-sight'. The fish symbolizes the auspiciousness of all living beings in a state of fearlessness without danger of drowning in the Samsaric Ocean of Suffering, and migrating from teaching to teaching freely and spontaneously just as fish swim.

They have religious significance in Hindu, Jain and Buddhist traditions but also in Christianity who is first signified by the sign of the fish, and especially referring to feeding the multitude in the desert. In the dhamma of Buddha the fish symbolize happiness as they have complete freedom of movement in the water. They represent fertility and abundance. Often drawn in the form of carp which are regarded in the Orient as sacred on account of their elegant beauty, size and life-span.

The name of the Canadian city of Coquitlam, British Columbia is derived from *Kwikwetlem*, which is said to be derived from a Coast Salish term meaning "little red fish".

A random assemblage of fish merely using some localised resource such as food or nesting sites is known simply as an *aggregation*. When fish come together in an interactive, social grouping, then they may be forming either a *shoal* or a *school* depending on the degree of organisation. A *shoal* is a loosely organised group where each fish swims and forages independently but is attracted to other members of the group and adjusts its behaviour, such as swimming speed, so that it remains close to the other members of the group. *Schools* of fish are much more tightly organised, synchronising their swimming so that all fish move at the same speed and in the same direction. Shoaling and schooling behaviour is believed to provide a variety of advantages.

*Examples:*

- Cichlids congregating at lekking sites form an *aggregation*. Many minnows and characins form *shoals*.
- Anchovies, herrings and silversides are classic examples of *schooling* fish.

While school and shoal have different meanings within biology, they are often treated as synonyms by non-specialists, with speakers of British English using "shoal" to describe any grouping of fish, while speakers of American English often using "school" just as loosely.

# Recreational Fishing

Recreational fishing, also called sport fishing, is fishing for pleasure or competition. It can be contrasted with commercial fishing, which is fishing for profit, or subsistençe fishing, which is fishing for survival.

The most common form of recreational fishing is done with a rod, reel, line, hooks and any one of a wide range of baits. Other devices, commonly referred to as *terminal tackle*, are also used to affect or complement the presentation of the bait to the targeted fish. Some examples of terminal tackle include weights, floats, and swivels. Lures are frequently used in place of bait. Some hobbyists make handmade tackle themselves, including plastic lures and artificial flies. The practice of catching or attempting to catch fish with a hook is known as angling. When angling, it is sometimes expected or required that the fish be released.

Big-game fishing is fishing from boats to catch large open-water species such as tuna, sharks and marlin. Noodling and trout tickling are also recreational activities. One method of growing popularity is kayak fishing. Kayak fisherman fish from sea kayaks in an attempt to level the playing field with fish and to further challenge their abilities. Kayaks are stealthy and allow anglers to reach areas not fishable from land or by conventional boat. Sport fishing is dominated by men, although women also participate in the sport.

The earliest English essay on recreational fishing was published in 1496, shortly after the invention of the printing press. The authorship of this was attributed to Dame Juliana Berners, the prioress of the Benedictine Sopwell Nunnery. The essay was titled *Treatyse of Fysshynge wyth an Angle*, and was published in the second *Boke of St Albans*, a treatise on hawking, hunting and heraldry. These were major interests of the nobility, and the publisher, Wynkyn de Worde, was concerned that the book should be kept from those who were not gentlemen, since their immoderation in angling might "utterly destroye it".

During the 16th century the work was much read, and was reprinted many times. *Treatyse* includes detailed information on fishing waters, the construction of rods and lines, and the use of natural baits and artificial flies. It also includes modern concerns about conservation and angler etiquette.

Recreational fishing for sport or leisure gained popularity during the 16th and 17th centuries, and coincides with the publication of Izaak Walton's *The Compleat Angler, or Contemplative Man's Recreation* in 1653. This book is the definitive work that champions the position of the angler who loves fishing for the sake of fishing.

More than 300 editions of *The Compleat Angler* have been published. The pastoral discourse is enriched with country fishing folklore, songs and poems, recipes and anecdotes, moral meditations and quotes from classic literature. The central character, Piscator, champions the art of angling, but also tranquilly relishes the pleasures of friendship, verse and song, good food and drink.

The early evolution of fishing as recreation is not clear. For example, there is anecdotal evidence for fly fishing in Japan as early as the ninth century BCE, and in Europe

Claudius Aelianus (175–235 CE) describes fly fishing in his work *On the Nature of Animals*, as "a Macedonian way of catching fish... They fasten red (crimson red) wool round a hook, and fix on to the wool two feathers which grow under a cock's wattles, and which in colour are like wax. Their rod is six feet long, and their line is the same length. Then they throw their snare, and the fish, attracted and maddened by the colour, comes straight at it..."

But for the early Japanese and Macedonians, fly fishing was likely to have been a means of survival, rather than recreation. It is possible that antecedents of recreational fly fishing arrived in England with the Norman conquest of 1066.

Although the point in history where fishing could first be said to be recreational is not clear, it is clear that recreational fishing had fully arrived with the publication of *The Compleat Angler*.

Big-game fishing started as a sport after the invention of the motorized boat. In 1898, Dr. Charles Frederick Holder, a marine biologist and early conservationist, invented this sport and went on to publish many articles and books on the subject noted for their combination of accurate scientific detail with exciting narratives.

Sport fishing methods vary according to the area fished, the species targeted, the personal strategies of the angler, and the resources available. It ranges from the aristocratic art of fly fishing elaborated in Great Britain, to the high-tech methods used to chase marlin and tuna. Sport fishing is usually done with hook, line, rod and reel rather than with nets or other aids.

The most common salt water game fish are marlin, tuna, tarpon, sailfish, shark, and mackerel.

In North America, freshwater fish include snook, redfish, salmon, trout, bass, pike, catfish, walleye and muskellunge. The smallest fish are called panfish, because they can fit in a normal cooking pan. Examples are perch and sunfish.

In the past, sport fishers, even if they did not eat their catch, almost always killed them to bring them to shore to be weighed or for preservation as trophies.

In order to protect recreational fisheries sport fishermen now often catch and release, and sometimes tag and release, which involves fitting the fish with identity tags, recording vital statistics, and sending a record to a government agency.

Most recreational fishers use a fishing rod with a fishing line and a hook at the end of the line. The rod may be equipped with a reel so the line can be reeled in, and some form of bait or a lure attached to the hook.

Fly fishing is a special form of rod fishing in which the reel is attached to the back end of the rod, and a whipping motion is used to imitate a fly with an artificial fly. Another less common technique is bowfishing using a regular bow or a crossbow. The "arrow" is a modified bolt with barbs at the tip, connected to a fishing line so the fish can be retrieved. Some crossbows are fitted with a reel.

The effective use of fishing techniques often depends on knowledge about the fish and their behaviour including migration, foraging and habitat.

### Fishing Tackle

Fishing tackle is a general term that refers to the equipment used by fishers. Almost any equipment or gear used for fishing can be called fishing tackle. Some examples are hooks, lines, sinkers, floats, rods, reels, baits, lures, spears, nets, gaffs, traps, waders and tackle boxes.

Tackle that is attached to the end of a fishing line is called terminal tackle. This includes hooks, sinkers, floats, leaders, swivels, split rings and wire, snaps, beads, spoons, blades, spinners and clevises to attach spinner blades to fishing lures.

Fishing tackle can be contrasted with fishing techniques. Fishing tackle refers to the physical equipment that is used when fishing, whereas fishing techniques refers to the ways the tackle is used when fishing.

### Rules and Regulations

Recreational fishing has conventions, rules, licensing restrictions and laws that limit the way in which fish may be caught. The International Game Fish Association (IGFA) makes and oversees a set of voluntary guidelines.

Typically, these prohibit the use of nets and the catching of fish with hooks not in the mouth. Enforceable regulations are put in place by governments to ensure sustainable practice amongst anglers. For example in the Republic of Ireland, the Central Fisheries Board oversees the implementation of all angling regulations, which include controls on angling lures, baits and number of hooks permissible, as well as licensing regimes and other conservation based restrictions.

### Fish Logs

In addition to capturing fish for food, recreational anglers may also keep a log of fish caught and submit trophy-sized fish to independent record keeping bodies. In the Republic of Ireland, the Irish Specimen Fish Committee verifies and publicizes the capture of trophy fish caught with rod and line by anglers in Ireland, both in freshwater and at sea. The Committee also ratifies Irish record rod caught fish. It also uses a set of 'fair play' regulations to ensure fish are caught in accordance with accepted angling norms.

### Competitions

Recreational fishing competitions (tournaments) are a recent innovation in which fishermen compete for prizes based on the total weight of a given species of fish caught within a predetermined time. This sport evolved from local fishing contests into large competitive circuits, especially in North America. Competitors are most often professional fishermen who are supported by commercial endorsements. Other competitions are based purely on length with mandatory catch and release. Either longest fish or total length is documented with a camera and a mandatory sticker or unique item, a practice used since it's hard to weigh a living fish accurately in a boat.

Sport fishing competitions involve individuals if the fishing occurs from land, and usually teams if conducted from boats, as well as specified times and areas for catching fish. A score is awarded for each fish caught. The points awarded depend on the fish's weight and species. Occasionally a score is divided by the strength of the fishing line used, yielding more points to those who use thinner, weaker line. In tag and release competitions, a flat score is awarded per fish species caught, divided by the line strength. Usually sport fishing competitions award a prize to the boat or team with the most points earned.

In Australia, a self-administered standard for the environmental assessment of tournament fishing has been proposed as an alternative and possible pathway to the ISO 14001 international standard. The standard assesses environmental, social, economic, and public risk factors. Tournament organizers may apply for voluntary certification. In some U.S. states, fishery agencies and competition organizers create their own codes of practice.

**Industry**

The recreational fishing industry consists of enterprises such as the manufacture and retailing of fishing tackle, the design and building of recreational fishing boats, and the provision of fishing boats for charter and guided fishing trips.

"Pay to fish" enterprises provide anglers with controlled access to stocked lakes, ponds or canals. These provide fishing opportunities outside of the permitted seasons and quotas applied to public waters. In the United Kingdom, commercial fisheries of this sort charge access fees. In North America, establishments usually charge for the fish caught, by length or by weight, rather than for access to the site although some establishments charge both types of fees.

Recreational fishing is a multi-billion dollar industry In the USA, about 12 million recreational saltwater fishers generate $30 billion in economic impact and support 350,000 jobs.

# 12

# Bass Fishing

Bass fishing is the activity of angling for the North American gamefish known colloquially as the *black bass*. There are numerous black bass species considered as gamefish in North America, including largemouth bass (*Micropterus salmoides*), smallmouth bass (*Micropterus dolomieui*), Spotted bass or Kentucky bass (*Micropterus punctatus*), Guadalupe bass (*Micropterus treculii*), and many other species and subspecies of the genus *Micropterus*. Though referred to as bass, all are actually members of the sunfish family (Centrarchidae: order Perciformes).

Modern bass fishing has evolved into a multi-billion dollar industry. The sport has changed drastically since its beginnings in the late 19th century. From humble beginnings, the black bass has become the second most specifically sought-after game fish in the United States. The sport has driven the development of all manner of fishing gear, including rods, reels, lines, lures, electronic depth and fish-finding instruments, drift boats, float tubes, and specialized bass boats.

All black bass are well-known as strong fighters, and are fished recreationally. Depending upon species and various other factors such as water quality and availability of food, black bass may be found in lakes, reservoirs, ponds, rivers, streams, creeks, even roadside ditches. Largemouth are known for their overall size and resistance when hooked, favoring short, powerful runs and escape to cover such as submerged logs or weedbeds. Largemouth bass are known for their wild jumps while Smallmouth bass are generally accepted as the hardest fighting black bass, pound for pound. Smallmouth bass tend to jump more and fight aggressively on the surface when hooked, in order to throw the hook. Large mouth bass tend to go after topwater and submerged baits with colors that closely resemble that of the bait-fish in their natural habitat. All bass are scent as well as visual predators so care should be taken to ensure no foreign scents, like tobacco, contaminate soft plastics. Largemouth bass anglers tend to catch and release. Bass are usually fileted when taken for the table, and the flesh is white and firm, with a delicate taste when cooked. Largemouth are not generally used for food because the meat has little taste. Largemouth bass offer the best striking ability of all bass and usually give the fisherman the most action. However, more bass anglers are adopting "catch and release" angling where the bass are returned to the water after being hooked and retrieved.

Bass fishing in the United States largely evolved on its own, and was not influenced by angling developments in Europe or other parts of the world. Indeed modern British sea bass fisherman look to the United States freshwater bass techniques for inspiration for lure fishing and to the USA, Japan and China for tackle. During the early-to-mid-19th century, wealthy sport anglers in the United States (mostly located in the northeastern portion of the country) largely confined themselves to trout and salmon fishing using fly rods. While smallmouth bass were sought by some fly fishermen, most bass fishing was done by sustenance anglers using poles and live bait. The working-class heritage of bass fishing strongly influenced the sport and is manifested even today in its terminology, hobbyist literature, and media coverage.

In the mid-19th century, the first artificial lure used for bass was developed in the form of an Artificial fly. At first, these artificial fly patterns were largely derivations of existing trout and salmon flies. As time went on, new fly patterns were specifically developed to fish for bass, as well as heavier spinner/fly lures that could be cast by the baitcasting and fixed-spool casting reels and rods available at the time. Floating wooden lures(plugs) or poppers of lightweight cork or balsa were introduced around 1900, sometimes combined with hooks dressed with artificial fur or feathers. Production of the plastic worm began in 1949, but it was not until the 1960's that its use became popular. The plastic worm revolutionized the sport of bass fishing.

In the United States, the sport of bass fishing was greatly advanced by the stocking of largemouth and smallmouth bass outside their native ranges in the latter portion of the 19th century. As the nation's railroad system expanded, large numbers of 'tank' ponds were built by damming various small creeks that intersected the tracks in order to provide water for steam engines; later, new towns often sprang up alongside these water stops. Shippers found that black bass were a hardy species that could be transported in buckets or barrels via the railroad, sometimes using the spigot from the railroad water tank to aerate the fingerlings.

Largemouth bass were often stocked in tank ponds and warmer lakes, while smallmouth bass were distributed to lakes and rivers throughout the northern and western United States, as far west as California. Smallmouth were transplanted east of the Appalachians just before the Civil War, and afterwards introduced into New England.

Largemouth bass populations boomed after the U.S. Department of Agriculture began to advise and assist farmers in constructing and stocking farm ponds with largemouth bass, even offering advice on managing various fish species. Soon, those who had stocked largemouth bass on their farm ponds began to pursue them on a burgeoning number of new reservoirs and impoundments built in the United States during the 1940s and 1950s. These impoundments coincided with a postwar fishing boom, additional funds from sales of fishing licenses for the first large-scale attempts at bass fisheries management. This was especially true in the southern United States, where the largemouth bass thrived in waters too warm or turbid for other types of gamefish.

With increased industrialization and development, many of the nation's eastern trout rivers were dammed, polluted, or allowed to silt up, raising water temperatures and killing off the native brook trout. Smallmouth bass were often introduced to northern rivers now too warm for native trout, and slowly became a popular gamefish with many anglers. Equally adaptable to large, cool-water impoundments and reservoirs, the smallmouth also spread far beyond its original native range. Later, smallmouth populations also began to decline after years of damage caused by overdevelopment and industrial and agricultural pollution, as well as a loss of river habitat caused by damming many formerly wild rivers in order to form lakes or reservoirs. In recent years, a renewed emphasis on preserving water quality and riparian habitat in the nation's rivers and lakes, together with stricter management practices, eventually benefited smallmouth populations and has caused a resurgence in their popularity with anglers.

By the early 20th century, bass fishing had been well established as a sport with its own following. Though the use of artificial lures for bass had begun with the Artificial fly and fly fishing tackle, the bait casting rod and reel soon came to dominate the sport. Although fixed-spool reels were introduced in use in the United States as early as the 1870s, spinning reels and rods did not gain wide acceptance as an angling tool until the 1950s. Since that time, most bass anglers have used bait casting or spinning tackle, using either artificial lures or live bait.

During the 1950s and 1960s, the development of specific angling tools for bass significantly increased angler bass catches and helped stimulate the development of the sport.

Some of these innovations include the invention of monofilament nylon fishing lines, the fiberglass (later graphite composite) fishing rod, the electric trolling motor, the fish finder/depth locator, and new artificial lures and baits made of various plastics. Recently, advanced electronics that mimic the sounds of schooling bait fish have been introduced, and a controversy has arisen over the proper use of these devices in bass tournament fishing.

Since the early 1990s, fly fishing for bass, particularly smallmouth bass, has again become popular, using fly patterns, rods, and fly lines suited for bass.

Fishermen, conservation groups, and governmental wildlife departments have introduced black bass of various species across the world for the sport of fishing. Outside North America, Japan and South Africa have active programs.

Bass fishing as a sport was helped along by the chase for the standing world record which has held for over 75 years. Though surrounded by controversy it is widely accepted that in 1932 a 22 pound 4 ounce bass was caught by George Perry in Montgomery Lake, Georgia. It is one of the longest standing records in the sport of fishing. This record was tied on July 2, 2009 when Aichi Japan resident Manabu Kurita caught a 22 pound 4 ounce largemouth bass in Lake Biwa.

The increasingly popularity of the sport combined with "catch and release" practices have in some cases led to an overpopulation of bass.

An overpopulated, stunted bass population can best be detected in the spring when all the bass are at least one year old. If virtually all the bass are 4 inches long or smaller, the population is probably stunted. Some indicators that a bass population is overpopulated:

*(a)* The largemouth bass caught are all less than 1 pound and are "skinny".

*(b)* The bluegills are ½ pound and larger (too large for the bass to eat). An overpopulation an/or stunting of bass may be caused by several factors including:

- Not enough bass being harvested.
- Too few bluegill or redear sunfish were stocked initially or they are failing to reproduce and the bass population does not have an adequate food supply.

It is posited that the easiest way to control an overpopulation of largemouth bass is by increasing the take of bass. This is clearly an effective method of thinning the bass population providing recreation at the same time - which is more important to American Bass anglers. It may take two to three years to bring the population back into balance. If forage fish are scarce, stock adult bluegill or redear sunfish (7 to 8 inches long). These fish will be too large to be eaten by the bass. The large panfish will spawn in the spring and produce a supply of forage.

Black bass should not be confused with a multitude of unrelated fish species found around the world and called "bass", such as the butterfly Peacock Bass (*Cichla ocellaris*), speckled Peacock bass (*Cichla temensis*), Papuan Black Bass (*Lutjanus goldiei*) (also called Niugini bass), Australian bass, Rock bass (*Ambloplites rupestris*), American Striped Bass, and British sea bass (*Dicentrarchus labrax*).

There are several major bass fishing competitions in the United States with the two most dominant circuit being Bassmasters and the FLW series.

The Bassmaster Tournament Trail is organized by the Bass Anglers Sportsman Society (B.A.S.S.). It was started by Ray Scott, the "father" of competitive bass fishing. First held in 1969, today, professionals like Michael Iaconelli, Kevin VanDam, Aaron Martens, Rick Clunn, and Luke Clausen are household names to many American sports fans. There are 12 events in which the top 50 anglers compete. The top prize in the Bassmaster Classic is $500,000.

The Wal-Mart FLW Tour was named after Forrest L. Wood of Ranger Boats fame. The top prize of the Forrest Wood Cup is $1 Million. Both tours are nationally televised on networks like ESPN and Fox Sports Net (ESPN actually owns and operates B.A.S.S.), and covered extensively by news media.

On the West Coast, WON BASS has been the main regional circuit in operation since the 1980s Annually, WON BASS conducts the U.S. Open of Bass Fishing at Lake Mead, Nevada which annually pays back nearly $500,000 per event. This is a test of both angling skill and endurance as the anglers compete for 3 days in the scorching hot sun and windy conditions of the Mohave desert. Renowned anglers Ricky Clunn, Byron Velvick, Aaron Martens, and Gary Klein have all been crowned champions during the Open's 25 year history.

In modern bass fishing competitions, caught bass are placed in a live well, and released as soon as caught and weighed by officials. Competitors are penalized heavily for dead fish and in some cases dead fish are not weighed. Fish turned in for weighing are immediately released or placed in tanks and treated for stress and glyco-protein (slime coat) injury, then released back into the water.

Competitive bass fishing has also spread to anglers in other countries such as Japan, Australia and South Africa. Takahiro Omori, a Japanese angler living in Texas, won the 2004 Bassmaster Classic title. Australian tournaments are based on a native freshwater fish called Australian bass that is unrelated to largemouth bass.

## Big-game Fishing

Big-game fishing, often referred to as offshore sportfishing, offshore gamefishing, or blue-water fishing is a form of recreational fishing, targeting large fish renowned for their sporting qualities, such as tuna and marlin. Big-game fishing started as a sport after the invention of the motor boat. Charles Frederick Holder, a marine biologist and early conservationist, is credited with founding the sport in 1898. He went on to publish many articles and books on the subject, noted for their combination of accurate scientific detail with exciting narratives. Purpose built game fishing boats appeared early in the 20th century. An example is the *Crete*, in use at Catalina Island, California, in 1915, and shipped to Hawaii the following year. According to a newspaper report at that time, the *Crete* had "... a deep cockpit, a chair fitted for landing big fish and leather pockets for placing the pole."

## Big-game Species

The billfish (broadbill swordfish, marlin and sailfish), larger tunas (bluefin, yellowfin, and bigeye) and sharks (mako, great white, tiger, hammerhead and other large species) are the main species recognized as big-game fish, with many anglers considering the Atlantic tarpon also a big-game species.

Smaller game fish, such as dolphinfish, wahoo, smaller tuna species such as albacore and skipjack tuna, plus barracuda, are commonly caught as by-catch or taken deliberately for use as live or dead bait.

## Locations

Historically most of the locations where the sport was developed, such as Avalon, California; Florida; Bimini in the Bahamas; Cairns, Queensland, Australia; northern New Zealand; Wedgeport in Nova Scotia and Kona in Hawaii, benefited from the presence of large numbers of gamefish relatively close to shore, within range of the boats of that era.

As the vessels used for sportfishing became larger, faster, longer-ranged and more seaworthy, big-game species are now pursued on grounds ranging from 60 or 70 miles' distance from port, such as the submarine canyons of the United States continental shelf, to hundreds of miles as in the case of the San Diego long range fishery, where large live-aboard vessels range far out into the Pacific searching for tuna schools.

Today big-game fishing is carried out from ports in tropical and temperate coasts practically worldwide.

## North America

The United States has the world's largest saltwater fishing industry and along the entire length of the East Coast, from

Key West to the Gulf of Maine, big-game anglers pursue a variety of tropical and temperate sportfish ranging from sailfish and dolphinfish in the Florida Keys to giant bluefin tuna in Massachusetts and in Canadian waters. The West Coast lacks the influence of the warm Gulf Stream current, and most big game species are mainly confined to California, a birthplace of the sport. Some of the same species that were fished for by the pioneers of the sport - Pacific bluefin tuna, broadbill swordfish and striped marlin - are still fished for today.

### Latin and South America

Billfish and tuna are pursued in almost all the Latin American coastal nations, many of which are renowned for the excellence of their fishing. Mexico, Panama, Costa Rica, Venezuela, Ecuador and Guatemala have the largest fleets of sport fishing boats.

### Land-based Game Fishing

In some areas big-game species can be caught by land-based anglers, with the rock platforms of Jervis Bay in New South Wales, Australia being probably the most well-known. Black marlin of up to 200 lbs have been caught here by anglers floating out baits on balloons.

### Boats

Big-game fishing requires a boat of sufficient seaworthiness and range to transport the crew to the fishing grounds and back. Boats that fit these requirements may be as small as the 18 to 21-foot trailerable boats commonly used along the Australian coast, in New Zealand and on the lee coasts of the Hawaiian Islands where they are known as the "mosquito fleet".

At the other extreme the 100-foot and larger vessels of the San Diego long range fleet and similar, although less refined "party boats" operating from New England, transport 25, 30 or more anglers in search of yellowfin, bluefin and bigeye tuna.

The cost of a suitable boat, electronics, tackle and the operating costs (fuels and other consumables, insurance, mooring fees and maintenance) can be very substantial. Consequently, many big-game anglers prefer to use charter services where they hire the use of a boat and equipment, and the fish-finding expertise of a captain, in preference to maintaining their own. Either way, big-game fishing can be an extremely expensive pursuit, and one in which the wealthy have tended to feature prominently.

### The Classic Sport Fisherman

Most of the features of the classic sport fisherman were gradually developed in the 1920s and 1930s as existing motor cruisers and commercial fishing vessels were adapted for fishing with outriggers, fighting chairs and other ancillaries such as bait boxes and flybridge helm stations. These boats, though crude by modern standards, scored many pioneering big game catches of huge bluefin tuna, broadbill swordfish and marlin.

Through the 1930s and 1940s sportfishermen in Florida, amongst them John Rybovich and Ernest Hemingway, continued to innovate and refine, and in 1946 the Rybovich yard launched the Miss Chevy II, a 34-footer that crystallized all the innovations that had gone before into a design whose features - raised foredeck, flybridge controls and roomy cockpit - are still closely followed by today's leading sportfish builders.

The need for greater range and speed as anglers sought gamefish further and further offshore resulted in the development of bigger boats powered by larger engines, but the basic layout of a dedicated big game fishing vessel has remained largely the same since the late 1940s.

### Smaller Sportfishing Boats

The development of outboard power opened up many big game fishing grounds to smaller craft in the 18 to 25 foot range.

### Electronics

Electronics technology developed for commercial fishermen has become increasingly used by recreational anglers. Fishfinders, also known as bottom machines or echo sounders, are now commonplace. Other electronics used to narrow down the search for fish may include radar, forward or side-scanning sonar, water temperature sensors and sea surface temperature imagery obtained from satellites.

### Trolling

Fish are enticed by trolling fishing lures (designed to resemble squid or other baitfish) or baits behind the boat. Multiple lines are often used. Outriggers were designed to spread the lines more widely.

### Chumming/Chunking

Chumming, or chunking, is the process of throwing pieces of bait fish overboard to attract larger game fish. This is called Berley in Australia.

### Fighting the Fish

Once a fish is properly hooked on a line, a somewhat tricky task as often initial nibbles only partly hook the fish, one of the fishermen attempts to reel it in. The captain assists by maneuvering the boat so that the fish remains astern (behind the boat), while other members of the crew race to reel in the other lines so as to avoid tangling with the angler reeling in the fish.

Most of the time, the fishing line used for sport fishing has a breaking strain less than the maximum force the fish can apply to the line. The fishing reels therefore have sophisticated drag mechanisms which allow the line to escape if the fish pulls on it, but keep the specified tension on the line.

When hooked, most fish will circulate in different directions, and when they are not pulling away from the boat the fisherman can take the opportunity to reel in some of the line. Eventually, if the fish tires and has not broken the line, they will be reeled in; however, the challenge does not end there.

Hauling a heavy, powerful, and still very much alive fish on board the boat represents a considerable challenge, unless the fish is tagged and released. Strategies include: gaffing, pulling it in with ones hands, and if it is a smallish game fish, a net.

The fish can be fought with or without a game-chair. With a game chair, the angler sits in a specially-designed chair at the stern of the boat, and places the butt of the rod into a gimbaled mount. Most rods used in this manner are quite long.

The older and more classic models had straight rod butts. More contemporary models have bent rod butts, which give a more convenient angle for fighting the fish when the rod is placed in the mount. With large fish, this can still represent a considerable challenge, but "stand-up" game fishing, without the assistance of a chair and with the seat mount replaced by a harness, requires a good deal of strength and endurance, as well as body mass.

# 13

# Overfishing

Overfishing occurs when fishing activities reduce fish stocks below an acceptable level. This can occur in any body of water from a pond to the oceans.

Ultimately overfishing can lead to resource depletion in cases of subsidised fishing, low biological growth rates and critical low biomass levels (e.g. by critical depensation growth properties). For example, overfishing of sharks has led to the upset of entire marine ecosystems.

The ability of a fishery to recover after overfishing depends on whether the ecosystem conditions are suitable for the recovery. Dramatic changes in species composition can result in an ecosystem shift, where other equilibrium energy flows involve species compositions other than those that had been present before. For example, once trout have been overfished, carp might take over in a way that makes it impossible for the trout to re-establish a breeding population. There are three recognized types of overfishing: growth overfishing, recruit overfishing and ecosystem overfishing.

*Growth overfishing* – is when fish are harvested at an average size that is smaller than the size that would produce the maximum yield per recruit. This makes the total yield less than it would be if the fish were allowed to grow to a reasonable size. It can be countered by reducing fishing mortality to lower levels and increasing the average size of the fish harvested to a length that will allow maximum yield per recruit.

*Recruit overfishing* – is when the mature adult (spawning biomass) population is depleted to a level where it no longer has the reproductive capacity to replenish itself. There are not enough adults to produce offspring. Increasing the spawning stock biomass to a target level is the approach taken by managers to restore an overfished population to sustainable levels. This is generally accomplished by placing moratoriums, quotas and minimum size limits on a fish population.

*Ecosystem overfishing* – is when the balance of the ecosystem is altered due to overfishing. Declines in the abundances of large predatory species declines and in turn small forage type species increase in abundance, causing a shift in the balance of the ecosystem towards smaller species of fish.

**Instances**

Examples of the outcomes from overfishing exist in areas such as the North Sea of Europe, the Grand Banks of North America and the East China Sea of Asia. In these locations, overfishing has not only proved disastrous to fish stocks but also to the fishing communities relying on the harvest. Like other extractive industries such as forestry and hunting, fishery is susceptible to economic interaction between ownership or stewardship and sustainability, otherwise known as the tragedy of the commons.

The Peruvian coastal anchovy fisheries crashed in the 1970s after overfishing, following an El Niño season which largely depleted anchovies from its waters. Anchovies had previously been a major natural resource in Peru; indeed, 1971 alone yielded 10.2 million metric tons of anchovies. However, in the following year, and the four after that, the Peruvian fleet's catch amounted to only about 4 million tons. This was a major loss to Peru's economy.

The collapse of the cod fishery off Newfoundland, and the 1992 decision by Canada to impose an indefinite moratorium on the Grand Banks, is a dramatic example of the consequences of overfishing.

The sole fisheries in the rish Sea, the west English Channel, and other locations have become overfished to the point of virtual collapse, according to the UK government's official Biodiversity Action Plan. The United Kingdom has created elements within this plan to attempt to restore this fishery, but the expanding global human population and the expanding demand for fish has reached a point where demand for food threatens the stability of these fisheries, if not the species' survival.

Many deep sea fish are at risk, such as orange roughy, Patagonian toothfish and sablefish. The deep sea is almost completely dark, near freezing and has little food. Deep sea fish grow slowly because of limited food, have slow metabolisms, low reproductive rates, and many don't reach breeding maturity for 30 to 40 years. A fillet of orange roughy at the store is probably at least 50 years old. Most deep sea fish are in international waters, where there are no legal protections. Most of these fish are caught by deep trawlers near seamounts, where they congregate because of food. Flash freezing allows the trawlers to work for days at a time, and modern fishfinders target the fish with ease.

According to a 2008 UN report, the world's fishing fleets are losing $50 billion USD each year through depleted stocks and poor fisheries management. The report, produced jointly by the World Bank and the UN Food and Agriculture Organization (FAO), asserts that half the world's fishing fleet could be scrapped with no change in catch. In addition, the biomass of global fish stocks have been allowed to run down to the point where it is no longer possible to catch the amount of fish that could be caught. Increased incidence of schistosomiasis in Africa has been linked to declines of fish species that eat the snails carrying the disease-causing parasites. Massive growth of jellyfish populations threaten fish stocks, as they compete with fish for food, eat fish eggs, and poison or swarm fish, and can survive in oxygen depleted environments where fish cannot; they wreak massive havoc on commercial fisheries. Overfishing eliminates a major jellyfish competitor and predator exacerbating the jellyfish population explosion.

### Acceptable Levels

The notion of overfishing hinges on what is meant by an acceptable level of fishing. More precise biological and bioeconomic terms define acceptable level as follows:

- *Biological overfishing* occurs when fishing mortality has reached a level where the stock biomass has negative marginal growth (slowing down biomass growth), as indicated by the red area in the figure. (Fish are being taken out of the water so quickly that the replenishment of stock by breeding slows down. If the replenishment continues to slow down for long enough, replenishment will go into reverse and the population will decrease.)
- *Economic or bioeconomic overfishing* additionally considers the cost of fishing when determining acceptable catches. Under this framework a fishery is considered to be overfished when catches exceed maximum economic yield where resource rent is at its maximum. Fish are being removed from the fishery so quickly that the profitability of the fishery is sub-optimal. A more dynamic definition of economic overfishing also considers the present value of the fishery using a relevant discount rate to maximise the flow of resource rent over all future catches.

A current model for predicting acceptable levels is the Harvest Control Rule (HCR), which is a variable over which management has some direct control as a function of some indicator of stock status. Constant catch and constant fishing mortality are two types of simple harvest control rules.

### Input and Output Orientations

Fishing capacity can also be defined following an input or an output orientation.

An input-oriented fishing capacity is defined as the maximum available capital stock in a fishery that is fully utilized at the maximum technical efficiency in a given time period, given resource and market conditions.

An output-oriented fishing capacity is defined as the maximum catch a vessel (fleet) can produce if inputs are fully utilized given the biomass, the fixed inputs, the age structure of the fish stock, and the present stage of technology.

Technical efficiency of each vessel of the fleet is assumed necessary to attain this maximum catch. The degree of capacity utilization results from the comparison of the actual level of output (input) and the capacity output (input) of a vessel or a fleet.

### Mitigation

With present and forecast levels of the world population it is not possible to solve the overfishing issue; however, there are mitigation measures that can save selected fisheries and forestall the collapse of others.

In order to meet the problems of overfishing, a precautionary approach and Harvest Control Rule (HCR) management principles have been introduced in the main fisheries around the world. The Traffic Light colour convention introduces sets of rules based on predefined critical values, which could be adjusted as more information is gained.

The "United Nations Convention on the Law of the Sea" treaty deals with aspects of overfishing in articles 61, 62 and 65.

- *Article 61* requires all coastal states to ensure that the maintenance of living resources in their exclusive economic zones is not endangered by over-exploitation. The same article addresses the maintenance or restoration of populations of species above levels at which their reproduction may become seriously threatened.

- *Article 62* provides that coastal states: "shall promote the objective of optimum utilization of the living resources in the exclusive economic zone without prejudice to Article 61".
- *Article 65* provides generally for the rights of, inter alia, coastal states to prohibit, limit, or regulate the exploitation of marine mammals.

Overfishing can be viewed as a case of the tragedy of the commons; in that sense, solutions would promote property rights, such as privatization and fish farming. Daniel K. Benjamin, in *Fisheries are Classic Example of the "Tragedy of the Commons"*, cites research by Grafton, Squires, and Fox to support the idea that privatization can solve the overfishing problem:

> According to recent research on the British Columbia halibut fishery, where the commons has been at least partly privatized, substantial ecological and economic benefits have resulted. There is less damage to fish stocks, the fishing is safer, and fewer resources are needed to achieve a given harvest.

Another possible solution, at least for some areas, is fishing quotas, so fishermen can only legally take a certain amount of fish. A more radical possibility is declaring certain areas of the sea "no-go zones" and make fishing there strictly illegal, so the fish in that area have time to recover and repopulate.

Controlling consumer behavior and demand is a key in mitigating action. Worldwide a number of initiatives emerged to provide consumers with information regarding the conservation status of the seafood available to them. The Guide to Good Fish Guides lists a number of these.

### Fishing Quotas

A model of the interaction between fish and fishers showed that when an area is closed to fishers, but there are no catch regulations such as individual transferable quotas, fish catches are temporarily increased but overall fish biomass is reduced, resulting in the opposite outcome than the one desired for fisheries. Thus, a displacement of the fleet from one locality to another will generally have little effect if the same quota is taken. As a result, management measures such as temporary closures or establishing a Marine Protected Area of fishing areas are ineffective when not combined with individual fishing quotas. An inherent problem with quotas is that fish populations vary from year to year. A study has found that fish populations rise dramatically after stormy years due to more nutrients reaching the surface and therefore greater primary production. To fish sustainably quotas need to be changed each year to take account of the population of fish but this is difficult to do.

### Individual Transferable Quotas

Individual transferable quotas (ITQs) are fishery rationalization instruments defined under the Magnuson-Stevens Fishery Conservation and Management Act as limited access permits to harvest quantities of fish. Fisheries scientists decide the optimal amount of fish (total allowable catch) to be harvested in a certain fishery, taking into account carrying capacity, regeneration rates and future values. Under ITQs, members of a fishery are granted rights to a percentage of the total allowable catch which can be harvested each year. These quotas can be fished, bought, sold, or leased allowing for the least cost vessels to be used. ITQs are used in New Zealand, Australia, Iceland, Canada and the United States. Only three ITQ programs have been implemented in the United States due to a moratorium supported by Ted Stevens.

In 2008 a large scale study of fisheries that used ITQ's and ones that didn't provided strong evidence that ITQ's can help to prevent collapses and restore fisheries that appear to be in decline.

### Fishing Suspension

China bans fishing in the South China Sea for a period each year.

## Benefits of Underfishing

Deliberately underfishing to increase long term fish stocks has been proposed as a way fisherman can maximize their yields in the long run.

## Resistance from Fishermen

There is always disagreement between fishermen and government scientists... Imagine an overfished area of the sea in the shape of a hockey field with nets at either end. The few fish left therein would gather around the goals because fish like structured habitats. Scientists would survey the entire field, make lots of unsuccessful hauls, and conclude that it contains few fish. The fishermen would make a beeline to the goals, catch the fish around them, and say the scientists do not know what they are talking about. The subjective impression the fishermen get is always that there's lots of fish - because they only go to places that still have them... fisheries scientists survey and compare entire areas, not only the productive fishing spots. *Fisheries scientist Daniel Pauly*

The fishing capacity problem is not only related to the conservation of fish stocks but also to the sustainability of fishing activity. Causes of the fishing problem can be found in property rights regime of fishing resources. Overexploitation and rent dissipation of fishermen arise in open-access fisheries as was shown in Gordon.

In open-access resources like fish stocks, in the absence of a system like individual transferable quotas, the impossibility of excluding others provokes the fishermen who want to increase catch to do so effectively by taking someone else' share, intensifying competition. This tragedy of the commons provokes a capitalization process that leads them to increase their costs until they are equal to their revenue, dissipating their rent completely. Removal of subsidies.

Several scientists have called for an end to subsidies paid to deep sea fisheries. In international waters beyond the 200 nautical mile exclusive economic zones of coastal countries, many fisheries are unregulated, and fishing fleets plunder the depths with state of the art technology. In a few hours, massive nets weighing up to 15 tons, dragged along the bottom by deep-water trawlers, can destroy deep-sea corals and sponge beds that have taken centuries or millennia to grow. The trawlers can target orange roughy, grenadiers or sharks. These fish are usually long-lived and late maturing, and their populations take decades, even centuries to recover.

Fisheries scientist Daniel Pauly and economist Ussif Rashid Sumaila have examined subsidies paid to bottom trawl fleets around the world. They found that $152 million US per year are paid to deep-sea fisheries. Without these subsidies, global deep-sea fisheries would operate at a loss of $50 million a year. A great deal of the subsidies paid to deep-sea trawlers is to subsidize the large amount of fuel required to travel beyond the 200 mile limit and drag weighted nets.

There is surely a better way for governments to spend money than by paying subsidies to a fleet that burns 1.1 billion litres of fuel annually to maintain paltry catches of old growth fish from highly vulnerable stocks, while destroying their habitat in the process.

Eliminating global subsidies would render these fleets economically unviable and would relieve tremendous pressure on over-fishing and vulnerable deep-sea ecosystems.

Sustainable seafood is a movement that has gained momentum as more people become aware about overfishing and environmentally destructive fishing methods. Sustainable seafood is seafood from either fished or farmed sources that can maintain or increase production in the future without jeopardizing the ecosystems from which it was acquired. In general, slow-growing fish that reproduce late in life, such as orange roughy, are vulnerable to overfishing. Seafood species that grow quickly and breed young, such as anchovies and sardines, are much more resistant to overfishing. Several organizations, including the Marine Stewardship Council (MSC), and Friend of the Sea, certify seafood fisheries as sustainable.

The Marine Stewardship Council (MSC) has developed an environmental standard for sustainable and well-managed fisheries. Environmentally responsible fisheries management and practices are rewarded with the use of its blue product ecolabel. Consumers concerned about overfishing and its consequences are increasingly able to choose seafood products which have been independently assessed against the MSC's environmental standard and labelled. This enables consumers to play a part in reversing the decline of fish stocks. As of April 2010, 69 fisheries around the world have been independently assessed and certified as meeting the MSC standard. Their where to buy page lists the currently available certified seafood - as of April 2010 nearly 4,000 MSC-labelled products are available in over 60 countries around the world. Fish & Kids is an MSC project to teach schoolchildren about marine environmental issues, including overfishing.

The Monterey Bay Aquarium's Seafood Watch Program, although not an official certifying body like the MSC, also provides guidance on the sustainability of certain fish species: Some seafood restaurants have begun to offer more sustainable seafood options.

The Seafood Choices Alliance is an organization whose members include chefs that serve sustainable seafood at their establishments. In the US, the Sustainable Fisheries Act defines sustainable practices through national standards. Although there is no official certifying body like the MSC, the National Oceanic and Atmospheric Administration has created FishWatch to help guide concerned consumers to sustainable seafood choices.

Environmental impact of fishing The environmental impact of fishing can be divided into issues that involve the availability of fish to be caught, such as overfishing, sustainable fisheries, and fisheries management; and issues that involve the impact of fishing on other elements of the environment, such as by-catch.

These conservation issues are part of marine conservation, and are addressed in fisheries science programs. There is a growing gap between how many fish are available to be caught and humanity's desire to catch them, a problem that gets worse as the world population grows.

Similar to other environmental issues, there can be conflict between the fishermen who depend on fishing for their livelihoods and fishery scientists who realise that if future fish populations are to be sustainable then some fisheries must reduce or even close.

The journal *Science* published a four-year study in November 2006, which predicted that, at prevailing trends, the world would run out of wild-caught seafood in 2048. The scientists stated that the decline was a result of overfishing, pollution and other environmental factors that were reducing the population of fisheries at the same time as their ecosystems were being degraded.

Yet again the analysis has met criticism as being fundamentally flawed, and many fishery management officials, industry representatives and scientists challenge the findings, although the debate continues. Many countries, such as Tonga, the United States, Australia and New Zealand, and international management bodies have taken steps to appropriately manage marine resources.

Some fishing techniques also may cause habitat destruction. Dynamite fishing and cyanide fishing, which are illegal in many places, harm surrounding habitat. Bottom trawling, the practice of pulling a fishing net along the sea bottom behind trawlers, removes around 5 to 25 per cent of an area's seabed life on a single run. A 2005 report of the UN Millennium Project, commissioned by UN Secretary-General Kofi Annan, recommended the elimination of bottom trawling on the high seas by 2006 to protect seamounts and other ecologically sensitive habitats.

In mid October 2006, U.S. President Bush joined other world leaders calling for a moratorium on deep-sea trawling, a practice shown to often have harmful effects on sea habitat and, hence, on fish populations.

Overfishing has also been widely reported due to increases in the volume of fishing hauls to feed a quickly growing number of consumers. This has led to the breakdown of some sea ecosystems and several fishing industries whose catch has been greatly diminished.

The extinction of many species has also been reported. According to an FAO estimate, over 70 per cent of the world's fish species are either fully exploited or depleted. According to Nitin Desai, Secretary General of the 2002 World Summit on Sustainable Development, "Overfishing cannot continue, the depletion of fisheries poses a major threat to the food supply of millions of people."

The cover story of the May 15, 2003 issue of the science journal *Nature* – with Dr. Ransom A. Myers, an internationally prominent fisheries biologist (Dalhousie University, Halifax, Canada) as the lead author – was devoted to a summary of the scientific information. The story asserted that, as compared with 1950 levels, only a remnant (in some instances, as little as 10%) of all large ocean-fish stocks are left in the seas.

These large ocean fish are the species at the top of the food chains (e.g., tuna, cod, among others). However, this article was subsequently criticized as being fundamentally flawed, although much debate still exists and the majority of fisheries scientists now consider the results irrelevant with respect to large pelagics (the open seas).

Fishing may disrupt food webs by targeting specific, in-demand species. There might be too much fishing of prey species such as sardines and anchovies, thus reducing the food supply for the predators. It may also cause the increase of prey species when the target fishes are predator species such as salmon and tuna. Fisheries can reduce fish stocks that cetaceans rely on for food.

By-catch is the portion of the catch that is not the target species. These are either kept to be sold or discarded. In some instances the discarded portion is known as discards.

Many governments and intergovernmental bodies have implemented fisheries management policies designed to curb the environmental impact of fishing. Fishing conservation aims to control the human activities that may completely decrease a fish stock or washout an entire aquatic environment.

These laws include the quotas on the total catch of particular species in a fishery, effort quotas (e.g., number of days at sea), the limits on the number of vessels allowed in specific areas, and the imposition of seasonal restrictions on fishing.

In 2008 a large scale study of fisheries that used individual transferable quotas and ones that didn't provided strong evidence that individual transferable quotas can help to prevent collapses and restore fisheries that appear to be in decline.

Fish farming has been proposed as a more sustainable alternative to traditional capture of wild fish. However, fish farming has been found to have negative impacts on nearby wild fish. Further, farming of predatory fish like salmon can rely on fish feed that is based on fish meal and oil from wild fish.

# 14

# Angling

Angling is a method of fishing by means of an "angle" (fish hook). The hook is usually attached to a fishing line and the line is often attached to a fishing rod. Fishing rods are usually fitted with a fishing reel that functions as a mechanism for storing, retrieving and paying out the line. The hook itself can be dressed with lures or bait. A bite indicator such as a float is sometimes used.

Angling is a principal method of sport fishing, but commercial fisheries also use angling methods such as longlining or trolling. Catch and release fishing is increasingly practiced by recreational fishermen. In many parts of the world, size limits apply to certain species, meaning fish below and/or above a certain size must, by law, be released.

The species of fish pursued by anglers vary with geography. Among the many species of salt water fish that are caught for sport are swordfish, marlin, tuna, salmon and halibut. In North America the most popular fresh water sport species include bass, pike, walleye, muskellunge, yellow perch, trout, salmon, catfish, crappie, bluegill and sunfish. In Europe a large number of anglers fish for species such as carp, pike, tench, rudd, roach, European perch and barbel (especially in stillwaters). Although some fish are sought for their value as food, others are pursued for their fighting abilities or for the difficulty of pursuit.

The use of the hook in angling is descended, historically, from what would today be called a "gorge." The word "gorge", in this context, comes from the French word meaning "throat." Gorges were used by ancient peoples to capture fish. A gorge was a long, thin piece of bone or stone attached by its midpoint to a thin line. The gorge would be fixed with a bait so that it would rest parallel to the lay of the line. When a fish would swallow the bait, a tug on the line would cause the gorge to orient itself at right angles to the line, thereby sticking in the fish's gullet.

Many people prefer to fish solely with lures, which are artificial baits designed to entice fish to strike. The artificial bait angler uses a man-made lure that may or may not represent prey. The lure may require a specialised presentation to impart an enticing action as, for example, in fly fishing. A common way to fish a soft plastic worm is the Texas Rig.

### Natural Baits

The natural bait angler, with few exceptions, will use a common prey species of the fish as an attractant. The natural bait used may be alive or dead. Common natural baits include worms, leeches, minnows, frogs, salamanders, and insects. Natural baits are effective due to the lifelike texture, odour and colour of the bait presented.

The common earthworm is a universal bait for fresh water angling. Grubs and maggots are also excellent bait when trout fishing. Grasshoppers, bees and even ants are also used as bait for trout in their season, although many anglers believe that trout or salmon roe is superior to any other bait. In lakes in southern climates such as Florida, USA, fish such as bream will take bread bait. Bread bait is a small amount of bread, often moistened by saliva, balled up to a small size that is bite size to small fish.

Roe is an excellent bait for trout, salmon and many other fresh water fish.

The capture, transportation and culture of bait fish can spread damaging organisms between ecosystems, endangering them. In 2007, several American states, including Michigan, enacted regulations designed to slow the spread of fish diseases, including viral hemorrhagic septicemia, by bait fish. Because of the risk of transmitting *Myxobolus cerebralis* (whirling disease), trout and salmon should not be used as bait.

Anglers may increase the possibility of contamination by emptying bait buckets into fishing venues and collecting or using bait improperly. The transportation of fish from one location to another can break the law and cause the introduction of fish alien to the ecosystem.

### Laws and Regulations

Laws and regulations managing angling vary greatly, often regionally, within countries. These commonly include permits (licences), closed periods (seasons) where specific species are unavailable for harvest, restrictions on gear types, and quotas.

Laws generally prohibit catching fish with hooks other than in the mouth (foul hooking, "snagging" or "jagging" or the use of nets other than as an aid in landing a captured fish. Some species, such as bait fish, may be taken with nets, and a few for food. Sometimes, (non-sport) fish are considered of lesser value and it may be permissible to take them by methods like snagging, bow and arrow, or spear. None of these techniques fall under the definition of angling since they do not rely upon the use of a hook and line.

### Fishing Season

Fishing seasons are set by countries or localities to indicate what kinds of fish may be caught during sport fishing (also known as angling) for a certain period of time. Fishing seasons are enforced to maintain ecological balance and to protect species of fish during their spawning period during which they are easier to catch.

Although most anglers keep their catch for consumption, catch and release fishing is increasingly practiced, especially by fly anglers. The general principle is that releasing fish allows them to survive, thus avoiding unintended depletion of the population. For species such as marlin and muskellunge but, also, among few bass anglers, there is a cultural taboo against killing fish for food. In many parts of the world, size limits apply to certain species, meaning fish below a certain size must, by law, be released. It is generally believed that larger fish have a greater breeding potential. Some fisheries have a slot limit that allows the taking of smaller and larger fish, but requiring that intermediate sized fish be released. It is generally accepted that this management approach will help the fishery create a number of large, trophy-sized fish. In smaller fisheries that are heavily fished, catch and release is the only way to ensure that catchable fish will be available from year to year.

The practice of catch and release is criticised by some who consider it unethical to inflict pain upon a fish for purposes of sport. Some of those who object to releasing fish do not object to killing fish for food. Adherents of catch and release dispute this charge, pointing out that fish commonly feed on hard and spiky prey items, and as such can be expected to have tough mouths, and also that some fish will re-take a lure they have just been hooked on, a behaviour that is unlikely if hooking were painful. Opponents of catch and release fishing would find it preferable to ban or to severely restrict angling. On the other hand, proponents state that catch-and-release is necessary for many fisheries to remain sustainable, is a practice that that generally has high survival rates, and consider the banning of angling as not reasonable or necessary.

In some jurisdictions, in the Canadian province of Manitoba, for example, catch and release is mandatory for some species such as brook trout. Many of the jurisdictions which mandate the live release of sport fish also require the use of artificial lures and barbless hooks to minimise the chance of injury to fish. Mandatory catch and release also exists in the Republic of Ireland where it was introduced as a conservation measure to prevent the decline of Atlantic salmon stocks on some rivers. In Switzerland, catch and release fishing is considered inhumane and was banned in September 2008.

Barbless hooks, which can be created from a standard hook by removing the barb with pliers or can be bought, are sometimes resisted by anglers because they believe that increased escapement results. Barbless hooks reduce handling time, thereby increasing survival. Concentrating on keeping the line taut while fighting fish, using recurved point or "triple grip" style hooks on lures, and equipping lures that do not have them with split rings can significantly reduce escapement.

Animal protection advocates have raised concerns about the possible suffering of fish caused by angling. In light of recent research, some countries, like Germany, have banned specific types of fishing and the British RSPCA now formally prosecutes individuals who are cruel to fish.

Experiments done by William Tavolga provide evidence that fish have pain and fear responses. For instance, in Tavolga's experiments, toadfish grunted when electrically shocked and over time they came to grunt at the mere sight of an electrode. Additional tests conducted at both the University of Edinburgh and the Roslin Institute, in which bee venom and acetic acid was injected into the lips of rainbow trout, resulted in fish rubbing their lips along the sides and floors of their tanks, which the researchers believe was an effort to relieve themselves of pain. One researcher argues about the definition of pain used in the studies.

In 2003, Scottish scientists at the University of Edinburgh performing research on rainbow trout concluded that fish exhibit behaviors often associated with pain, and the brains of fish fire neurons in the same way human brains do when experiencing pain. James D. Rose of the University of Wyoming critiqued the study, claiming it was flawed, mainly since it did not provide proof that fish possess "conscious awareness, particularly a kind of awareness that is meaningfully like ours". Rose argues that since the fish brain is rather different from ours, fish are probably not conscious (in the manner humans are), whence reactions similar to human reactions to pain instead have other causes. Rose had published his own opinion a year earlier arguing that fish cannot feel pain as they lack the appropriate neocortex in the brain. However, animal behaviorist Temple Grandin argues that fish could still have consciousness without a neocortex because "different species can use different brain structures and systems to handle the same functions.

Sometimes considered within the broad category of angling is where contestants compete for prizes based on the total length or weight of a fish, usually of a pre-determined species, caught within a specified time (fishing tournaments). Such contests have evolved from local fishing contests into large competitive circuits, where professional anglers are supported by commercial endorsements. Professional anglers are not engaged in commercial fishing, even though they gain an economic reward. Similar competitive fishing exists at the amateur level with fishing derbies. In general, derbies are distinguished from tournaments; derbies normally require fish to be killed. Tournaments normally deduct points if fish can not be released alive.

### Motivation

A ten-year-long survey of US fishing club members, completed in 1997, indicated that motivations for recreational angling have shifted from relaxation, an outdoor experience and the experience of the catch, to the importance of family recreation. Anglers with higher family incomes fished more frequently and were less concerned about obtaining fish as food.

A German study indicated that satisfaction derived from angling was not dependent on the actual catch, but depended more on the angler's expectations of the experience.

A 2006 study by the Louisiana Department of Wildlife and Fisheries tracked the motivations of anglers on the Red

River. Included among the most often stated responses were the fun of catching fish, the experience, to catch a lot of fish or a very large fish, for challenge, adventure and more. Use as food was not investigated as a motivation for angling.

### Fishing Lure

A fishing lure is an object attached to the end of a fishing line which is designed to resemble and move like the prey of a fish. The purpose of the lure is to use movement, vibration, and colour to catch the fish's attention so it bites the hook. Lures are equipped with one or more single, double, or treble hooks that are used to hook fish when they attack the lure.

Lures are usually used with a fishing rod and fishing reel. When a lure is used for casting, it is continually cast out and retrieved, the retrieve making the lure swim or produce a popping action. A skilled angler can explore many possible hiding places for fish through lure casting such as under logs and on flats.

In early times, fishing lures were made from bone or bronze. The Chinese and Egyptians used fishing rods, hooks, and lines as early as 2,000 B.C. though most of the first fishermen used handlines. The first hooks were made out of bronze which was strong but still very thin and less visible to the fish. The Chinese were the first to make fishing line, spun from fine silk. The modern fishing lure was made commercially in the United States in the early 1900s by the firm of Heddon and Pflueger in Michigan. Before this time most fishing lures were made by individual craftsman. Commercial-made lures were based on the same ideas that the individual craftsmen were making but on a larger scale.

### Methods

The fishing lure is either tied with a knot, such as the improved clinch knot, or connected with a tiny safety pin-like device called a "swivel" onto the fishing line which is in turn connected to the reel via the arbor. The reel is attached to a rod. The motion of the lure is made by winding line back on to the reel, by sweeping the fishing rod, jigging movements with the fishing rod, or by being pulled behind a moving boat (trolling). exceptions included are artificial flies, commonly called *flies* by fly fishers, which either float on the water surface, slowly sink or float underwater, and represent some form of insect fish food.

### Types

There are many types of fishing lures. They are all manufactured in different ways to resemble prey for the fish in most cases, but are sometimes engineered to appeal to a fishes sense of territory, curiosity or aggression. Most lures are made to look like dying, injured, or fast moving fish. They include the following types:

- A jig is a weighted hook with a lead head opposite the sharp tip. They are often covered with a minnow or crawfish or even a plastic worm to get the fish's attention. The operator moves the rod to make the jig move.
- Surface lures are also known as top water lures. They float and resemble prey that is on top of the water. They can make a popping sound from a concave-cut head, a burbling sound from "side fins" or scoops or a buzzing commotion from one or several propellers. A few have only whatever motion the fisherman applies through the rod itself, though if skillfully used, they can be very effective.
- Spoon lures are made to resemble the inside of a table spoon. They flash in the light while wobbling or darting due to their shape, and attract fish.
- Plugs are also known as crankbaits. These lures have a fishlike body shape and they are run through the water where they can make a variety of different movements caused by instability due to the scoop under the head.
- Artificial flies are designed to resemble all manner of fish prey and are used with a fly rod and reel in fly fishing.
- Soft plastic baits are made of plastic or rubber, and are designed to resemble worms, lizards, frogs, leeches and other creatures.

- Spinnerbait are pieces of wire bent at about a 60 degree angle with a hook on the lower end and a flashy spinner mechanism on the upper end.
- Swimbait is a minnow- like soft plastic bait that is reeled like a plug. Some of these have a swimming tail.

These fishing lures can be made of wood, plastic, rubber, metal, cork, and materials like feathers, animal hair, string, tinsel and others. They can have many moving parts or no moving parts. They can be retrieved fast or slow. Some of the lures can be used by alone, or with another lure.

One advantage of use of artificial lures is a reduction in use of bait. This contributes to resolving one of the marine environment's more pressing problems; the undermining of marine food webs by overharvesting "bait" species which tend to occur lower in the food chain. Another advantage of lures is that their use promotes improved survival of fish during catch and release fishing. This is because lures reduce the incidence of deep hooking which has been correlated to fish mortality in many studies. Mortality by swallowing hooks is mostly caused by the handling stress and damage resulting from removing the hook from the gut or throat. The best course of action when a fish is gut-hooked is to leave the hook and cut the line as soon as possible. Hooks will then be encapsulated or evacuated from the body. Use of non corroding steel is not recommended because a corroding hook will be easier to for the fish to expel.

**Daisy Chain**

A daisy chain is a "chain" of plastic lures, however they do not have hooks - their main purpose is to merely attract a school of fish closer to the lures with hooks.

Typically, the main line of the daisy chain is clear monofilament line with crimped on droppers that connect the lure to the main line. The last lure can be rigged with a hook or unrigged. The unrigged versions are used as teasers while the hooked versions are connected to a rod and reel. The lures used on a daisy chain are made from cedar plugs, plastic squids, jets, and other soft and/or hard plastic lures.

In some countries (e.g. New Zealand, Australia) daisy chains can sometimes refer to a rig which is used to catch baitfish in a similar arrangement to a 'flasher rig' or a 'sabiki rig'; a series of hooks with a small piece of colourful material/ feather/plastic attached to each hook.

15

# Fly Fishing

Fly fishing is an angling method in which an artificial 'fly' is used to catch fish. The fly is cast by using a fly rod, reel, and a plastic coated line which is heavier than regular monofilament. Casting the nearly weightless fly or 'lure' requires a special casting technique and an especially light rod. Fly fishermen use hand tied *flies* that resemble natural invertebrates or other food organisms, or 'lures' to provoke the fish to strike.

Fly fishing can be done in fresh or salt water. North Americans usually distinguish freshwater fishing between cold-water species (trout, salmon, steelhead) and warm-water species, notably bass. In Britain, where natural water temperatures vary less, the distinction is between game fishing for trout or salmon and coarse fishing for other species. Techniques for freshwater fly fishing also differ with habitat (lakes, small streams and big rivers.)

In fly fishing, fish are caught by using Artificial flies that are cast with a fly rod and a fly line. The fly line (today, almost always coated with plastic) is heavy enough to send the fly to the target. There is a main difference between fly fishing and spin or bait fishing. In fly fishing the weight of the line carries the hook through the air, whereas in spin and bait fishing the weight of the lure or sinker at the end of the monofilament line gives casting distance. Artificial flies are of several types; some imitating an insect (either flying or swimming), others a bait fish or crustacean, others *attractors* are known to attract fish although they look like nothing in nature. Flies can be made either to float or sink, and range in size from a few millimeters to 30 cm long; most are between 1 and 5 cm.

Artificial flies are made by fastening hair, fur, feathers, or other materials, both natural and synthetic, onto a hook. The first flies were tied with natural materials, but synthetic materials are now very popular and prevalent. The flies are tied in sizes, colors and patterns to match local terrestrial and aquatic insects, baitfish, or other prey attractive to the target fish species.

**Fish Species**

Fly fishing is most renowned as a method for catching trout and salmon, but it is also used for a wide variety of species including pike, bass, panfish, grayling and carp, as well as marine species, such as redfish, snook, tarpon, bonefish and striped bass. Many fly anglers catch unintended species such as chub, bream and rudd while fishing for 'main target' species such as trout. A growing population of anglers attempt to catch as many different species as possible with the fly. With the advancement of technology and development of stronger rods and reels, larger predatory saltwater species such as wahoo, tuna, marlin and sharks have become target species on fly. Realistically any fish can be targeted and captured on fly as long as the main food source is effectively replicated by the fly itself and the gear used is suitable.

Many credit the first recorded use of an artificial fly to the Roman Claudius Aelianus near the end of the 2nd century. He described the practice of Macedonian anglers on the Astraeus river:

> ...they have planned a snare for the fish, and get the better of them by their fisherman's craft. ... They fasten red ... wool round a hook, and fit on to the wool two feathers which grow under a cock's wattles, and which in color are like wax. Their rod is six feet long, and their line is the same length. Then they throw their snare, and the fish, attracted and maddened by the color, comes straight at it, thinking from the pretty sight to gain a dainty mouthful; when, however, it opens its jaws, it is caught by the hook, and enjoys a bitter repast, a captive.

In his book *Fishing from the Earliest Times*, however, William Radcliff (1921) gave the credit to Martial (*Marcus valerius* Martialis), born some two hundred years before Aelian, who wrote:

> ...Who has not seen the scarus rise, decoyed and killed by fraudful flies...

The last word, somewhat indistinct in the original, is either "mosco" (moss) or "musca" (fly) but catching fish with fraudulent moss seems unlikely.

### Great Britain

Other than a few fragmented references little was written on fly fishing until *The Treatyse on Fysshynge with an Angle* was published (1496) within *The Boke of St. Albans* attributed to Dame Juliana Berners. The book contains, along with instructions on rod, line and hook making, dressings for different flies to use at different times of the year. The earliest English poetical treatise on Angling by John Dennys, said to have been a fishing companion of Shakespeare, was published in 1613, The Secrets of Angling, of which 6 verses were quoted in the better known book Izaak Walton's Compleat Angler (1653), of which the latter two chapters were actually written by his friend Charles Cotton, and described the fishing in the Derbyshire Wye.

British fly-fishing continued to develop in the 19th Century, with the emergence of fly fishing clubs, along with the appearance of several books on the subject of fly tying and fly fishing techniques. In southern England, dry-fly fishing acquired an elitist reputation as the only acceptable method of fishing the slower, clearer rivers of the south such as the River Test and the other chalk streams concentrated in Hampshire, Surrey, Dorset and Berkshire (see Southern England Chalk Formation for the geological specifics). The weeds found in these rivers tend to grow very close to the surface, and it was felt necessary to develop new techniques that would keep the fly and the line on the surface of the stream. These became the foundation of all later dry-fly developments. However, there was nothing to prevent the successful employment of wet flies on these chalk streams, as George Edward MacKenzie Skues proved with his nymph and wet fly techniques. To the horror of dry-fly purists, Skues later wrote two books, *Minor Tactics of the Chalk Stream*, and *The Way of a Trout with a Fly*, which greatly influenced the development of wet fly fishing. In northern England and Scotland, many anglers also favored wet-fly fishing, where the technique was more popular and widely practiced than in southern England. One of Scotland's leading proponents of the wet fly in the early-to-mid 19th century was W.C. Stewart, who published "The Practical Angler" in 1857.

In Scandinavia and the United States, attitudes toward methods of fly fishing were not nearly as rigidly defined, and both dry- and wet-fly fishing were soon adapted to the conditions of those countries.

**Japan**

The traditional Japanese method of fly-fishing is known as "Tenkara" (literally: "from heaven"). The first reference to tenkara fly-fishing was in 1878 in a book called *"Diary of climbing Mt. Tateyama"*.

Tenkara is the only fly-fishing method in Japan that is defined by using a fly and casting technique where the line is what is actually being cast. Tenkara originated in the mountains of Japan as a way for professional fishermen and inn-keepers to harvest the local fish, Ayu, trout, char for selling and providing a meal to their guests. Primarily a small-stream fishing method that was preferred for being highly efficient, where the long rod allowed the fisherman to place the fly where the fish would be.

Another style of fishing in Japan is Ayu fishing. As written by historian Andrew Herd, in the book *"The Fly"*:

> "Fly fishing became popular with Japanese peasants from the twelfth century onward...fishing was promoted to a pastime worthy of Bushi (warriors), as part of an official policy to train the Bushi's mind during peacetime."

This refers primarily to Ayu fishing, which commonly uses a fly as lure, uses longer rods, but there is no casting technique required, it's more similar to dapping. Ayu was practiced in the lowlands (foothills), where the Bushi resided, tenkara practiced in the mountains. Fishing flies are thought to have first originated in Japan for Ayu fishing over 430 years ago. These flies were made with needles that were bent into shape and used as fishing hooks, then dressed as a fly. The rods along with fishing flies, are considered to be a traditional local craft of the Kaga region.

In the West, fly-fishing rods were primarily made of wood, which is heavy, so having long rods to reach spots where fish may be was tricky. Anglers started devising running line systems, where they could use shorter rods and longer lines. Eventually this led to the development of reels and the widespread use of shorter rods and reels. In Japan, bamboo, a very light material, was readily available, so anglers could make very long rods without much concern for weight. Fly-fishing remained more pure, as it was in its origins, anglers in Japan could continue using the long rods and did not feel the need to invent running line systems and reels.

### North America

In the United States, fly anglers are thought to be the first anglers to have used artificial lures for bass fishing. After pressing into service the fly patterns and tackle designed for trout and salmon to catch largemouth and smallmouth bass, they began to adapt these patterns into specific bass flies. Fly anglers seeking bass developed the spinner/fly lure and bass popper fly, which are still used today.

In the late 19th century, American anglers, such as Theodore Gordon, in the Catskill Mountains of New York began using fly tackle to fish the region's many brook trout-rich streams such as the Beaverkill and Willowemoc Creek. Many of these early American fly anglers also developed new fly patterns and wrote extensively about their sport, increasing the popularity of fly fishing in the region and in the United States as a whole. One such man was Charles F. Orvis, who through his actions helped to popularize fly fishing by designing and distributing novel reel and fly designs. His 1874 fly reel was described by reel historian Jim Brown as the "benchmark of American reel design," the first fully modern fly reel. The founding of The Orvis Company helped institutionalize fly fishing within America and supplied angling equipment and accessories to the homes of millions of Americans. His elegantly printed tackle catalogs, distributed to a small but devoted customer list in the late 1800s, are now highly collectible as early forerunners of today's enormous direct-mail outdoor products industry. The Junction Pool in Roscoe, where the Willowemoc flows into the Beaver Kill, is the center of an almost ritual pilgrimage every April 1, when the season begins. Albert Bigelow Paine, a New England author, wrote about fly fishing in *The Tent Dwellers*, a book about a three week trip he and a friend took to central Nova Scotia in 1908.

Participation in fly fishing peaked in the early 1920s in the eastern states of Maine and Vermont and in the Midwest in the spring creeks of Wisconsin. Along with deep sea fishing, Ernest Hemingway did much to popularize fly fishing through his works of fiction, including The Sun Also Rises. It was the development of inexpensive fiberglass rods, synthetic fly lines, and monofilament leaders, however, in the early 1950s, that revived the popularity of fly fishing, especially in the United States.

In recent years, interest in fly fishing has surged as baby boomers have discovered the sport. Movies such as Robert Redford's film *A River Runs Through It*, starring Craig Sheffer and Brad Pitt, cable fishing shows, and the emergence of a competitive fly casting circuit have also added to the sport's visibility.

**Australia**

Brown trout were first introduced to Australia by the efforts of Edward Wilson's Acclimatisation Society of Victoria with the aim to "provide for manly sport which will lead Australian youth to seek recreation on the river's bank and mountainside rather than in the Cafe and Casino. " The first successful transfer of Brown Trout ova (from the Itchen and Wye) was aboard the Norfolk in 1864. Rainbow Trout were not introduced until 1894.

**Gear Improvements**

Lines made of silk replaced those of horse hair and were heavy enough to be cast in the modern style. George Cotton and his predecessors fished their flies with long rods, and light lines allowing the wind to do most of the work of getting the fly to the fish. The introduction of new woods to the manufacture of fly rods, first greenheart and then bamboo, made it possible to cast flies into the wind on silk lines. These early fly lines proved troublesome as they had to be coated with various dressings to make them float and needed to be taken off the reel and dried every four hours or so to prevent them from becoming waterlogged.

American rod builders such as Hiram Leonard developed superior techniques for making bamboo rods: thin strips were cut from the cane, milled into shape, and then glued together to form light, strong, hexagonal rods with a solid core that were superior to anything that preceded them.

Fly reels were soon improved, as well. At first they were rather mechanically simple; more or less a storage place for the fly line and backing. In order to tire the fish, anglers simply applied hand pressure to the rim of the revolving spool, known as 'palming' the rim. . In fact, many superb modern reels still use this simple design, often with a "click-check" mechanism which makes both an audible noise and provides light spool braking to prevent over-runs.

## Casting

Unlike other casting methods, fly fishing can be thought of as a method of casting *line* rather than lure. Non-flyfishing methods rely on a lure's weight to pull line from the reel during the forward motion of a cast. By design, a fly is too light to be cast, and thus simply follows the unfurling of a properly cast fly line, which is heavier and tapered and therefore more castable than lines used in other types of fishing.

The physics of flycasting can be described by the transfer of impulse, the product of mass and speed through the rod from base to top and from the transfer of impulse through the fly line all the way to the tip of the leader. Because both the rod and the fly line are tapered the smaller amount of mass will reach high speeds as the waves in rod and line unfurl. The waves that travel through the fly line are called *loops*. Determining factors in reaching the highest speeds are the basal frequency of a rod and the transfer of the speed from the tip of the rod to the fly line. At the moment the rod tip reaches its highest velocity the direction of the cast is determined.

The type of cast used when fishing varies according to the conditions. The most common cast is the forward cast, where the angler whisks the fly into the air, back over the shoulder until the line is nearly straight, then forward, using primarily the forearm. The objective of this motion is to "load" (bend) the rod tip with stored energy, then transmit that energy to the line, resulting in the fly line (and the attached fly) being cast for an appreciable distance. Casting without landing the fly on the water is known as 'false casting', and may be used to pay out line, to dry a soaked fly, or to reposition a cast. Other casts are the roll cast, the single- or double-haul, the tuck cast, and the side- or curve-cast.

Dropping the fly onto the water and its subsequent movement on or beneath the surface is one of fly fishing's most difficult aspects; the angler is attempting to cast in such a way that the line lands smoothly on the water and the fly appears as natural as possible. At a certain point, if a fish does not strike, depending upon the action of the fly in the wind or current, the angler picks up the line to make another presentation. On the other hand, if a fish strikes, the angler pulls in line while raising the rod tip. This "sets" the hook in the fish's mouth. The fish is played either by hand, where the angler continues to hold the fly line in one hand to control the tension applied to the fish, or by reeling up any slack in the line and then using the hand to act as a drag on the reel. Most modern fly reels have an adjustable, mechanical drag system to control line tension during a fish's run.

Beginners tend to point with the rod to where they want to throw, but the movement of the hand has to be a controlled speed-up and then come to an abrupt stop. The rod will then start to unfurl and the tip of the rod will reach a high speed in the required direction. The high speed of the rod tip toward the target gives the impulse to make the cast, the abrupt stop and retreat of the rod tip is essential for the formation of a loop. Experienced fishermen also improve the speed of the line leaving the rod tip by a technique called *hauling*, applying a quick fast pull with the hand holding the line. At the end of the cast when the line is stretched the line as a whole will still have speed and the fisherman can let some extra line through his fingers making a false throw, either forward or backward or to finish the cast and start fishing.

There are a great number of special casts meant to evade problems like trees behind the angler (roll cast), the pulling of the line on the fly by the action of the stream, or to make the fly land more softly.

## Spey Casting

Spey casting is a casting technique used in fly fishing. Spey casting requires a longer, heavier two-handed fly rod, referred to as a Spey rod. Spey casting is essentially a large roll cast, developed on the Scottish River Spey where high banks do not allow space for the usual back cast.

Spey casting is used for fishing large rivers for salmon and large trout such as steelhead and sea trout. Spey technique is also used in saltwater surf casting. All of these situations require the angler to cast larger flies long distances. The two-handed Spey technique allows more powerful casts and avoids obstacles on the shore by keeping most of the line in front of the angler.

## Fly Fishing for Trout

Fly fishing for trout is a very popular sport, which can be done using any of the various methods and any of the general types of flies. Many of the techniques and presentations of fly fishing were first developed in fishing for trout. There is a misconception that all fly fishing for trout is done on the surface of the water with "dry flies." In most places, especially heavily fished trout areas, success usually comes from fly fishing using flies that were designed to drift on the bottom of the water. A trout feeds below the water's surface nearly 90 per cent of the time. Trout usually only come to the surface when there is a large bug hatch (when aquatic insects grow wings and leave the water to mate and lay eggs). There are exceptions to this rule, however, particularly during the summer months and on smaller mountain streams.

## Fishing in Cold Water

In order to deceive wary trout, or to reach deep runs where he/she believes salmon lie, the fly angler often needs to wade to the right casting position. He/she therefore requires sure footing and insulation from cold water, both provided by hip boots or chest-high waders. The latter are of two main types, one-piece "boot foot" waders and "stocking foot" waders, which require external boots.

Formerly of latex rubber, "stocking foot" waders now are made of neoprene, usually 3 mm thick, which provide additional warmth. In the mid-20th century American anglers developed felt boot soles for a better grip in rocky rivers: but felt is now prohibited in some US states, as a vector of fish and plant diseases that damage sport fisheries. Manufacturers now offer wading boots with special rubber treads or metal studs. Breathable Gore-Tex waders provide ventilation when hiking along the water, but do not provide flotation in the event of slipping or falling into deep water. In deep water streams, an inflatable personal flotation device (PFD), or a Type III Kayak fishing vest, adds a degree of safety.

Some "catch and release" anglers flatten the barb of their hook. Such "barbless hooks" are much easier to remove from the fish (and from the angler, in the event of mishap). Many rivers with special regulations mandate that fishermen use barbless hooks in an effort to conserve a healthy fish population.

### Dry Fly Trout Fishing

Dry fly fishing is done with line and flies that float, joined by a leader, usually made of fine polyamide monofilament line. The tapered leader is 3 to 5 meters long, thus nearly invisible where the fly is knotted, and the angler can replace the last meter of nylon as required. Unlike sinking fly (nymph) fishing, the "take" on dry flies is visible, explosive and exciting. While trout typically consume about 90 per cent of their diet from below-water sources, the 10 per cent of surface-level consumption by trout is more than enough to keep most anglers busy. Additionally, beginning fly anglers generally prefer dry fly fishing because of the relative ease of detecting a strike and the instant gratification of seeing a trout strike their fly. Nymph fishing may be more productive, but dry fly anglers soon become addicted to the surface strike.

Dry flies may be "attractors", such as the Royal Wulff, or "natural imitators", such as the elk hair caddis, a caddisfly imitation A beginner may wish to begin with a fly that is easy to see such as a Royal Wulff attractor or a mayfly imitation such as a Parachute Adams. The "parachute" on the Parachute Adams makes the fly land as softly as a natural on the water and has the added benefit of making the fly very visible from the surface. Being able to see the fly is especially helpful to the beginner. The fly should land softly, as if dropped onto the water, with the leader fully extended from the fly line. Due to rivers having faster and slower currents often running side by side, the fly can over take or be overtaken by the line, thus disturbing the fly's drift. Mending is a technique where by one lifts and moves the part of the line that requires re-aligning with the fly's drift, thus extending the drag free drift. The mend can be upstream or down stream depending on the currents carrying the line or fly. To be effective, any mending of the fly line should not disturb the natural drift of the fly. Learning to mend is often much easier if the angler can see the fly.

Once a fish has been caught and landed, the fly may no longer float well. A fly can sometimes be dried and made to float again by "false" casting, casting the fly back and forth in the air. In some cases, the fly can be dried with a small piece of reusable absorbent towel, an amadou patch or chamoisand after drying placed and shaken in a container full of fly "dressing"; a hydrophobic solution. A popular solution to a dry fly which refuses to float is simply to replace it with another, similar or identical fly until the original can fully dry, rotating through a set of flies.

Dry fly fishing on small, clear-water streams can be especially productive if the angler stays as low to the ground and as far from the bank as possible, moving upstream with stealth. Trout tend to face upstream and most of their food is carried to them on the current. For this reason, the fish's attention is normally focused into the current; most anglers move and fish "into the current", fishing from a position downstream of the fish's suspected lie. Trout tend to strike their food at current "edges", where faster- and slower-moving waters mix. Obstructions to the stream flow, such as large rocks or nearby pools, provide a "low energy" environment where fish sit and wait for food without expending much energy. Casting upstream to the "edge" of the slower water, the angler can see the fly land and drift slowly back downstream. The challenge in stream fishing is placing the fly with deadly accuracy, within inches of a protective rock for instance, not long range casting. Done properly, the fly seems to be just floating along in the current with a "perfect drift" as if not connected to the fly line. The angler must remain vigilant for the "take" in order to be ready to raise the rod tip and set the hook.

### Nymphing for Trout

Trout tend mostly to feed underwater. Especially when fishing deeper waters such as rivers or lakes, putting a fly down to the trout may be more successful than fishing on the surface, especially in the absence of any surface insect activity or hatch. The nymph itself can be weighted, as is the popular bead headed hare's ear nymph or bead headed pheasant tail nymph. Alternatively, the angler can use an attractor pattern such as a Prince Nymph. Weights can be added to the leader. Probably the best weight to use is twist on lead or other metal strips because it has a much less detrimental effect on the casting ability. A sinking tip fly line can also serve to sink the fly. The most common nymphing and general overall fly fishing technique that even beginners can master is a "dead drift" or tight line fishing technique, casting directly across the river, letting the fly line drift downriver while keeping any slack out of the line. If the Nymph is drifting too fast then you should perform an upstream mend. If the nymph is drifting too slowly you should mend downstream. A beginner need simply to point the rod at the fly, lifting the rod in the event of a strike. This is a "downstream technique", where the angler moves in a downstream direction. More advanced techniques make use of a highly visible strike indicator attached to the leader above the sinking fly.

It is also possible to use standard sinking fly lines. Especially if the current is strong and if it is difficult to get down to the correct level to catch the trout.

## Still Water Trout Fishing

Fishing for trout in lakes requires different tactics. A canoe, pontoon boat or a float tube allows an angler to cover a lot more water than waders. Trout may congregate in cooler water near an inflowing stream or an underwater spring and may be lured to bite on a streamer fly. An often successful tactic is to pull a streamer such as a woolly bugger using clear sinking line, behind the watercraft. The somewhat erratic motion of the oars or fins tends to give the streamer an enticing action. Trout also tend to "cruise" transitional areas (*e.g.* dropoffs, weed bed edges, subsurface river flow at inlets, etc.) Watching for cruising trout and casting well ahead of any visible fish is often successful.

## Playing Trout

Once hooked, a small trout can be easily retrieved "on the reel" or by simply pulling in the fly line with the reel hand while pinching the line between the rod handle and the index finger of the rod hand. It is important to keep the rod tip high, allowing the bend of the rod to absorb the force of the fish's struggles against the line. Larger trout will often take line in powerful runs before they can be landed. Unlike spin fishing where the line is already on the reel, playing a large fish with fly line and a fly reel can present a special challenge. Usually, when a fish is hooked, there will be extra fly line coiled between the reel and the index finger of the rod hand. The challenge is to reel up the loose fly line onto the reel without breaking off a large fish (or getting the line wrapped up around the rod handle, one's foot, a stick or anything else in the way). With experience, really large trout can be put on the reel simply by applying light pressure on the outgoing line using the fisher's fingers. Once the extra line is on the reel, an angler can use the reel's drag system to tire the fish. It is important to use heavier tippet material if it won't spook the fish. The reason why this is important is an exhausted fish can easily die if released too soon. Heavier tippet material enables the angler to land the fish while not over exhausting it.

**Releasing Trout**

Releasing wild trout helps preserve the quality of a fishery. Trout are more delicate than most fish and require careful handling. When a trout has been caught but the hook is still embedded, wet your hands before handling the fish. Dry hands stick to the adhesive slime coating the fish and can pull off its scales. It is preferred for the fish to remain in the water when removing the hook, but holding the trout out of the water will not be lethal, provided the hook is removed quickly and the trout is returned immediately.

Small trout caught on a barb-less hook can be released simply by: grasping the eyelet of the fly, and rotating the eyelet toward the bend (the U-bend). This pulls the point backwards, back through the way it entered. Push the eyelet directly toward the bend until the point is removed from the fish. Large trout can be grasped gently and forceps can be used to grip the bend and push backwards, away from the direction the hook currently points. If necessary, squirming trout can be held on their backs. This often subdues the fish and provides enough time to remove the hook.

Once the hook has been removed, return the trout into the water.Support the trout until it stabilizes. This includes holding the fish in water deep enough to submerge its gills. After long fights, it may be necessary to manually move water past its gills. This can be done either by holding the trout in moving water with its head facing upstream, or, in calm water, moving the trout backwards and forwards repeatedly. Once stabilized, the trout will swim off on its own. If released prematurely, the trout, not having enough energy to move, will sink to the bottom of the river and suffocate. Take however long is necessary to revive a trout.

## Saltwater Flyfishing

Saltwater flyfishing is typically done with heavier tackle than that which is used for freshwater trout fishing, both to handle the larger, more powerful fish, and to accommodate the casting of larger and heavier flies. Salt water fly fishing typically employs the use of wet flies resembling baitfish, crabs, shrimp and other forage. However, saltwater fish can also be caught with "poppers," and other surface lure similar to those used for freshwater bass fishing, though much larger. Saltwater species sought and caught with fly tackle include: bonefish, redfish or red drum, permit, snook, spotted sea trout, tuna, dorado (mahi-mahi), sailfish, tarpon, striped bass, salmon and marlin. Offshore saltwater species are usually attracted to the fly by "chumming" with small baitfish, or "teasing" the fish to the boat by trolling a large hookless lure (Billfish are most often caught using this latter method).

Many saltwater species, particularly large, fast and powerful fish, are not easily slowed down by "palming" the hand on the reel. Instead, a purpose-made saltwater reel for these species must have a powerful drag system. Furthermore, saltwater reels purpose-made for larger fish must be larger, heavier, and corrosion-resistant - a typical high-quality saltwater reel costs 500.00 USD or more. Corrosion-resistant equipment is key to durability in all types of saltwater fishing, regardless of the size and power of the target species.

Saltwater fly fishing is most often done from a boat, either a shallow draft flats boat used to pursue species such as bonefish, redfish, permit and tarpon in shallow waters, from larger offshore boats for pursuing sailfish, tuna, dorado, marlin and other pelagics and may be done from shore, such as wading flats for bonefish or redfish or surf fishing for striped bass and other assorted fish. Typically, most trout fly fisherman need to practice new skills to catch saltwater fish on a fly rod. Ocean fish are usually harder to catch. They can be extremely spooky, and much larger. Trout fisherman need to practice with at least an 8 weight fly rod and accurately cast the line 30–90 feet if they are going to have success—particularly in the flat areas fishing for bonefish, redfish, permit, tarpon, jacks and more.

Hooks for saltwater flies must also be extremely durable and corrosion resistant. Most saltwater hooks are made of stainless steel, but the strongest (though less corrosion resistant) hooks are of high-carbon steel. Typically, these hooks vary from size #8 to #2 for bonefish and smaller nearshore species, to size #3/0 to #5/0 for the larger offshore species.

### Fly Fishing Tackle

Fly fishing tackle comprises the fishing tackle or equipment typically used by fly anglers. Fly fishing tackle includes:

- A wide variety of Fly rods of different weights, lengths and material are used to present artificial flies to target species of fish as well as fight and land fish being caught.
- A wide variety of Fly reels are used to store fly line and provide a braking mechanism (drag) for fighting heavy or fast moving fish.
- A wide variety of general use and specialized fly lines are used to cast artificial flies under a wide variety of fresh and saltwater conditions.
- Terminal tackle is used to connect the artificial fly to the fly line and allow the appropriate presentation of the fly to the fish.
- There are a wide variety of accessories—tools, gàdgets, clothing and apparel used by the fly angler for maintenance and preparation of tackle, dealing the fish being caught as well as personal comfort and safety while fly fishing. Includes fly boxes used to store and carry artificial flies.

Fly rods are typically between 1.8 m (6 ft) long in freshwater fishing and up to 4.5 m (15 ft) long for two-handed fishing for salmon or steelhead, or in tenkara fishing in small streams. The average rod for fresh and salt water is around 9 feet (2.7 m) in length and weighs from 3-5 ounces, though a recent trend has been to lighter, shorter rods for fishing smaller streams. Another trend is to longer rods for small streams. The choice of rod lengths and line weights used varies according to local conditions, types of flies being cast, and/or personal preference.

When actively fishing, the angler may want to keep the fly line lightly pressed against the rod handle with the index finger of the casting arm. The free arm is used to pull line from the reel or to retrieve line from the water. If a fish strikes, the angler can pinch the line with the index finger against the rod handle and lift the rod tip, setting the hook.

### Artificial Flies

In broadest terms, flies are categorized as either imitative or attractive. Imitative flies resemble natural food items. Attractive flies trigger instinctive strikes by employing a range of characteristics that do not necessarily mimic prey items. Flies can be fished floating on the surface (dry flies), partially submerged (emergers), or below the surface (nymphs, streamers, and wet flies). A dry fly is typically thought to represent an insect landing on, falling on (terrestrials), or emerging from, the water's surface as might a grasshopper, dragonfly, mayfly, ant, beetle, stonefly or caddisfly. Other surface flies include poppers and hair bugs that might resemble mice, frogs, etc. Sub-surface flies are designed to resemble a wide variety of prey including aquatic insect larvae, nymphs and pupae, baitfish, crayfish, leeches, worms, etc. Wet flies, known as streamers, are generally thought to imitate minnows, leeches or scuds.

Artificial flies, constructed of furs, feathers, and threads bound on a hook were created by anglers to imitate fish prey. The first known mention of an artificial fly was in 200AD in Macedonia. Most early examples of artificial flies imitated common aquatic insects and baitfish. Today, artificial flies are tied with a wide variety of natural and synthetic materials (like mylar and rubber) to represent all manner of potential freshwater and saltwater fish prey to include aquatic and terrestrial insects, crustaceans, worms, baitfish, vegetation, flesh, spawn, small reptiles, amphibians, mammals and birds, etc.

A few knots have become more or less standard for attaching the various parts of the fly lines and backing, etc., together. A detailed discussion of most of these knots is available in any good book on fly fishing. Some of the knots that are in most every fly angler's arsenal are: the improved clinch knot which is commonly used to attach the fly to the leader, the overhand slip knot or arbor knot which is used to attach the backing to the spool, the albright knot which can be used to attach the fly line to the backing. A loop can also be put in fly line backing using a bimini twist. Often, a loop is added to the business end of the fly line to facilitate the connection to the leader. This loop may take one of several forms. It may be formed by creating a loop in the end of the fly line itself or by adding a braided loop or a loop of monofilament nylon (as in *Gray's Loop*). Alternatively, a single length of monofilament nylon, or fluorocarbon, may be tied to the end of the fly line using a nail or *tube knot* or a *needle knot*. A loop can then be tied at the end of this monofilament butt length using a double surgeon's knot or a perfection loop, to which the tapered or untapered leader, also looped using a double surgeon's knot or a perfection loop, may in turn be connected via a loop to loop connection. The use of loop to loop connections between the fly line and the leader provides a quick and convenient way to change or replace a tapered leader. Many commercially-produced tapered leaders come with a pre-tied loop connection.

### Trolling (Fishing)

Trolling is a method of fishing where one or more fishing lines, baited with lures or bait fish, are drawn through the water. This may be behind a moving boat, or by slowly winding the line in when fishing from a static position, or even sweeping the line from side-to-side, e.g. when fishing from a jetty. Trolling is used to catch pelagic fish such as salmon, mackerel and kingfish.

Trolling can be phonetically confused with trawling, a different method of fishing where a net (trawl) is drawn through the water instead of lines. Trolling is used both for recreational and commercial fishing whereas trawling is used mainly for commercial fishing.

Trolling from a moving boat involves moving quite slowly through the water. This can be accomplished with the use of a special trolling motor. Multiple lines are often used, and outriggers can be used to spread the lines more widely and reduce their chances of tangling. Downriggers can also be used to keep the lures or baits trailing at a desired depth.

Outriggers are poles which allow a boat to troll multiple lines in the water without tangling. A boat which trolls enough lines can simulate a school of fish.

Downrigger are devices used while trolling to keep a bait or lure at the desired depth. In practice, fish swim at different depths according to factors such as the temperature and amount of light in the water, and the speed and direction of water currents. A downrigger consists of a one or two metre horizontal pole which supports a weight, typically about three kilograms of lead, on a steel cable. A clip called a "line release" attaches the fishing line to the weight, and the bait or lure is attached to the release. The fishing line is reeled in by a spool powered either by manual cranking or by an electric motor. Using a downrigger can be hazardous. For example, man-made reservoirs can contain submerged trees and other structures beneath the surface which downriggers can snag.

Paravanes (underwater kites) are sometimes used as depth controlling devices, particularly in commercial tuna fishing operations. These kites have various shapes, such as arrowhead paravanes, flexi-wing paravanes, and bi-wing paravanes. The devices can place the lure or bait at designated depths and positions; and in this way multiple devices can be towed at the same time without the devices and bait interfering with each other.

"Spreaders" allow multiple baited hooks or lures to be trolled from a single line. There are many inventive spreader designs, such as devices which cause the baited hooks or lures to move in helical patterns, in a sophisticated emulation of the schooling behaviour of a group of fish.

### Baits and Lures

To be effective, trolling baits and lures must have the visual ability to attract fish and intrigue them with the way they move through the water. Most trolling lures are designed to look and behave like dying, injured, or fast moving fish. They include:

- Surface lures, also known as top water lures. They float and resemble prey that is on top of the water. They can make a popping sound from a concave-cut head, a burbling sound from "side fins" or scoops or a buzzing commotion from one or several propellers.
- Plugs are also known as crankbaits. These lures have a fishlike body shape and as they troll through the water they make various movements caused by instability due to a scoop under their heads.
- Swimbait, a minnow-like soft plastic bait that is reeled like a plug. Some have swimming tails.
- Spoon lures resemble the inside of a table spoon. They flash in the light while randomly wobbling or darting due to their shape.
- Spinnerbait, pieces of wire bent at about a 60 degree angle with a hook on the lower end and a flashy spinner mechanism on the upper end.

Trolling baits and lures are either tied with a knot, such as the improved clinch knot, or connected with a tiny safety pin-like device called a "snap" onto the fishing line which is in turn connected to the reel. The reel is attached to a rod. The motion is of the lure is made by winding line back on to the reel, by sweeping the fishing rod, jigging movements with the fishing rod, or by trolling behind a moving boat. Lures can be contrasted with artificial flies, commonly called *flies* by fly fishers, which either float on the water surface, slowly sink or float underwater, in imitation some form of insect fish food. However some flies, such as the trolling tandem streamer fly, are designed for trolling behind a moving boat.

As an example, marlin lures are typically 7-14 inches or more long with a shaped plastic or metal head and a plastic skirt. The design of the lure head, particularly its face, gives the lure its individual action when trolled through the water. Lure actions range from an active side-to-side swimming pattern to pushing water aggressively on the surface to, most commonly, tracking along in a straight line with a regular surface pop and bubble trail. Besides the shape, weight and size of the lure head, the length and thickness of skirting, the number and size of hooks and the length and size of the leader used in lure rigging all influence the action of the lure: how actively it will run and how it will respond to different sea conditions. Experienced anglers fine tune their lures to get the action they want.

A pattern of four or more lures can be trolled at varying distances behind the boat. Lures may be fished either straight from the rod tip ("flat lines"), or from outriggers.

In addition to attaching a lure to the fishing line, an oval piece of metal (often hammered or curved for reflective purposes) called a dodger is often used to attract fish from greater distances. Lures designed for trolling with downriggers include metal "spoons" that are often decorated with colour tape, and plastic or rubber "squids" with various colours.

A daisy chain is a chain of plastic lures which have no hooks. Their purpose is to function as teasers which attract a school of fish closer to the lures that do have hooks.

### Trolling Speed

Baits and lures are typically trolled at speeds up to 9 knots, though speeds up to 15 knots can be used, particularly when boats are travelling to different fishing areas. The speed at which the lure is pulled through the water impacts on the fishing success. The optimum trolling speed varies with different species of fish, with weather conditions and the time of year, and other conditions. Chinook salmon can be successfully trolled at higher speeds than more docile lake trout. For these reasons fishermen use devices that accurately track speed. Trolling motors calibrate speed more accurately than large outboard motors. Trolling plates are also used with larger motors to slow the boat to the desired speed, although some anglers experience mixed results with plates.

Trolling can be effective at surprisingly low speeds. Kayaks fitted with a deck-mounted bracket for holding a rod can be paddled to troll effectively for salmon.

### Recreational Fishing

In marine environments trolling is used in big-game fishing to catch large offshore or open-water species such as tuna and marlin. Saltwater anglers also troll for inshore species such as bluefish, kingfish and various jacks.

Rock fishermen can use an umbrella rig as a method of trolling without using a boat. Typically, an umbrella rig consists of four plastic neon green lures with a lead dragging behind. An additional lure is attached to the lead. Only the lure behind the lead need have hooks attached because this lure can appear to a stalking fish as a wounded or sick laggard in a school, making it a more likely target.

A pattern of multiple baits or lures can be trolled at varying distances behind a boat. Lures can be fished straight from the rod tip (flat line), or from outriggers. Purpose designed sinkers exist to control the trolling depth on freshwater lakes.

Freshwater anglers can also find trolling effective. Recreational fishermen can successfully troll lakes and reservoirs for salmon and trout. It can be the method of choice for catching the elusive muskie, and a useful technique for catching walleye, black bass and striped bass. For light and medium freshwater gamefishing, any reasonably robust casting or spinning rod can be used as a trolling rod. Effective trolling rods should be fairly stiff with a relatively fast action, since "whippy" slow action rods are frustrating to troll with.

Commercial trolling vessels catch fish by towing astern one of more trolling lines. The trolling lines are fishing lines with natural or artificial baited hooks trailed by a vessel near the surface or at a certain depth. Several lines can be towed at the same time using outriggers to keep the lines apart. The lines can be hauled in manually or by small winches. A length of rubber is often included in each line as a shock absorber. The trolling line is towed at a speed depending on the target species, from 2.3 knots up to at least 7 knots. Trollers range from small open boats to large refrigerated vessels 30 meters long. In many tropical artisanal fisheries, trolling is done with sailing canoes with outriggers for stability. With properly designed vessels, trolling is an economical and efficient way of catching tuna, mackerel and other pelagic fish swimming close to the surface. Purpose built trollers are usually equipped with two or four trolling booms raised and lowered by topping lifts, held in position by adjustable stays. Electrically powered or hydraulic reels can be used to haul in the lines. Drawing.

Commercial trolling for tuna is more successful near offshore banks than in open water areas, and is also enhanced in the vicinity of a fish aggregation device (FAD).

Historically, in Alaska, hand hook and line trolling were used to catch king and silver salmon in salt water. This method required minimal gear-boat, lines and hooks—and was used to catch fish that were still feeding in open water before returning to spawn. Trolling was very successful in southeast Alaska and historically the catch was used by the fresh and mild-cured fish packing industries. Power boats located near feeding grounds conducted most of the trolling. Each boat had four to ten lines, extending from tall poles hung outboard when fishing; each line carried several hooks, with heavy lead sinkers and spoons or baits as lures. Trolling lengthened the fishing season, allowing fishermen to fish in early spring before spawning runs.

# 16

# Fishing Weir

A fishing weir, or fish weir, is an obstruction placed in tidal waters or wholly or partially across a river, which is designed to hinder the passage of fish. Traditionally they were built from wood or stones. They can be used to trap fish. For example, salmon and other fish can be trapped when they attempt to swim upstream, or eels can be trapped when they attempt to migrate downstream.

Alternatively, fish weirs can be used to redirect fish elsewhere, such as to a fish ladder.

As fish traps, fishing weirs date back to the Bronze Age in Sweden and to Roman times in the UK. They were used by native North Americans and early settlers to catch fish for trade and to feed their communities.

In medieval Europe, large fishing weir structures were constructed from wood posts and wattle fences. 'V' shaped structures in rivers could be as long as 60 m and worked by directing fish towards fish traps or nets. Such fish traps were evidently controversial in medieval England. The Magna Carta includes a clause requiring that they be removed:

All fish-weirs shall be removed from the Thames, the Medway, and throughout the whole of England, except on the sea coast.

Basket weir fish traps were widely used in ancient times. They are shown in medieval illustrations and surviving examples have been found. Basket weirs are about 2 m long and comprise two wicker cones, one inside the other—easy to get into and hard to get out.

In the U.K. the traditional form was one or more rock weirs constructed in tidal races with a small gap that could be blocked by wattle fences when the tide turned to flow out again. Surviving examples, but no longer in use, can be seen in the Menai Strait. Because they were so effective they reduced inshore fish stocks and in 1861 Parliament banned their use except where they could be shown to have been in use prior to the Magna Carta. An example of such a fishing weir was at Rhos Fynach in North Wales, which survived in use until Ist World War.

An enormous series of fish weirs, canals and artificial islands was built by an unknown pre-Columbian culture in the Baures region of Bolivia, part of the Amazonian savannah. These earthworks cover over 500 square kilometres (190 sq mi), and appear to have supported a large and dense population around 3000 BCE. An approximate location for these sites is 63.4128° W, 13.4812° S.

In North America, fishing weirs are constructed using wooden stakes woven together to create a barrier that traps fish while letting water pass through. The pattern of wooden stakes depends on the location and nature of the waters being fished.

In the Back Bay area of Boston, Massachusetts, wooden stake remains of the Boylston Street Fishweir have been documented during excavations for subway tunnels and building foundations. The Boylston Street Fishweir was actually a series of fish weirs built and maintained near the tidal shoreline between 3,700 and 5,200 years ago.

Natives in Nova Scotia use weirs that stretch across the entire river to retain shad during their seasonal runs up the Shubenacadie, Nine Mile, and Stewiacke rivers, and use nets to scoop the trapped fish. Various weir patterns were used on tidal waters to retain a variety of different species, which are still used today. V-shaped weirs with circular formations to hold the fish during high tides are used on the Bay of Fundy to fish herring, which follow the flow of water. Similar V-shaped weirs are also used in British Columbia to corral salmon to the end of the "V" during the changing of the tides.

**Fish Trap**

A fish trap is a trap used for fishing. Fish traps may have the form of a fishing weir or a lobster trap. A typical trap might consist of a frame of thick steel wire in the shape of a heart, with chicken wire stretched around it. The mesh wraps around the frame and then tapers into the inside of the trap. When a fish swims inside through this opening, it cannot get out, as the chicken wire opening bends back into its original narrowness. In earlier times, traps were constructed of wood and fibre.

Traps are culturally almost universal and seem to have been independently invented many times. There are essentially two types of trap, a permanent or semi-permanent structure placed in a river or tidal area and pot-traps that are baited to attract prey and periodically lifted.

The prehistoric Yaghan people who inhabited the Tierra Del Fuego area constructed stonework in shallow inlets that would effectively confine fish at low tide levels. Some of this extant stonework survives at Bahia Wulaia at the Bahia Wulaia Dome Middens archaeological site.

In southern Italy, during the 17th century, a new fishing technique began to be used. The trabucco is an old fishing machine typical of the coast of Gargano protected as historical monuments by the homonym National Park. This giant trap, built in structural wood, is spread along the coast of southern Adriatic especially in the province of Foggia and also in some parts of the coast of southern Tyrrhenian Sea.

Indigenous Australians were, prior to European colonisation, most populous in Australia's better-watered areas such as the Murray-Darling river system of the south-east. Here, where water levels fluctuate seasonally, indigenous people constructed ingenious stone fish traps. Most have been completely or partially destroyed. The largest and best-known are those on the Barwon River at Brewarrina, New South Wales, which are at least partly preserved. The Brewarrina fish traps caught huge numbers of migratory native fish as the Barwon River rose in flood and then fell. In southern Victoria, indigenous people created an elaborate system of canals, some more than 2 km long. The purpose of these canals was to attract and catch eels, a fish of short coastal rivers (as opposed to rivers of the Murray-Darling system). The eels were caught by a variety of traps including stone walls constructed across canals with a net placed across an opening in the wall. Traps at different levels in the marsh came into operation as the water level rose and fell. Somewhat similar stone-wall traps were constructed by native American Pit River people in north-eastern California.

A technique called dam fishing is used by the Baka pygmies. This involves the construction of a temporary dam resulting in a drop in the water levels downstream— allowing fish to be easily collected.

The manner in which fish traps are used depends on local conditions and the behaviour of the local fish. For example, a fish trap might be placed in shallow water near rocks where pikes like to lie. If placed correctly, traps can be very effective. It is usually not necessary to check the trap daily, since the fish remain alive inside the trap, relatively unhurt. Because of this, the trap also allows for the release of undersized fish as per fishing regulations.

The Wagenya people, in the Congo, build a huge system of wooden tripods across the river. These tripods are anchored on the holes naturally carved in the rock by the water current. To these tripods are anchored large baskets, which are lowered in the rapids to "sieve" the waters for fish. The baskets are designed and sized to trap only large fish. The Wagenya lift the baskets twice daily to check for fish, which are retrieved by swimmers.

In the Great Lakes Region of the United States, fishermen submerse a long, visible mesh wall running perpendicular to the shoreline that guides fish (who instinctively swim towards deeper water when coming upon a large obstacle) into a maze that ends in a large mesh "pot", that can be raised up to the boat to haul the fish in. This method of fishing results in fish staying alive until the time they are hauled into the boat, as against being entangled and killed in a gill net. This method also allows for sportfish and other protected species to be released without harm.

In Finland, the portable fish trap called *katiska* is made from chicken wire. It is lightweight and enables easy portability of the traps. The trap can either be collapsible or rigid, and is easily placed at any depth, as it needs no anchoring.

# 17

# Lobster Fishing

Lobster fishing, sometimes called lobstering is the commercial or recreational harvesting of marine lobsters, spiny lobsters or crayfish.

### Tools and Technology

Lobster fishing is part of the larger fishing industry. It uses tools such as boats, navigation, and other fishing technology. Fishing technology specific to the lobster industry generally includes traps, either rectangular-shaped or half-cylinders, once made from oak (coated with tar), but are now primarily made from wire mesh covered with a thick layer of plastic to reduce oxidation of the metal. Lobster traps, or pot warp, are connected to each other and to a buoy with rope. Ground lines are normally made of floating rope, or have a small buoyancy "toggle", to prevent the rope from snagging up on rocks and the bottom. Thus held off the bottom, they may be a danger to whales, and there are moves to forbid the use of floating rope for this purpose. It is currently illegal to use floating rope as ground line in the waters off north east America and Georges Bank.

A lobster trap must have in it a $2^3/_8 \times 11½$ inch-sized escape hole to allow under-sized lobsters to escape the trap.

Every trap must also have a "self-destruction device" to allow its door to fall open after it has been out too long. Traps are sunk to the ocean bottom with weights and are baited with dead fish. Attached to every trap is a buoy labelled with the license number and name or initials of the fisherman who has set the trap.

Using lobster traps allows a fisher to harvest far more lobsters in the same amount of time than does scuba diving to catch lobster by hand. A fisher with one boat can set, pull, and reset well over 100 traps a day, making trapping a much more efficient means than diving. With the use of traps, a fisher could collect anywhere from 100 to 1000 lobsters per day. Moreover, using traps is not held back by some of the limits of scuba diving - water depth, the time a diver can remain underwater, and the water conditions during diving.

### North America

Areas in North America where lobster fishing is common include southern California, New England, portions of the Caribbean Sea, and the Canadian Maritimes.

In the United States, as with all U.S. fishing industries, individual states manage lobster fishing within their three-mile boundaries. In Maine, this job is done by the Maine Department of Marine Resources. Since lobsters caught near shore and offshore look exactly the same when they are loaded onto the dock, it is important that interstate and federal regulations complement each other. An organization called the Atlantic States Marine Fisheries Commission, formed in 1942, helps to do this.

A compact of 15 eastern seaboard states, the Commission has three representatives from each state. These people include the Director of the state's marine resources management agency, a state legislator, and a fisheries representative appointed by the Governor. The member states are responsible for implementing the Commission Plan. The federal partners in lobster management are also part of the Commission process and work to complement the states efforts. Through the auspices of the National Marine Fisheries Service, federal regulations are adopted for lobster harvesting between three and 200 miles from shore, the United States' "economic zone".

Currently, the American lobster is managed under Amendment 4.5 of the Commission's American Lobster Management Plan. In Maine, lobsters can only be legally caught in lobster traps, also called pots. Inshore lobstermen have a limit of 800 pots per license, and regularly pull between 200-400 pots per day. Lobster caught in this region must be fished for only between sunrise and sunset, although this regulation is rarely enforced in the hour before dawn. Commercial lobstering season is year-round, with the exception of some self-managed zones around several islands off the Maine coast. Offshore lobstermen on the Eastern seaboard until recently had no trap limits, and traditionally fished between 2,000 and 3,000 pots per boat.

Inshore lobster boats on the eastern seaboard range from 22-42 feet on average, while offshore boats are considerably larger. The Maine lobster industry harvests more lobster annually than any other state in New England. Commercial U.S. fishers, while not bound to abide by any particular legal quota, must fish during lobster season, which starts on the first Wednesday in October through to the first Wednesday after the 15th of March. All commercial fishers must also keep a log of the exact number of legal and illegal lobster they catch.

Recreational lobster fishers in California must abide by a legal catch limit of seven lobsters per day and a minimal catch size of 3¼ inch long body measured from the eye socket to the edge of the carapace. The sport season for California spiny lobster starts on the Saturday preceding the first Wednesday in October through to the first Wednesday after the 15th of March. In southern California, lobster fishing for California spiny lobster is lucrative due to a huge market demand for lobster. Most commercial fishers use lobster traps. Their use is considered to be better than other collection techniques.

Nova Scotia limit the number pots per boat to between 250 and 375, depending on the district, and restricts the season. There is no limit to the number of lobster caught per trap, but there are size restrictions. Undersized lobsters must be returned to the water. Main article: Fishing industry in New Zealand.

### New Zealand

New Zealand implements the Quota Management System (QMS) to limit catches of fish and shellfish. Under QMS, a limit of 2,807,364 kilograms (6,189,180 lb) for the rock lobster *Jasus edwardsii*, and 1,291,000 kg (2,850,000 lb) for the New Zealand scampi, *Metanephrops challengeri*, were in place in 2011. Recreational fishers may only use lobster pots, while commercial fishers catch lobsters by trawling. The total catch in 2011 was 2,539,946 kg (5,599,620 lb) of *J. edwardsii*, 350,194 kg (772,050 lb) of *M. challengeri*, and 23,086 kg (50,900 lb) of *Sagmariasus verreauxi*.

### Lobster

Clawed lobsters comprise a family (Nephropidae, sometimes also Homaridae) of large marine crustaceans. Lobsters are economically important as seafood, forming the basis of a global industry that nets more than US$1 billion annually.

Though several groups of crustaceans are known as "lobsters," the clawed lobsters are most often associated with the name. They are also revered for their flavor and texture. Clawed lobsters are not closely related to spiny lobsters or slipper lobsters, which have no claws (*chelae*), or squat lobsters. The closest relatives of clawed lobsters are the reef lobsters and the three families of freshwater crayfish.

Lobsters were more diverse in the Cretaceous period (53 species) than in the Tertiary (16 or 18 species), which has been postulated to have been caused by mass extinction at the K–T boundary. However, diversity rebounded in the Eocene, and it may be that the lower Tertiary diversity was mainly due to lobsters abandoning shelf depths in the late

Eocene/early Oligocene, as fossils of deep-dwelling lobsters are rare. It is nevertheless clear that shelf-dwelling lobsters were more diverse during the Cretaceous.

Lobsters are invertebrates, with a hard protective exoskeleton. Like most arthropods, lobsters must molt in order to grow, which leaves them vulnerable. During the molting process, several species change color. Lobsters have 10 walking legs; the front three pairs bear claws, the first of which are larger than the others. Although, like most other arthropods, lobsters are largely bilaterally symmetrical, they often possess unequal, specialized claws, like the king crab.

Lobster anatomy includes the cephalothorax which fuses the head and the thorax, both of which are covered by the chitinous carapace and the abdomen. The lobster's head bears antennae, antennules, mandibles, the first and second maxillae, and the first, second, and third maxillipeds. Because lobsters live in a murky environment at the bottom of the ocean, they mostly use their antennae as sensors. The lobster eye has a reflective structure above a convex retina. In contrast, most complex eyes use refractive ray concentrators (lenses) and a concave retina. The abdomen includes swimmerets and its tail is composed of uropods and the telson.

Lobsters, like snails and spiders, have blue blood due to the presence of haemocyanin, which contains copper. (In contrast, mammals and many other animals have red blood from iron-rich haemoglobin.) Lobsters possess a green hepatopancreas, called the tomalley by chefs, which functions as the animal's liver and pancreas.

In general, lobsters are 25-50 centimetres (10-20 in) long and move by slowly walking on the sea floor. However, when they flee, they swim backwards quickly by curling and uncurling their abdomen. A speed of 5 metres per second (11 mph) has been recorded. This is known as the caridoid escape reaction.

**Longevity**

Recent research suggests that lobsters may not slow down, weaken, or lose fertility with age. In fact, older lobsters are more fertile than younger lobsters. This longevity may be due to telomerase, an enzyme that repairs DNA sequences of the form "TTAGGG". This sequence is often referred to as the telomeres of the DNA. It has been argued that lobsters may exhibit negligible senescence and some scientists have claimed that they could effectively live indefinitely, barring injury, disease, capture, etc. ; however, this claim is highly speculative. Their undoubted longevity allows them to reach impressive sizes. According to the Guinness World Records, the largest lobster was caught in Nova Scotia, Canada, and weighed 20.15 kilograms (44.4 lb).

### *Symbion*

Animals of the genus *Symbion*, the only member of the animal phylum Cycliophora, live exclusively on lobster gills and mouthparts.

### *Ecology*

Lobsters are found in all oceans. They live on rocky, sandy, or muddy bottoms from the shoreline to beyond the edge of the continental shelf. They generally live singly in crevices or in burrows under rocks.

Lobsters are omnivores, and typically eat live prey such as fish, mollusks, other crustaceans, worms, and some plant life. They scavenge if necessary, and may resort to cannibalism in captivity; however, this has not been observed in the wild. Although lobster skin has been found in lobster stomachs, this is because lobsters eat their shed skin after molting.

## Gastronomy

Lobster recipes include Lobster Newberg and Lobster Thermidor. Lobster is used variously, for example in soup, bisque, lobster rolls, and cappon magro. Lobster meat may be dipped in clarified butter, resulting in a sweetened flavour.

Cooks boil live lobsters in water or steam. The lobster simmers for seven minutes for the first pound and three minutes for each additional pound.

According to the United States Food and Drug Administration (FDA), the mean level of mercury in American lobster is 0.31 ppm.

### History

In North America, the American lobster did not achieve popularity until the mid-19th century, when New Yorkers and Bostonians developed a taste for it; not until the invention of a special boat, the lobster smack, did a commercial fishery flourish. Prior to this time, lobster was considered a mark of poverty or as a food for indentured servants or lower members of society in Maine, Massachusetts and the Canadian Maritimes, and servants specified in employment agreements that they would not eat lobster more than twice per week. American lobster was initially deemed worthy only of being used as fertilizer or fish bait, and it was not until well into the twentieth century that it was viewed as more than a low-priced canned staple food.

Caught lobsters are graded as new-shell, hard-shell and old-shell and, because lobsters that have recently shed their shells are the most delicate, there is an inverse relationship between the price of American lobster and its flavor. New-shell lobsters have paper-thin shells and a worse meat-to-shell ratio, but what meat exists is very sweet. However, the lobsters are so delicate that even transport to Boston almost kills them, making the market for new-shell lobsters strictly local to the fishing towns where they are offloaded. Hard-shell lobsters with firm shells but with less sweet meat can survive shipping to Boston, New York and even Los Angeles so command a higher price than new-shell lobsters. Meanwhile, old-shell lobsters, which have not shed since the previous season and have a coarser flavor, can be air-shipped anywhere in the world and arrive alive, making them the most expensive. One seafood guide notes that an eight dollar lobster dinner at a restaurant overlooking fishing piers in Maine is consistently delicious, while "the eighty-dollar lobster in a three-star Paris restaurant is apt to be as much about presentation as flavour."

### *Animal Welfare Issues*

The most common way of killing a lobster is by placing it, live, in boiling water, or by splitting: severing the body in half, lengthwise. Lobsters may also be killed or rendered insensate immediately before boiling through a stab into the brain, in the belief that this will stop suffering. However, a lobster's brain operates from not one but several ganglia and disabling only the frontal ganglion does not usually result in death or unconsciousness.

The boiling method is illegal in some places, such as in Reggio Emilia, Italy, where offenders face fines of up to €495.

# 18

# Diversity of Fish

Fish are very diverse and are categorized in many ways. This article is an overview of some of the more common types of fish. Although most fish species have probably been discovered and described, about 250 new ones are still discovered every year. According to Fishbase, 31,900 species of fish had been described by November 2010. That is more than the combined total of all other vertebrates: mammals, amphibians, reptiles and birds.

## By Species

Fish systematics is the formal description and organisation of fish taxa into systems. It is complex and still evolving. Controversies over "arcane, but important, details of classification are still quietly raging."

The term "fish" describes any non-tetrapod chordate, (i.e., an animal with a backbone), that has gills throughout life and has limbs, if any, in the shape of fins. Unlike groupings such as birds or mammals, fish are not a single clade but a paraphyletic collection of taxa, including jawless, cartilaginous and skeletal types.

### Jawless Fish

Jawless fish are the most primitive fish. There is current debate over whether these are really fish at all. They have no jaw, no scales, no paired fins, and no bony skeleton. Their skin is smooth and soft to the touch, and they are very flexible. Instead of a jaw, they possess an oral sucker. They use this to fasten on to other fish, and then use their rasp-like teeth to grind through their host's skin into the viscera. Jawless fish inhabit both fresh and salt water environments. Some are anadromous, moving between both fresh and salt water habitats.

Extant jawless fish are either lamprey or hagfish. Juvenile lamprey feed by sucking up mud containing micro-organisms and organic debris. The lamprey has well developed eyes, while the hagfish has only primitive eyespots. The hagfish coats itself and carcasses it finds with noxious slime to deter predators, and periodically ties itself into a knot to scrape the slime off. It is the only invertebrate fish and the only animal which has a skull but no vertebral column. It has four hearts, two brains, and a paddle-like tail.

### Cartilaginous Fish

Cartilaginous fish have a cartilaginous skeleton. However, their ancestors were bony animals, and were the first fish to develop paired fins. Cartilaginous fish don't have swim bladders. Their skin is covered in placoid scales (dermal denticles) that are as rough as sandpaper. Because cartilaginous fish do not have bone marrow, the spleen and special tissue around the gonads produces red blood cells. Their tails can be asymmetric, with the upper lobe longer than the lower lobe. Some cartilaginous fishes possess an organ called Leydig's Organ which also produces red blood cells.

### Bony Fish

Bony fish include the lobe finned fish and the ray finned fish. The lobe finned fish is the class of fleshy finned fishes, consisting of lungfish, and coelacanths. They are bony fish with fleshy, lobed paired fins, which are joined to the body by a single bone. These fins evolved into the legs of the first tetrapod land vertebrates, amphibians. Ray finned fishes are so-called because they possess lepidotrichia or "fin rays", their fins being webs of skin supported by bony or horny spines ("rays").

There are three types of ray finned fishes: the chondrosteans, holosteans, and teleosts. The chondrosteans and holosteans are primitive fishes sharing a mixture of characteristics of teleosts and sharks. In comparison with the other chondrosteans, the holosteans are closer to the teleosts and further from sharks.

### Teleosts

Teleosts are the most advanced or "modern" fishes. They are overwhelmingly the dominant class of fishes (or for that matter, vertebrates) with nearly 30,000 species, covering about 96 per cent of all extant fish species. They are ubiquitous throughout fresh water and marine environments from the deep sea to the highest mountain streams. Included are nearly all the important commercial and recreational fishes.

Teleosts have a movable maxilla and premaxilla and corresponding modifications in the jaw musculature. These modifications make it possible for teleosts to protrude their jaws outwards from the mouth. The caudal fin is homocercal, meaning the upper and lower lobes are about equal in size. The spine ends at the caudal peduncle, distinguishing this group from those in which the spine extends into the upper lobe of the caudal fin.

The smallest species is *Paedocypris progenetica*, a type of minnow. It is also the smallest vertebrate. The smallest mature female had a standard length of 7.9 millimeters (0.3 in). The largest individual is 10.3 millimeters (0.4 in). They live in the dark–colored peat swamps of the Indonesian island of Sumatra.

Other contenders for smallest fish are the male anglerfish, *Photocorynus spiniceps*, and the stout infantfish, a type of goby. According to the Guinness Book of World Records, the sinarapan, another type of goby, is the world's smallest commercially harvested fish. Found in the Philippines, they have an average length of 12.5 millimeters (0.5 in), and are threatened by overfishing.

The largest is the whale shark. It is a slow moving filter feeding shark with a maximum published length of 20 meters (66 ft) and a maximum weight of 34 tonnes. Whale sharks can live up to 70 years.

The heaviest bony fish is the ocean sunfish. It can weigh up to 2,300 kg (5,100 lb). It is found in all warm and temperate oceans. The longest bony fish is the king of herrings. Its total length can reach 11 metres (36 ft), and it can weigh up to 272 kilograms (600 lb). It is a rarely seen oarfish found in all the world's oceans, at depths of between 20 metres (66 ft) and 1,000 metres (3,300 ft).

**By Lifespan**

The shortest lived is the seven-figure pygmy goby, which lives for at most 59 days. This is the shortest lifespan for any vertebrate. Short lived fish have particular value in genetic studies on aging. In particular, the ram cichlid is used in laboratory studies because of its ease of breeding and predictable aging pattern.

The longest–lived fish is the 205 years reported for the rougheye rockfish, *Sebastes aleutianus,* found offshore in the North Pacific at 25-900 metres (14-490 fathoms). This fish exhibits negligible senescence.

There are stories about Japanese Koi goldfish passed from generation to generation for 300 years. Scientists are sceptical. Counting growth lines on the scales of fish confined to ponds or bowls is unreliable, since they lay down extra lines.

The longest living commercial fish may be the orange roughy, with a maximum reported age of 149 years. One of the longest living sport fish is the Atlantic tarpon, with a maximum reported age of 55 years."

Some of the longest living fish are living fossils, such as the green sturgeon. This species is among the longest living species found in freshwater, with a maximum reported age of 60 years. They are also among the largest fish species found in freshwater, with a maximum reported length of 2.5 meters (8 ft) and a maximum reported weight of {{kg to lb}159}}. Another living fossil is the Australian lungfish. One individual has lived in an aquarium for 75 years, and is the oldest fish in captivity. According to fossil records, the Australian lungfish has hardly changed for 380 million years.

**By Habitat**

Fish can also be demersal or pelagic. Demersal fish live on or near the bottom of oceans and lakes, while pelagic fish inhabit the water column away from the bottom. Habitats can also be vertically stratified. Epipelagic fish occupy sunlit waters down to 200 metres (110 fathoms), mesopelagic fish occupying deeper twilight waters down to 1,000 meters (3,281 ft), and bathypelagic fish inhabiting the cold and pitch black depths.

Most oceanic species (78%, or 44% of all fish species), live near the shoreline. These coastal fish live on or above the relatively shallow continental shelf. Only 13 per cent of all fish species live in the open ocean, off the shelf. Of these, 1 per cent are epipelagic, 5 per cent are pelagic, and 7 per cent are deep water.

Fish are found in nearly every aquatic habitat. Most fish, whether by species count or abundance, live in warmer environments with relatively stable temperatures. However, some species can survive temperatures up to 44.6 °C (112.3 °F), while others can cope with salinity greater than 10 per cent. The world's deepest living fish, *Abyssobrotula galatheae*, a species of cusk eel, lives in the Puerto Rico Trench at a depth of 8,372 meters (27,467 ft). At the other extreme, the Tibetan stone loach lives at altitudes over 5,200 meters (17,060 ft) in the Himalayas.

Some marine pelagic fish range over vast areas, such as the blue shark that lives in all oceans. At the other extreme are fish confined to single, small living spaces, such as isolated cave fish like *Lucifuga* in the Bahamas and Cuba, or equally isolated desert pupfish living in small desert spring systems in Mexico and the southwest U.S., or bythitid vent fish like *Thermichthys hollisi*, living around thermal vents 2,400 metres (1,300 fathoms) down.

### By Breeding Behaviour

Grouper are protogynous hermaphrodites, who school in *harems* of three to fifteen females. When no male is available, the most aggressive and largest females shift sex to male, probably as a result of behavioural triggers.

In very deep waters, it is not easy for a fish to find a mate. There is no light, so some species depend on bioluminescence. Others are hermaphrodites, which doubles their chances of producing both eggs and sperm when an encounter does occur. The female anglerfish releases pheromones to attract tiny males. When a male finds her, he bites on to her and never lets go. When a male of the anglerfish species *Haplophryne mollis* bites into the skin of a female, he release an enzyme that digests the skin of his mouth and her body, fusing the pair to the point where the two circulatory systems join up. The male then atrophies into nothing more than a pair of gonads. This extreme sexual dimorphism ensures that, when the female is ready to spawn, she has a mate immediately available.

Some sharks, such as hammerheads are able to breed parthogenetically.

### By Booding Behaviour

Fish adopt a variety of strategies for nurturing their brood. Sharks, for example, variously follow three protocols with their brood. Most sharks, including lamniformes are ovoviviparous, bearing their young after they nourish themselves after hatching and before birth, by consuming the remnants of the yolk and other available nutrients. Some such as hammerheads are viviparous, bearing their young after nourishing hatchlings internally, analgously to mammalian gestation. Finally catsharks and others are, oviparous, laying their eggs to hatch in the water.

Some animals, predominantly fish such as cardinalfish practice mouthbrooding, caring for their offspring by holding them in the mouth of a parent for extended periods of time. Mouthbrooding has evolved independently in several different families of fish.

### By Feeding Behaviour

Others, such as seahorse males, practice pouch-brooding, analogous to Australia's kangaroos, nourishing their offspring in a pouch in which the female lays them.

There are three basic methods by which food is gathered into the mouths of fish: by suction feeding, by ram feeding, and by manipulation or biting. Nearly all fish species use one of these styles, and most use two.

Early fish lineages had inflexible jaws limited to little more than opening and closing. Modern telosts have evolved protusible jaws that can reach out to engulf prey. An extreme example is the protusible jaw of the slingjaw wrasse. Its mouth extends into a tube half as long as its body, and with a strong suction it catches prey. The equipment tucks away under its body when it is not in use.

In practice, feeding modes lie on a spectrum, with suction and ram feeding at the extremes. Many fish capture their prey using both suction pressure combined with a forward motion of the body or jaw.

The cookiecutter shark is a small dogfish which derives its name from the way it removes small circular plugs, looking as though cut with a cookie cutter, from the flesh and skin of cetaceans and larger fish, including other sharks. The cookiecutter attaches to its larger prey with its suctorial lips, and then protrudes its teeth to remove a symmetrical scoop of flesh.

Other fish have developed extreme specializations. Silver arowana, also called *monkey fish*, can leap two meters out of the water to capture prey. They usually swim near the surface of the water waiting for potential prey. Their main diet consist of crustaceans, insects, smaller fishes and other animals that float on the water surface, for which its draw-bridge-like mouth is exclusively adapted for feeding. The remains of small birds, bats, and snakes have also been found in their stomachs.

Archerfish prey on land–based insects and other small animals by literally shooting them down with water droplets from their specialized mouths. Archerfish are remarkably accurate; adults almost always hit the target on the first shot. They can bring down insects such as grasshoppers, spiders and butterflies on a branch of an overhanging tree, 3 m above the water's surface. This is partially due to good eyesight, but also the ability to compensate for light refraction when aiming. Triggerfish also use jets of water, to uncover sand dollars buried in sand or overturn sea urchins.

**By Locomotion**

The slowest-moving fishes are the sea horses. The slowest of these, the dwarf seahorse, attains about five feet per hour.

Among the fasted sprinters are the Indo-Pacific sailfish and the black marlin. Both have been recorded in a burst at over 110 kilometres per hour (68 mph). For the sailfish, that is equivalent to 12 to 15 times their own length per second. The wahoo is perhaps the fastest fish for its size, attaining a speed of 19 lengths per second, reaching 78 kilometres per hour (48 mph).

The shortfin mako shark is fast enough and agile enough to chase down and kill an adult swordfish, but they don't always win. Sometimes in the struggle with a shark a swordfish can kill it by ramming it in the gills or belly. The shortfin mako's speed has been recorded at 50 kilometres per hour (31 mph), and there are reports that it can achieve bursts of up to 74 kilometres per hour (46 mph). It can jump up to 9 meters (30 ft) in the air. Due to its speed and agility, this high-leaping fish is sought as game worldwide. This shark is highly migratory. Its exothermic constitution partly accounts for its relatively great speed.

A number of species jump while swimming near the surface, skimming the water. Flying fish have unusually large pectoral fins, which enable the fish to take short gliding flights above the surface of the water, in order to escape from predators. Their glides are typically around 50 meters (160 ft), but they can use updrafts at the leading edge of waves to cover distances of at least 400 meters (1,300 ft). In May 2008, a flying fish was filmed off the coast of Japan . The fish spent 45 seconds aloft, and was able to stay aloft by occasionally beating the surface of the water with its caudal (tail) fin. The previous record was 42 seconds.

Walking fish are often amphibious and can travel over land for extended periods of time. Able to spend longer times out of water, these fish may use a number of means of locomotion, including springing, snake-like lateral undulation, and tripod-like walking. The mudskipper is probably the best land-adapted of contemporary fish and is able to spend days moving about out of water and can even climb mangroves, although to only modest heights. There are some species of fish that can "walk" along the sea floor but not on land. One such animal is the flying gurnard, which can walk on the sea floor.

**By Toxicity**

Toxic fish produce strong poisons in their bodies. Both poisonous fish and venomous fish, contain toxins, but deliver them differently.

Venomous fish bite, sting, or stab, causing an envenomation. Venomous fish don't necessarily cause poisoning if they are eaten, since the digestive system often destroys the venom. By contrast, the digestive system does not destroy poisonous fish toxins, making them poisonous to eat.

The most poisonous fish is the puffer fish. It is the second most poisonous vertebrate after the golden dart frog. It paralyzes the diaphragm muscles of human victims, who can die from suffocation. In Japan, skilled chefs use parts of a closely related species, the blowfish to create a delicacy called "fugu", including just enough toxin for that "special flavour".

The spotted trunkfish is a reef fish which secretes a colourless ciguatera toxin from glands on its skin when touched. The toxin is only dangerous when ingested, so there's no immediate harm to divers. However, predators as large as nurse sharks can die as a result of eating a trunkfish.

The giant moray is a reef fish at the top of the food chain. Like many other apex reef fish, it is likely to cause ciguatera poisoning if eaten. Outbreaks of ciguatera poisoning in the 11th to 15th centuries from large, carnivorous reef fish, caused by harmful algal blooms, could be a reason why Polynesians migrated to Easter Island, New Zealand, and possibly Hawaii.

A 2006 study found that there are at least 1200 species of venomous fish. There are more venomous fish than venomous snakes. In fact, there are more venomous fish than the combined total of all other venomous vertebrates. Venomous fish are found in almost all habitats around the world, but mostly in tropical waters. They wound over 50,000 people every year.

They carry their venom in venom glands and use various delivery systems, such as spines or sharp fins, barbs, spikes and fangs. Venomous fish tend to be either very visible, using flamboyant colors to warn enemies, or skilfully camouflaged and maybe buried in the sand. Apart from the defense or hunting value, venom help bottom dwelling fish by killing the bacteria that try to invade their skin. Few of these venoms have been studied. They are yet to be tapped resource for bioprospecting to find drugs with medical uses.

The most venomous fish is the reef stonefish. It has a remarkable ability to camouflage itself amongst rocks. It is an ambush predator that sits on the bottom waiting for prey to approach. Instead of swimming away if disturbed, it erects 13 venomous spines along its back. For defense, it can shoot venom from each or all of these spines. Each spine is like a hypodermic needle, delivering the venom from two sacs attached to the spine. The stonefish has control over whether to shoot its venom, and does so when provoked or frightened. The venom results in severe pain, paralysis and tissue death, and can be fatal if not treated. Despite its formidable defenses, stonefish have predators. Some bottom feeding rays and sharks with crushing teeth feed on them, as does the Stokes' seasnake.

Unlike stonefish, lionfish can only release venom when something strikes its spines. Although not native to the U.S. coast, lionfish have appeared around Florida and have spread up the coast to New York. They are attractive aquarium fish, sometimes used to stock ponds, and may have been washed into the sea during a hurricane. Lionfish can aggressively dart at scuba divers and attempt to puncture their facemask with their venomous spines.

The stargazer buries itself and can deliver electric shocks as well as venom. It is a delicacy in some cultures (cooking destroys the venom), and can be found for sale in some fish markets with the electric organ removed. They have been called "the meanest things in creation".

Stingray envenomations can occur to people who wade in shallow water and tread on them. This can be avoided by shuffling through the sand or stamping on the bottom, as the rays detect this and swim away. The stinger usually breaks off in the wound. It is barbed, so it can easily penetrate but not so easily be removed. The stinger causes local trauma from the cut itself, pain and swelling from the venom, and possible later infection from bacteria. Occasionally severed arteries or death can result.

Treatment for venom stings usually includes the application of heat, using water at temperatures of about 45°C (113°F), since heat breaks down most complex venom proteins.

Fish are sought by humans for their value as commercial food fish, recreational sport fish, decorative aquarium fish and in tourism, attracting snorkelers and SCUBA divers.

Throughout human history, important fisheries have been based on forage fish. Forage fish are small fish which are eaten by larger predators. They usually school together for protection. Typical ocean forage fish feed near the bottom of the food chain on plankton, often by filter feeding. They include the family Clupeidae (herrings, sardines, menhaden, hilsa, shad and sprats), as well as anchovies, capelin and halfbeaks.

Important herring fisheries have existed for centuries in the North Atlantic and the North Sea. Likewise, important traditional for anchovy and sardine fisheries have operated in the Pacific, the Mediterranean, and the southeast Atlantic. The world annual catch of forage fish in recent years has been around 25 million tonnes, or one quarter of the world's total catch.

Higher in the food chain, Gadidae (cod, pollock, haddock, saithe, hake and whiting also support important fisheries. Concentrated initially in the North Sea, Atlantic cod was one of Europe's oldest fisheries, later extending to the Grand Banks, Declining numbers led to international "cod wars" and eventually the virtual abandonment of these fisheries.

**By Vulnerability**

Fish hold the records for the relative brain weights of vertebrates. Most vertebrate species have similar brain-to-body weight ratios. The deep sea bathopelagic cusk-eel *Acanthonus armatus*, has the smallest ratio of all known vertebrates. At the other extreme, the elephantnose fish, an African freshwater fish, has the largest ratio of all known vertebrates.

*Sarpa salpa*, a species of bream are recognizable by the golden stripes running the length of its body and can induce LSD-like hallucinations if it is eaten. These widely distributed coastal fish became a recreational drug during the Roman Empire, and are called "the fish that make dreams" in Arabic. Other hallucinogenic fish are *Siganus spinus*, called "the fish that inebriates" in Reunion Island, and *Mulloidichthys samoensis*, called "the chief of ghosts" in Hawaii.

These days the Alaska pollock supports an important fishery in the Bering Sea and the north Pacific, yielding about 6 million tonnes, while cod amounts to about 9 million tonnes.

### Four-eyed Fish

Four-eyed fish have eyes raised above the top of the head and divided in two different parts, so that they can see below and above the water surface at the same time.

Four-eyed fish actually have only two eyes, but their eyes are specially adapted for their surface-dwelling lifestyle. The eyes are positioned on the top of the head, and the fish floats at the water surface with only the lower half of each eye underwater. The two halves are divided by a band of tissue and the eye has two pupils, connected by part of the iris. The upper half of the eye is adapted for vision in air, the lower half for vision in water. The lens of the eye also changes in thickness top to bottom to account for the difference in the refractive indices of air versus water. These fish spend most of their time at the surface of the water. Their diet mostly consists of the terrestrial insects which are available at the surface.

## SEA LAMPREY

The sea lamprey (*Petromyzon marinus*) is a parasitic lamprey found on the Atlantic coasts of Europe and North America, in the western Mediterranean Sea, and in the Great Lakes. It is brown or gray on its back and white or gray on the underside and can grow to be up to 90 cm (35.5 in) long.

Sea lampreys prey on a wide variety of fish. The lamprey uses its suction-cup like mouth to attach itself to the skin of a fish and rasps away tissue with its sharp probing tongue and teeth. Secretions in the lamprey's mouth prevent the victim's blood from clotting. Victims typically die from excessive blood loss or infection.

### Life-cycle

The life cycle of sea lampreys is anadromous, like that of salmon. The young are born in inland rivers, live in the ocean as adults, and return to the rivers to breed. Young emerge from the egg as larvae, blind and toothless, and live that way for 3 to 7 years, buried in mud and filter-feeding.

Once they have grown to a certain length, they metamorphosize into their parasitic form, after which they migrate to the sea. Parasitic lampreys feed on the tissue and blood of teleost fish. After several years they become sexually mature and stop feeding. Sexually mature lampreys return to freshwater rivers and streams and spawn, after which they die.

### Attacks on Humans

While lamprey attacks on humans remain few and far between, they have been known to occur. Most recently in the early hours of 28 August 2010, a swimmer participating in a relay swim of the English Channel, was attacked by a lamprey which attached itself to the athlete's lower back. It remained there until the swimmer returned to the pilot boat at the end of his swim, where it was removed and returned to the water. The swimmer made a full recovery.

### Invasion of Great Lakes

Sea lampreys are considered a pest in the Great Lakes region. The species is native to the inland Finger Lakes and Lake Champlain in New York and Vermont. It is not clear whether it is native to Lake Ontario, where it was first noticed in the 1830s, or whether it was introduced through the Erie Canal, which opened in 1825. It is thought that improvements to the Welland Canal in 1919 allowed its spread from Lake Ontario to Lake Erie, and while it was never abundant in either lake, it soon spread to Lake Michigan, Lake Huron, and Lake Superior, where it decimated indigenous fish population in the 1930s and 1940s.

They have created a problem with their aggressive parasitism on key predator species and game fish, such as lake trout, lake whitefish, chub, and lake herring. Elimination of these predators allowed the alewife, another invasive species, to explode in population, having adverse effects on many native fish species. The lake trout plays a vital role in the Lake Superior ecosystem.

The lake trout is considered an apex predator which means that the entire system relies on its presence to be diverse and healthy. With the removal of an apex predator from a system, the entire system feels the effects all the way down the food chain. The sea lamprey is an aggressive predator by nature which gives it a competitive advantage in a lake system where it has no predators, and its prey lacks defenses against it. The sea lamprey played a large role in the destruction of the Lake Superior lake trout population. Lampreys are not entirely to blame for the crash of Great Lake fisheries, but their introduction, along with poor unsustainable fishing practices caused the lake trout populations to decline drastically.

This resulted in the relationship between predators and prey in the Great Lakes' Ecosystem became unbalanced. Control efforts, including electric current, chemical lampricides, and barriers, have met with varied success. The control programmes are carried out under the Great Lakes Fishery Commission, a joint Canada-US body, specifically by the agents of the GLFC, Fisheries and Oceans Canada, and the United States Fish and Wildlife Service.

### Efforts at Control

Genetic researchers have begun mapping the sea lamprey's genome in the hope of finding out more about evolution; scientists trying to eliminate the Great Lakes problem are co-ordinating with these genetic scientists, hoping to find out more about its immune system and fitting it into its place in the phylogenetic tree.

Several scientists in this field work directly for Fisheries and Oceans Canada or the United States Fish and Wildlife Service. Researchers from Michigan State University have teamed up with others from the Universities of Minnesota, Guelph, Wisconsin, as well as many others in a massive research effort into newly synthesized pheromones. These are believed to have independent influences on the sea lamprey behaviour.

One pheromone serves a migratory function in that odor emitted from larva are thought to lure maturing adults into streams with suitable spawning habitat; other, a sex pheromone, is emitted from males and is capable of luring females long distances to very specific locations - even in complete darkness and even though many lampreys at this stage in their life have strongly degraded eyesight. These two pheromones are actually both several different compounds that are thought to elicit different behaviours that collectively influence the lamprey to exhibit migratory behaviours or spawning behaviours.

Effort is being made to characterize the function of each pheromone, each part of each pheromone, and if they can be used in a targeted effort at environmentally friendly lamprey control. It is the hope of the Great Lakes Fishery Commission that at least some of this work into sea lamprey genetics as well as pheromones will pan out into a successful, effective management technique that could one day drastically reduce the need for TFM treatments of spawning grounds.

Despite millions put into research however, the most effective control measures are still being undertaken by control agents of State and Federal Agencies but involve the somewhat publicly unacceptable dumping of TFM into rivers.

Another technique used in the prevention of lamprey population growth is the use of barriers in major reproduction streams of high value to the lamprey. The barriers are placed in areas downstream of highly productive lamprey spawning grounds. The purpose is to block upstream migration of the lampreys to allow for minimal reproduction.

The issue with these barriers is that other aquatic species are also inhibited by this barrier. Fish that use tributaries are impeded from travelling upstream to spawn. To account for the issue, barriers have been altered and designed to allow the passage of most fish species but still impede others.

This is another indirect negative impact that the sea lamprey has on Lake Superior, and the entire Great Lakes

Ecosystem as a whole. Today the lamprey population in Lake Superior is in check, but there is still a prevalent population. Lake trout numbers have increased dramatically due to natural reproduction and intense stocking programmes.

The future of the Lake Superior ecosystem is unknown and much research is being conducted to find new ways to eliminate the sea lamprey. The lake ecosystem will never be how it once was because of new exotic species entering the lake at an alarming rate. However new regulation and a sense of urgency have led to strong movements to return the lake to the diverse, healthy ecosystem it was in the past.

# Fish Locomotion

The prevailing type of fish locomotion is swimming in water. In addition, some fish can "walk", i.e., move over land, burrow in mud, and glide through the air.

## Swimming

Fish swim by exerting force against the surrounding water. There are exceptions, but this is normally achieved by the fish contracting muscles on either side of its body in order to generate waves of flexion that travel the length of the body from nose to tail, generally getting larger as they go along. The vector forces exerted on the water by such motion cancel out laterally, but generate a net force backwards which in turn pushes the fish forward through the water.

Most fishes generate thrust using lateral movements of their body & caudal fin. But there are also a huge number of species that move mainly using their median and paired fins. The latter group profits from the gained manoeuvrability that is needed when living in coral reefs for example. But they can't swim as fast as fish using their bodies & caudal fins.

### Body/Caudal Fin Propulsion

There are four groups that differ in the fraction of their body that is displaced laterally.

### Anguilliform Locomotion

In some long, slender fish – eels, for example – there is little increase in the amplitude of the flexion wave as it passes along the body.

### Sub-carangiform Locomotion

Here, there is a more marked increase in wave amplitude along the body with the vast majority of the work being done by the rear half of the fish. In general, the fish body is stiffer, making for higher speed but reduced maneuverability. Trout use sub-carangiform locomotion.

### Carangiform Locomotion

Fish in this group are stiffer and faster-moving than the previous groups. The vast majority of movement is concentrated in the very rear of the body and tail. Carangiform swimmers generally have rapidly oscillating tails.

### Thunniform Locomotion

The final group is reserved for the high-speed long-distance swimmers, like tuna (new research shows that the thunniform locomotion is an autapomorphy of the tunas. Here, virtually all the lateral movement is in the tail and the region connecting the main body to the tail (the peduncle). The tail itself tends to be large and crescent shaped.

### Median/Paired Fin Propulsion

Not all fish fit comfortably in the above groups. Ocean sunfish, for example, have a completely different system, and many small fish use their pectoral fins for swimming as well as for steering and dynamic lift. Fish with electric organs, such as those in Gymnotiformes, swim by undulating their fins while keeping the body still, presumably so as not to disturb the electric field that they generate.

## Dynamic Lift

Bone and muscle tissues of fish are denser than water. To maintain depth some fish increase buoyancy by means of a gas bladder or by storing oils or lipids. Fish without these features use dynamic lift instead. It is done using their pectoral fins in a manner similar to the use of wings by aeroplanes and birds. As these fish swim, their pectoral fins are positioned to create lift which allows the fish to maintain a certain depth.

Sharks are a notable example of fish that depend on dynamic lift; notice their well-developed pectoral fins.

The two major drawbacks of this method are that these fish must stay moving to stay afloat and that they are incapable of swimming backwards or hovering. Burrowing

Many fishes, particularly eel-shaped fishes such as true eels, moray eels, and spiny eels, are capable of burrowing through sand or mud. Ophichthids are capable of digging backwards using a sharpened tail.

## Walking Fish

Walking fish, sometimes called ambulatory fish, is a general term that refers to fish that are able to travel over land for extended periods of time. The term may also be used for some other cases of nonstandard fish locomotion, e.g., when describing fish "walking" along the sea floor.

Most commonly this term is applied to amphibious fish. Able to spend longer times out of water, these fish may use a number of means of locomotion, including springing, snake-like lateral undulation, and tripod-like walking. The mudskippers are probably the best land-adapted of contemporary fish and are able to spend days moving about out of water and can even climb mangroves, although to only modest heights. The Climbing gourami is often specifically referred to as a "walking fish", although it does not actually "walk", but rather moves in a jerky way by supporting itself on the extended edges of its gill plates and pushing itself by its fins and tail. Some reports indicate that it can also climb trees.

There are a number of fish that are less adept at actual walking, such as the walking catfish. Despite being known for "walking on land", this fish usually wriggles and may use its pectoral fins to aid in its movement. Walking Catfish have a respiratory system that allows them to live out of water for several days. Some are invasive species. A notorious case in the United States is the Northern snakehead. Polypterids have rudimentary lungs and can also move about on land, though rather clumsily.

There are some species of fish that can "walk" along the sea floor but not on land; one such animal is the flying gurnard (it does not actually fly, and should not be confused with flying fish). The batfishes of the Ogcocephalidae family (not to be confused with Batfish of Ephippidae) are also capable of walking along the sea floor.

The axolotl, an aquatic salamander native to Mexico, is colloquially known as the "Mexican walking fish", although it is not a fish, but an amphibian.

In modern fish the "walking" ability differs from that of *tetrapods* (four-legged animals). The theory of evolution suggests that life originated in the oceans and later moved onto land, and paleontologists have long been looking for a missing evolutionary link between ocean-living and land-living animals. Of recent finds, reported in *Nature* (April 2006) is *Tiktaalik roseae,* which has many features of wrist, elbow, and neck that are akin to those of tetrapods. It belonged to a group of lobe-finned fish called *Rhipidistia,* which according to some recent theories were the ancestors of all tetrapods.

# 20

# Traditional Fishing Boat

Traditionally, many different kinds of boats have been used as fishing boats to catch fish in the sea, or on a lake or river. Even today, many traditional fishing boats are still in use. According to the United Nations Food and Agriculture Organization (FAO), at the end of 2004, the world fishing fleet consisted of about 4 million vessels, of which 2.7 million were undecked (open) boats. While nearly all decked vessels were mechanized, only one-third of the undecked fishing boats were powered, usually with outboard engines. The remaining 1.8 million boats were traditional craft of various types, operated by sail and oars.

This chapter is about the boats used for fishing that are or were built from designs that existed before engines became available.

Early fishing vessels included rafts, dugout canoes, reed boats, and boats constructed from a frame covered with hide or tree bark, such as coracles. The oldest boaats found by archaeological excavation are dugout canoes dating back to the Neolithic Period around 7,000-9,000 years ago. These canoes were often cut from coniferous tree logs, using simple stone tools. A 7000 year-old sea going boat made from reeds and tar has been found in Kuwait. These early vessels had limited capability; they could float and move on water, but were not suitable for use any great distance from the shoreline. They were used mainly for fishing and hunting.

The development of fishing boats took place in parallel with the development of boats built for trade and war. Early navigators began to use animal skins or woven fabrics for sails. Affixed to a pole set upright in the boat, these sails gave early boats more range, allowing voyages of exploration

According to the FAO, at the end of 2004, the world fishing fleet included 1.8 million traditional craft of various types which were operated by sail and oars. These figures for small fishing vessels are probably under reported. The FAO compiles these figures largely from national registers. These records often omit smaller boats where registration is not required or where fishing licences are granted by provincial or municipal authorities. Indonesia reportedly has about 700,000 current fishing boats, 25 per cent of which are dugout canoes, and half of which are without motors. The Philippines have reported a similar number of small fishing boats.

Traditional fishing boats are usually characteristic of the stretch of coast along which they operate. They evolve over time to meet the local conditions, such as the materials available locally for boat building, the type of sea conditions the boats will encounter, and the demands of the local fisheries.

Artisan fishing is a term used to describe small scale commercial or subsistence fishing practises. The term particularly applies to coastal or island ethnic groups using traditional fishing techniques and traditional boats. The term can also be applied to heritage groups involved in customary fishing practices. Small traditional fishing boats are usually used by artisan fishers. Artisan fishing boats are often open (undecked), many have sails, but they do not usually use much, or any mechanised or electronic gear. Large numbers of artisan fishing boats are still in use, particularly in developing countries with long productive marine coastlines.

### Rafts

A raft is a structure with a flat top that floats. It is the most basic boat design, characterized by the absence of a hull. The classic raft is constructed by lashing several logs, placed side by side, to two or more additional logs placed transverse to the others. In many Asian countries, the rafts are similarly constructed using bamboo.

In shallow waters, rafts can be punted with a push pole. They can be used as stealthy platforms for fishing shallow waters around lakes. In sheltered coastal waters, anchored or drifting rafts can become effective fish aggregating devices. Payaos were traditional bamboo rafts used in Southeast Asia as aggregating device. Fishermen on the top of the raft used handlines to catch tuna.

Pontoon boats, and to some degree the punt, can be viewed as modern derivatives of rafts.

Boats, rafts and even small floating islands have been made from reeds. Reed rafts can be distinguished from reed boats, since the rafts are not made watertight.

The earliest known boat made with reeds (and tar) is a 7000 year-old sea going boat found in Kuwait.

The Uros are an indigenous people pre-dating the Incas. They live, still today, on man-made floating islands scattered across Lake Titicaca. These islands are constructed from totora reeds. Lake Titicaca, part belonging to Bolivia and the rest to Peru, is 3810 meters above sea level. Each floating island supports between three and ten houses, also built of reeds. The Uros also build their boats from bundled dried reeds. These days some Uros boats, used for fishing and hunting seabirds, have motors.

Reed boats were constructed in Easter Island with a markedly similar design to those used in Peru. Apart from Peru and Bolivia, reed boats are still used in Ethiopia and were used until recently in Corfu.

### Coracles

Coracles are light boats shaped like a bowl, typically with a frame of woven grass or reeds, or strong saplings covered with animal hides. The keel-less, flat bottom evenly spreads the weight across the structure reducing the required depth of water often to only a few inches. Coracles have been used, and to a degree are still used, in India, Vietnam, Iraq, Tibet, North America and Britain.

Coracles in Iraq are called *quffa*. Their history goes back to antiquity where they appear on sculptured panels in Assyrian palaces constructed between 700 and 900 BC. These panels are now in the British Museum. Herodotus visited Babylon in the 5th century BC, and wrote a long description of the coracles he encountered there. Traditionally, quffa were framed with willow or juniper and covered with hides. The outside was coated with hot bitumen for waterproofing. These coracles have been in use, at least until recently, around Baghdad and on the Tigris. Some of the Iraq coracles are very large.

Coracles are known to have been in use in Britain in 49BC when Julius Caesar encountered them. They are still used in Wales, where they were traditionally framed with split and interwoven willow rods, tied with willow bark. The outer layer was an animal skin, such as horse or bullock hide, with a thin layer of tar for water proofing. Today tarred calico or canvas, or simply fibreglass can be used. Different Welsh rivers have their own designs, tailored to the flow of the river. The Teifi coracle, for instance, is flat bottomed, as it is designed to negotiate shallow rapids, common on the river in the summer, while the Carmarthen coracle is rounder and deeper, because it is used in tidal waters on the Tywi, where there are no rapids.

Coracles can be effective fishing vessels. When operated skilfully, they hardly disturb the water or the fish. Welsh coracle fishing is performed by two men, each seated in his coracle and with one hand holding the net while with the other he plies his paddle. When a fish is caught, each hauls up his end of the net until the two coracles touch and the fish are secured. Many coracles are so light and portable that they can easily be carried on the fisherman's shoulders.

In Tibet, coracles, used for fishing and ferrying people, are made by stretching yak hide over juniper frames, and fastened with leather thongs. They are shaped like the Iraq coracles. Yack butter is used for waterproofing. Again, different rivers have their own designs. Sometimes two coracles are strapped together for added stability.

In North America, American Indians and frontiersmen made coracles, called bull boats, by covering a willow frame with buffalo hide. The buffalo hair was left on the hide because it inhibited the craft from spinning, and the tails were also left intact and used to tie bull boats together.

Indian coracles commonly operate on the rivers Kaveri and Tungabhadra in Southern India. The smaller ones are about 6.2 feet (1.9 metres) in diameter, and are used primarily for fishing. Indian coracles have been used since prehistoric times.

In Vietnam, elegant coracles constructed with bamboo, are still used from many beaches, such as at Nha Trang, Phan Thiat and Mui Ne. The coracles are towed in a line behind a motor boat, like beads on a string, to their fishing ground. There the fisherman lay fishing nets in the sea before another tow returns them with their catch..

## Canoes

A canoe is a small narrow boat, usually pointed at both bow and stern and normally open on top, though they can be covered. A dugout is a canoe hollowed from a tree trunk. The oldest known canoe is the dugout canoe of Pesse (the Netherlands). According to C14 dating analysis it was constructed somewhere between 8200 and 7600 BC. This canoe is exhibited in the Drents Museum in Assen, Netherlands. Another dugout, almost as old, has been found at Noyen-sur-Seine. The oldest known canoe found in Africa is the Dufuna canoe, constructed about 6000 BC. It was discovered by Fulani herdsman in Nigeria in 1987.

During the Iron Age residents of Great Britain used dugouts for fishing and transport. Two ancient dugouts discovered in Newport, Shropshire are on display at Harper

Adams University College Newport. In 1964, a dugout was uncovered in Poole Harbour, Dorset. The Poole Logboat, dated to 300 BC, was large enough to accommodate 18 people and was constructed from a large oak tree.

Best known are the canoes of the Eastern North American Indians. These, often elegant canoes, were not dugouts, but were made of a wooden frame covered with bark of a birch tree, pitched to make it waterproof.

Typically canoes are propelled with paddles, often with two people. Paddlers face in the direction of travel, either seated on supports in the hull, or kneeling directly upon the hull. Paddles can be single-bladed or double-bladed.

A pirogue is a small, flat-bottomed boat of a design associated particularly with West African fishermen and the Cajuns of the Louisiana marsh. These are usually dugouts, and are light and small enough to be easily taken onto land. The design allows the pirogue to move through the very shallow water of marshes and be easily turned over to drain any water that may get into the boat. The pirogue is usually propelled by paddles with one blade. It can also be punted with a push pole in shallow water. Small sails can also be used. Outboard motors are increasingly being used in many regions.

The log canoe of Chesapeake Bay is in the modern sense not a canoe at all, though it evolved through the enlargement of dugout canoes.

For stability in rougher waters, canoes can be fitted with outriggers. One or two small logs are mounted parallel to the main hull by long poles. In the case of two outriggers, one is mounted to either side of the hull. These are called outrigger canoes.

Many of the fishing boats in Indonesia and the Philippines are double-outrigger craft, consisting of a narrow main hull with two attached outriggers, commonly known as *jukung* in Indonesia and *banca* in the Philippines.

The jukung is of Balinese origin, one of many genre of Pacific/Asian outrigger canoes. The considerable stability provided by the outriggers means that the jukung copes well with a lateen (triangular) sail. While the lateen sail presents some difficulties in tacking into the wind, requiring a jibe, the jukung is superb in its reaching ability and jybe-safe running. They are usually highly decorated and bear a marlin-like prow.

A traditional catamaran consists of two canoes, or vakas, joined by a frame, formed of akas. Catamarans were used by the ancient Tamil Chola dynasty as early as the 5th century AD for moving their invasion fleets. Since then, they have been widely used for fishing in South East Asia and Polynesia.

Kayaks are generally differentiated from canoes by the sitting position of the paddler and the number of blades on the paddle. In a kayak the paddler faces forward, legs in front, using a double bladed paddle. In a canoe the paddler faces forward and sits or kneels in the boat, using a single bladed paddle. In some parts of the world, such as the United Kingdom, kayaks are considered a subtype of canoes. Continental European and British canoeing clubs and associations of the 19th Century used craft similar to kayaks, but referred to them as canoes.

### Ropes and Lines

Ropes and lines are made of fibre lengths, twisted or braided together to provide tensile strength. They are used for pulling, but not for pushing.

Fossilised fragments of "probably two-ply laid rope of about 7 mm diameter" have been found in one of the caves at Lascaux, dated about 15,000 BC. Egyptian rope dates back to 4000 to 3500 BC and was generally made of water reed fibers. Other rope in antiquity was made from the fibers of date palms, flax, grass, papyrus, leather, or animal hair. Rope made of hemp fibres was in use in China from about 2800 BC.

The availability of reliable and durable ropes and lines has had many consequences for the development and utility of traditional fishing boats. They can be used to lash planks and frames together, as stay lines for masts, as anchor lines to secure the boat, and as fishing lines for making fishing nets.

### Propulsion

Before engines became available, boats could be propelled manually or by the wind. Boats could be propelled by the wind by attaching sails to masts set upright in the boat. Manual propulsion could be done in shallow water by punting with a push pole, and in deeper water by paddling with a paddle or rowing with oars. The difference between paddling and rowing is that when rowing the oars have a mechanical connection with the boat, while when paddling the paddles are hand-held with no mechanical connection. Canoes were traditionally paddled, with the paddler facing the bow of the boat. Small boats that use oars are called rowboats, and the rower typically faces the stern.

Around 4000 B.C., Egyptians were building long narrow boats powered by many oarsmen. Over the next 1,000 years, they made a series of remarkable advances in boat design. They developed cotton-made sails to help their boats go faster with less work. Then they built boats large enough to cross the oceans. These boats had sails and oarsmen, and were used for war and trade. Some ancient vessels were propelled by either oars or sail, depending on the speed and direction of the wind (see trireme and bireme). The Chinese were using sails around 3000 BC, of a type that can still be seen on traditional fishing boats sailing off the coast of Vietnam in Ha Long Bay.

A jangada is an elegant planked fishing boat used in northern Brazil. It has been claimed the jangada dates back to ancient Greek time. It uses a triangular (lateen) sail, which allows it to sail against the wind.

A felucca is a traditional wood-planked sailing boat used in protected waters of the Red Sea and eastern Mediterranean including Malta, and particularly along the Nile in Egypt. Its rig consists of one or two lateen sails.

## Planking

Building boats from planks meant boats could be more precisely constructed along the line of large canoes than hollowing tree trucks allowed. It is possible that planked canoes were developed as early as 8,500 years ago in Southern California.

By 3000 BC, the Egyptians knew how to assemble planks of wood into a ship hull. They used woven straps to lash planks together, and reeds or grass stuffed between the planks to seal the seams. An example of their skill is the Khufu ship, a vessel 143 feet (44 m) in length entombed at the foot of the Great Pyramid of Giza around 2500 BC and found intact in 1954.

A further development was the use of timber frames, to which the planks could be lashed, stitched or nailed. With the use of frames, it is possible to develop carvel-style and clinker-style planking (in the USA the term *lapstrake* is used instead of *clinker*). Scandinavians were using clinker construction by at least 350 BC.

Carvel construction dates back even earlier. The design of the luzzu is believed to date back at least to Phoenician times. A luzzu is a double-ended carvel-built fishing boat from the Maltese islands. Traditionally, they are brightly painted in shades of yellow, red, green and blue, and the bow is normally pointed with a pair of eyes. These eyes may be the modern survival of an ancient Phoenician custom (also practiced by the ancient Greeks); they are sometimes (and probably inaccurately) referred to as the Eye of Horus or of Osiris. The luzzu has survived because it tends to be a sturdy and stable boat even in bad weather. Originally, the luzzu was equipped with sails although nowadays almost all are motorised, with onboard diesel engines being the most common.

Boats in South East Asia and Polynesia centred on canoes, outriggers and multihull boats. By contrast, boats in Europe centred on framed and keeled monohulls.

The Scandinavians were building innovative boats millennia ago, as shown by the many petroglyph images of Nordic Bronze Age boats. The oldest archaeological find of a wooden Nordic boat is the Hjortspring boat, built about 350 BC. This is the oldest known boat to use clinker planking, where the planks overlap one another. It was designed as a large canoe, 19 m long and crewed by 22-23 men using paddles. Scandinavians continued to develop better boats, incorporating iron and other metal into the design, adding keels, and developing oars for propulsion.

21

# Fishing Vessel

A fishing vessel is a boat or ship used to catch fish in the sea, or on a lake or river. Many different kinds of vessels are used in commercial, artisanal and recreational fishing.

According to the FAO, there are four million commercial fishing vessels (2004). About 1.3 million of these are decked vessels with enclosed areas. Nearly all of these decked vessels are mechanised, and 40,000 of them are over 100 tons. At the other extreme, two-thirds (1.8 million) of the undecked boats are traditional craft of various types, powered only by sail and oars. These boats are used by artisan fishers.

It is difficult to estimate the number of recreational fishing boats. They range in size from small dingies to large charter cruisers, and unlike commercial fishing vessels, are often not dedicated just to fishing.

Prior to the 1950s there was little standardisation of fishing boats. Designs could vary between ports and boatyards. Traditionally boats were built out of wood, but wood is not often used now because of cost and the difficulty in obtaining suitable timber. Fibreglass is used increasingly in smaller fishing vessels up to 25 metres (100 tons), while steel is usually used on vessels above 25 metres.

## History

Early fishing vessels included rafts, dugout canoes, and boats constructed from a frame covered with hide or tree bark, along the lines of a coracle. The oldest boats found by archaeological excavation are dugout canoes dating back to the Neolithic Period around 7,000-9,000 years ago. These canoes were often cut from coniferous tree logs, using simple stone tools. A 7000 year-old sea going boat made from reeds and tar has been found in Kuwait. These early vessels had limited capability; they could float and move on water, but were not suitable for use any great distance from the shoreline. They were used mainly for fishing and hunting.

The development of fishing boats took place in parallel with the development of boats built for trade and war. Early navigators began to use animal skins or woven fabrics for sails. Affixed to a pole set upright in the boat, these sails gave early boats more range, allowing voyages of exploration.

Around 4000 B.C., Egyptians were building long narrow boats powered by many oarsmen. Over the next 1,000 years, they made a series of remarkable advances in boat design. They developed cotton-made sails to help their boats go faster with less work. Then they built boats large enough to cross the oceans. These boats had sails and oarsmen, and were used for travel and trade. By 3000 BC, the Egyptians knew how to assemble planks of wood into a ship hull. They used woven straps to lash planks together, and reeds or grass stuffed between the planks to seal the seams. An example of their skill is the Khufu ship, a vessel 143 feet (44 m) in length entombed at the foot of the Great Pyramid of Giza around 2,500 BC and found intact in 1954.

At about the same time, the Scandinavians were also building innovative boats. People living near Kongens Lyngby in Denmark, came up with the idea of segregated hull compartments, which allowed the size of boats to gradually be increased. A crew of some two dozen paddled the wooden Hjortspring boat across the Baltic Sea long before the rise of the Roman Empire. Scandinavians continued to develop better ships, incorporating iron and other metal into the design and developing oars for propulsion.

The oldest Nordic shipfind is the Nydam boat, found preserved in the Nydam Mose bog in Sundeved, Denmark. It has been dendro dated to A.D. 310-320 and is the oldest known boat to use clinker planking, where the planks overlap one another. Built of oak, it is 23 metres long and about 4 metres wide. It originally weighed over three tonnes and was rowed by thirty men.

By A.D. 1000 the Norsemen were pre-eminent on the oceans. They were skilled seamen and boat builders, with clinker-built boat designs that varied according to the type of boat. Trading boats, such as the knarrs, were wide to allow large cargo storage. Raiding boats, such as the longship, were long and narrow and very fast. The vessels they used for fishing were scaled down versions of their cargo boats. The Scandinavian innovations influenced fishing boat design long after the Viking period came to an end. For example, yoles from the Orkney island of Stroma were built in the same way as the Norse boats.

In the 15th century, the Dutch developed a type of sea-going herring drifter that became a blueprint for European fishing boats. This was the Herring Buss, used by Dutch herring fishermen until the early 19th centuries. The ship type buss has a long history. It was known around 1000 AD in Scandinavia as a *buza*, a robust variant of the Viking longship. The first herring buss was probably built in Hoorn around 1415. The last one was built in Vlaardingen in 1841. The ship was about 20 meters long and displaced between 60 and 100 tons. It was a massive round-bilged keel ship with a bluff bow and stern, the latter relatively high, and with a gallery. The busses used long drifting gill nets to catch the herring. The nets would be retrieved at night and the crews of eighteen to thirty men would set to gibbing, salting and barrelling the catch on the broad deck. The ships sailed in fleets of 400 to 500 ships to the Dogger Bank fishing grounds and the Shetland isles. They were usually escorted by naval vessels, because the English considered they were "poaching". The fleet would stay at sea for weeks at a time. The catch would sometimes be transferred to special ships (called *ventjagers*), and taken home while the fleet would still be at sea (the picture shows a *ventjager* in the distance).

During the 17th century, the British developed the dogger, an early type of sailing trawler or longliner, which commonly operated in the North Sea. The dogger takes its name from the Dutch word *dogger*, meaning a fishing vessel which tows a trawl. Dutch trawling boats were common in the North Sea, and the word *dogger* was given to the area where they often fished, which became known as the Dogger Bank. Doggers were slow but sturdy, capable of fishing in the rough conditions of the North Sea. Like the herring buss, they were wide-beamed and bluff-bowed, but considerably smaller, about 15 meters long, a maximum beam of 4.5 meters, a draught of 1.5 meters, and displacing about 13 tonnes. They could carry a tonne of bait, three tonnes of salt, half a tonne each of food and firewood for the crew, and return with six tonnes of fish. Decked areas forward and aft probably provided accommodation, storage and a cooking area. An anchor would have allowed extended periods fishing in the same spot, in waters up to 18 meters deep. The dogger would also have carried a small open boat for maintaining lines and rowing ashore.

Dories are small, shallow-draft boats, usually about five to seven metres (15 to 22 feet) long. They are lightweight versatile boats with high sides, a flat bottom and sharp bows, and are easy to build because of their simple lines. The dory first appeared in New England fishing towns sometime after the early 18th century. A precursor to the dory type was the early French bateau type, a flat bottom boat with straight sides used as early as 1671 on the Saint Lawrence River. The common coastal boat of the time was the wherry and the merging of the wherry design with the simplified flat bottom of the bateau resulted in the birth of the dory. Antecdotal evidence exists of much older precursors throughout Europe.

England, France, Italy, and Belgium have small boats from medieval periods that could reasonably be construed as predecessors of the Dory.

The Banks dories appeared in the 1830s. They were designed to be carried on mother ships and used for fishing cod at the Grand Banks. Adapted almost directly from the low freeboard, French river bateaus, with their straight sides and removable thwarts, bank dories could be nested inside each other and stored on the decks of fishing schooners, such as the *Gazela Primeiro*, for their trip to the Grand Banks fishing grounds.

In the 19th century, a more effective design for sailing trawlers was developed at the English fishing port, Brixham. These elegant wooden sailing boats spread across the world, influencing fishing fleets everywhere. Their distinctive sails inspired the song Red Sails in the Sunset, written aboard a Brixham sailing trawler called the *Torbay Lass*. In the 1890s there were about 300 trawling vessels there, each usually owned by the skipper of the boat. Several of these old sailing trawlers have been preserved.

Throughout history, local conditions have led to the development of a wide range of types of fishing boats. The Lancashire nobby was used down the north west coast of England as a shrimp trawler from 1840 until World War II. The Manx nobby was used around the Isle of Man as a herring drifter. The fifie was also used as a herring drifter along the east coast of Scotland from the 1850s until well into the 20th century.

The bawley and the smack were used in the Thames Estuary and off East Anglia, while trawlers and drifters were use on the east coast. Herring fishing started in the Moray Firth in 1819. The peak of the fishing at Aberdeen was in 1937 with 277 steam trawlers, though the first diesel drifter was introduced in 1926. In 1870 paddle tugs were being used to tow luggers and smacks to sea. Steam trawlers were introduced in 1881, mainly at Grimsby and Hull. In 1890 it was estimated that there were 20,000 men on the North Sea.

The steam drifter was not used in the herring fishery until 1897. The first trawlers fished over the side but in 1961 the first stern trawler was used at Lowestoft for fishing in Arctic waters. By 1981 only 27 of 130 deep sea trawlers were still going to sea. Many were converted to oil rig safety vessels.

Trawler designs adapted as the way they were powered changed from sail to coal-fired steam by World War I, and then to diesel and turbines by the end of World War II. During World War I and World War II, many fishing trawlers were commissioned as naval trawlers to be used as minesweepers, the activities being similar, with the crew and layout already suited to the task. Likewise, many commercial drifters were commissioned as naval drifters to be used for maintaining and monitoring anti-submarine nets. Since World War II, commercial fishing vessels have been increasingly equipped with electronic aids, such as radio navigation aids and fish finders. During the Cold War, some countries fitted fishing trawlers with additional electronic gear so they could be used as spy ships to monitor the activities of other countries.

**Commercial Vessels**

The 200-mile fishing limit has changed fishing patterns and, in recent times, fishing boats are becoming more specialised and standardised. In the United States and Canada more use is made of large factory trawlers, while the huge blue water fleets operated by Japan and the Soviet-bloc countries have contracted. In western Europe, fishing vessel design is focused on compact boats with high catching power.

Commercial fishing is a high risk industry, and countries are introducing regulations governing the construction and operation of fishing vessels. The International Maritime Organization, convened in 1959 by the United Nations, is responsible for devising measures aimed at the prevention of accidents, including standards for ship design, construction, equipment, operation and manning.

Of the decked vessels, 86 per cent are found in Asia, 7.8 per cent in Europe, 3.8 per cent in North and Central America, 1.3 per cent in Africa, 0.6 per cent in South America and

0.4 per cent in Oceania. Most commercial fishing boats are small, usually less than 30 metres (98 ft) but up to 100 metres (330 ft) for a large purse seiner or factory ship.

Commercial fishing vessels can be classified by architecture, the type of fish they catch, the fishing method used, or geographical origin. The following classification follows the FAO, who classify commercial fishing vessels by the gear they use.

**Trawlers**

A trawler is a fishing vessel designed to use trawl nets in order to catch large volumes of fish.

- *Outrigger trawlers* - use outriggers to tow the trawl. These are commonly used to catch shrimp. One or two otter trawls can be towed from each side. Beam trawlers, employed in the North sea for catching flatfish, are another form of outrigger trawler. Medium sized and high powered vessels, these tow a beam trawl on each side at speeds up to 8 knots.
- *Beam trawlers* - use sturdy outrigger booms for towing a beam trawl, one warp on each side. Double-rig beam trawlers can tow a separate trawl on each side. Beam trawling is used in the flatfish and shrimp fisheries in the North Sea. They are medium sized and high powered vessels, towing gear at speeds up to 8 knots. To avoid the boat capsizing if the trawl snags on the sea floor, winch brakes can be installed, along with safety release systems in the boom stays. The engine power of bottom trawlers is also restricted to 2000 HP (1472 KW) for further safety.
- *Otter trawlers* - deploy one or more parallel trawls kept apart horizontally using otter boards. These trawls can be towed in midwater or along the bottom.
- *Pair trawlers* - are trawlers which operate together towing a single trawl. They keep the trawl open horizontally by keeping their distance when towing. Otter boards are not used. Pair trawlers operate both midwater and bottom trawls.

- *Side trawlers* - have the trawl set over the side with the trawl warps passing through blocks which hang from two gallows, one forward and one aft. Until the late sixties, side trawlers were the most familiar vessel in the North Atlantic deep sea fisheries. They evolved over a longer period than other trawler types, but are now being replaced by stern trawlers.
- *Stern trawlers* - have trawls which are deployed and retrieved from the stern. Larger stern trawlers often have a ramp, though pelagic and small stern trawlers are often designed without a ramp. Stern trawlers are designed to operate in most weather conditions. They can work alone when midwater or bottom trawling, or two can work together as pair trawlers.
- *Freezer trawlers* - The majority of trawlers operating on high sea waters are freezer trawlers. They have facilities for preserving fish by freezing. They are medium to large size trawlers, with the same general arrangement as stern or side trawlers.
- *Wet fish trawlers* - are trawlers where the fish is kept in the hold in a fresh/wet condition. They must operate in areas not far distant from their landing place, and the fishing time of such vessels is limited.

**Seiners**

Seiners use surrounding and seine nets. This is a large group ranging from open boats as small as 10 metres in length, to ocean going vessels. There are also specialised gears that can target demersal species.

- *Purse seiners* - are very effective at targeting aggregating pelagic species near the surface. The seiner circles the shoal with a deep curtain of netting, possibly using bow thrusters for better manoeuvrability. Then the bottom of the net is pursed (closed) underneath the fish shoal by hauling a wire running from the vessel through rings along the bottom of the net and then back to the vessel. The most important part of the fishing operation is searching for the fish shoals and assessing their size and direction of movement. Sophisticated electronics, such as echosounders, sonar, and track plotters, may be used are used to search for and track schools; assessing their size and movement and keeping in touch with the school while it is surrounded with the seine net. Crows nests may be built on the masts for further visual support. Large vessels can have observation towers and helicopter landing decks. Helicopters and spotter planes are used for detecting fish schools. The main types of purse seiners are the American seiners, the European seiners and the Drum seiners.

- *American seiners* - have their bridge and accommodation placed forward with the working deck aft. American seiners are most common on both coasts of North America and in other areas of Oceania. The net is stowed at the stern and is set over the stern. The power block is usually attached to a boom from a mast located behind the superstructure. American seiners use Triplerollers. A purse line winch is located amidships near the hauling station, near the side where the rings are taken onboard.
- *European seiners* - have their bridge and accommodation located more to the after part of the vessel with the working deck amidships. European seiners are most common in waters fished by European nations. The net is stowed in a net bin at the stern, and is set over the stern from this position. The pursing winch is normally positioned at the forward part of the working deck.
- *Drum seiners* - have the same layout as American seiners except a drum is mounted on the stern and used instead of the power block. They are mainly used in Canada and U.S.A.
- *Tuna purse seiners* - are large purse seiners, normally over 45 meters, equipped to handle large and heavy purse seines for tuna. They have the same general arrangement as the American seiner, with the bridge and accommodation placed forward. A crows nest or tuna

tower is positioned at the top of the mast, outfitted with the control and manoeuvre devices. A very heavy boom which carries the power block is fitted at the mast. They often carry a helicopter to search for tuna schools. On the deck are three drum purse seine winches and a power block, with other specific winches to handle the heavy boom and net. They are usually equipped with a skiff.

- *Seine netters* - the basic types of seine netters are the Anchor seiners and Scottish seiner in northern Europe and the Asian seiners in Asia.
- *Anchor seiners* - have the wheelhouse and accommodation aft and the working deck amidships, thus resembling side trawlers. The seine net is stored and shot from the stern, and they may carry a power block. Anchor seiners have the coiler and winch mounted transversally amidships.
- *Scottish seiners* - are basically configured the same as anchor seiners. The only difference is that, whereas the anchor seiner has the coiler and winch mounted transversally amidships, the Scottish seiner has them mounted transversally in the forward part of the vessel.
- *Asian seiners* - In Asia the seine netter usually has the wheelhouse forward and the working deck aft, in the manner of a stern trawler. However, in regions where the fishing effort is a labour intensive, low technology approach, they are often undecked and may be powered by outboards motors, or even by sail.

**Line Vessels**

- *Longliners* - use one or more long heavy fishing lines with a series of hundreds or even thousands of baited hooks hanging from the main line by means of branch lines called "snoods". Hand operated longlining can be operated from boats of any size. The number of hooks and lines handled depends on the size of vessel, the number of crew, and the level of mechanisation. Large purpose built longliners can be designed for single species fisheries such as tuna. On such larger vessels the bridge is usually placed aft, and the gear is hauled from the bow or from the side with mechanical or hydraulic line haulers. The lines are set over the stern. Automatic or semi-automatic systems are used to bait hooks and shoot and haul lines. These systems include rail rollers, line haulers, hook separators, dehookers and hook cleaners, and storage racks or drums. To avoid ncidental catches of seabirds, an outboard setting funnel is used to guide the line from the setting position on the stern down to a depth of one or two metres. Small scale longliners handle the gear by hand. The line is stored into baskets or tubs, perhaps using a hand cranked line drum.

- Bottom Longliners.
- *Midwater longliners* - are usually medium sized vessels which operate worldwide, purpose built to catch large pelagics. The line hauler is usually forward starboard, where the fish are hauled through a gate in the rail. The lines are set from the stern where a baiting table and chute are located. These boats need adequate speed to reach distant fishing grounds, enough endurance for continued fishing, adequate freezing storage, suitable mechanisms for shooting and hauling longlines quickly, and proper storage for fishing gears and accessories.
- *Freezer longliners* - are outfitted with freezing equipment. The holds are insulated and refrigerated. Freezer longliners are medium to large with the same general characteristics of other longliners. Most longliners operating on the high seas are freezer longliners.
- *Factory longliners* - are generally equipped with processing plant, including mechanical gutting and filleting equipment accompanied by freezing facilities, as well as fish oil, fish meal and sometimes canning plants. These vessels have a large buffer capacity. Thus, caught fish can be stored in refrigerated sea water tanks and piks in the catch can also be used. Freezer longliners are large ships, working the high seas with the same general characteristics of other large longliners.

- *Wet-fish longliners* - keep the caught fish in the hold in the fresh/wet condition. The fish is stored in boxes and covered with ice, or stored with ice in the fish hold. The fishing time of such vessels is limited, so they operate close to the landing place.
- *Pole and line vessels* - are used mainly to catch tuna and skipjack. The fishers stand at the railing or on special platforms and fish with poles and lines. The lines have hooks which are baited, preferably with live bait. Caught tuna are swung on board, by two to three fishermen if the tuna is big, or with an automated swinging mechanism. The tuna usually release themselves from the barbless hook when they hit the deck. Tanks with live bait are placed round the decks, and water spray systems are used to attract the fish. The vessels are 15 to 45 metres o/a. On smaller vessels fishers fish from the main deck right around the boat. With larger vessels, there are two different deck styles: the American style and the Japanese style.
- *Japanese style* - Fishers stands at the rail in the forepart of the vessel. The vessel drifts during fishing operations.
- *American style* - fishers stand on platforms arranged over the side abaft amidships and around the stern. The vessel moves ahead during fishing operation.
- *Trollers* - catch fish by towing astern one of more trolling lines. A trolling line is a fishing line with natural or artificial baited hooks trailed by a vessel near the surface or at a certain depth. Several lines can be towed at the same time using outriggers to keep the lines apart. The lines can be hauled in manually or by small winches. A length of rubber is often included in each line as a shock absorber. The trolling line is towed at a speed depending on the target species, from 2.3 knots up to at least 7 knots. Trollers range from small open boats to large refrigerated vessels 30 meters long. In many tropical artisanal fisheries, trolling is done with sailing canoes with outriggers for

stability. With properly designed vessels, trolling is an economical and efficient way of catching tuna, mackerel and other pelagic fish swimming close to the surface. Purpose built trollers are usually equipped with two or four trolling booms raised and lowered by topping lifts, held in position by adjustable stays. Electrically powered or hydraulic reels can be used to haul in the lines.

- *Jiggers* - there are two types of jiggers: specialised squid jiggers which work mostly in the southern hemisphere and smaller vessels using jigging techniques in the northern hemisphere mainly for catching cod.
- *Squid jiggers* - have single or double drum jigger winches lined along the rails around the vessel. Strong lamps, up to 5000 W each, are used to attract the squid. These are arranged 50-60 centimetres apart, either as one row in the centre of the vessel, or two rows on each side. As the squid are caught they are transferred by chutes to the processing plant of the vessel. The jigging motion can be produced mechanically by the shape of the drum or electronically by adjustment to the winch motor. Squid jiggers are often used during the day as midwater trawlers and during the night as jiggers.

*Cod jiggers* - use single jigger machines and do not use lights to attract the fish. The fish are attracted by the jigging motion and artificial bait.

### Other Vessels

- *Dredgers* - use a dredge for collecting molluscs from the seafloor. There are three types of dredges:
  - *(a)* The dredge can be dragged along the seabed, scooping the shellfish from the ground. These dredges are towed in a manner similar to beam trawlers, and large dredgers can work three or more dredges on each side.
  - *(b)* Heavy mechanical dredging units are operated by special gallows from the bow of the vessel.

(c) The dredger employs a hydraulic dredge which uses a powerful water pump to operates water jets which flush the molluscs from the bottom.

Dredgers don't have a typical deck arrangement, the bridge and accommodation can be aft or forward. Derricks and winches may be installed for lowering and lifting the dredge. Echosounders are used for determining depths.

- *Gillnetters* - On inland waters and inshore, gillnets can be operated from open boats and canoes. In coastal waters, they are operated by small decked vessels which can have their wheelhouse either aft or forward. In coastal waters, gillnetting is often used as a second fishing method by trawlers or beam trawlers, depending on fishing seasons and targeted species. For offshore fishing, or fishing on the high seas, medium sized vessels using drifting gillnets are called drifters, and the bridge is usually located aft. The nets are set and hauled by hand on small open boats. Larger boats use hydraulic or occasionally mechanical net haulers, or net drums. These vessels can be equipped with an echosounder, although locating fish is more a matter of the fishermen's personal knowledge of the fishing grounds rather than depending on special detection equipment.
- *Set netters* - also operate gillnets. However, during fishing operations the vessel is not attached to the nets. The size of the vessels varies from open boats to large specialised drifters operating on the high seas. The wheelhouse is usually located aft, and the front deck is used for handling gear. Normally the nets are set at the stern by steaming ahead. Hauling is done over the side at the forepart of the deck, usually using hydraulic driven net haulers. Wet fish is packed in containers chilled with ice. Larger vessels might freeze the catch.
- *Lift netters* - are equipped to operate lift nets, which are held from the vessel's side and raised and lowered by means of outriggers. Lift netters range from open boats

about 10 meters long to larger vessels with open ocean capability. Decked vessels usually have the bridge amidships. Larger vessels are often equipped with winches and derricks for handling the lifting lines, as well as outriggers and light booms. They can be fitted with powerful lights to attract and aggregate the fish to the surface. Open boats are usually unmechanized or use hand operated winches. Electronic equipment, such as fish finders, sonar and echo sounders are used extensively on larger boats.

- *Trap setters* - are used to set pots or traps for catching fish, crabs, lobsters, crayfish and other similar species. Trap setters range in size from open boats operating inshore to larger decked vessels, 20 to 50 metres long, operating out to the edge of the continental shelf. Small decked trap setters have the wheelhouse either forward or aft with the fish hold amidships. They use hydraulic or mechanical pot haulers. Larger vessels have the wheelhouse forward, and are equipped with derricks, davits or cranes for hauling pots aboard. Locating fish is often more a matter of the fishermen's knowledge of the fishing grounds rather than the use of special detection equipment. Decked vessels are usually equipped with an echosounder, and large vessels may also have a Loran or GPS.
- *Handliners* - are normally undecked vessels used for handlining (fishing with a line and hook). Handliners include canoes and other small or medium sized vessels. Traditional handliners are less than 12 metres o/a, and do not have special gear handling, there is no winch or gurdy. Locating fish is left to the fishermen's personal knowledge of fishing grounds rather than the use of special electronic equipment. Non traditional handliners can set and haul using electrical or hydraulic powered reels. These mechanised reels are normally fastened to the gunwale or set on stanchions close to or overhanging the gunwale. They operate all over the world, some in

shallow waters, some fishing up to 300 meters deep. No typical deck arrangement exists for handliners.

- *Multipurpose vessels* - are vessels which are designed so they can deploy more than one type of fishing gear without major modifications to the vessels. The fish detection equipment present on board also changes according to which fishing gear is being used.
- *Trawler/Purse seiners* - are designed so the deck arrangement and equipment, including a suitable combination winch, can be used for both methods. Rollers, blocks, trawl gallows and purse davits need to be arranged so they control the lead of warps and pursing lines in such a way as to reduce the time needed to convert from one type to the other. Typical fish detection equipment includes a sonar and an echosounder. These vessels are usually designed as trawlers, since the power requirement for trawling is higher.
- *Research vessels* - a fisheries research vessel (FRV) requires platforms which are capable of towing different types of fishing nets, collecting plankton or water samples from a range of depths, and carrying acoustic fish-finding equipment. Fisheries research vessels are often designed and built along the same lines as a large fishing vessel, but with space given over to laboratories and equipment storage, as opposed to storage of the catch. An example of a fisheries research vessel is FRV *Scotia*.

## Artisan Vessels

Artisan fishing is a term used to describe small scale commercial or subsistence fishing practises. The term particularly applies to coastal or island ethnic groups using traditional fishing techniques and traditional boats. The term can also be applied to heritage groups involved in customary fishing practices.

Artisan fishing boats are usually small traditional fishing boats, appropriately designed for use on their local inland waters or coasts. Many localities around the world have developed their own traditional types of fishing boats, adapted to use local materials suitable for boat building and to the specific requirements of the fisheries and sea conditions in their area. Artisan boats are often open (undecked). Many have sails, but they do not usually use much, or any mechanised or electronic gear. Large numbers of artisan fishing boats are still in use, particularly in developing countries with long productive marine coastlines. For example, Indonesia has reported about 700,000 fishing boats, 25 per cent of which are dugout canoes, and half of which are without motors. The Philippines have reported a similar number of small fishing boats. Many of the boats in this area are double-outrigger craft, consisting of a narrow main hull with two attached outriggers, commonly known as *jukung* in Indonesia and *banca* in the Philippines.

**Recreational Vessels**

Recreational fishing is done for pleasure or sport, and not for profit or survival. Just about anything that will stay afloat can be called a recreational fishing boat, so long as a fisher periodically climbs aboard with the intent to catch a fish. Usually some form of fishing tackle is brought onboard, such as hooks, lines, sinkers or nets. Fish are caught for recreational purposes from boats which range from dugout canoes, kayaks, rafts, pontoon boats and small dingies to runabouts, cabin cruisers and cruising yachts to large, hi-tech and luxurious big game rigs. Larger boats, purpose-built with recreational fishing in mind, usually have large, open cockpits at the stern, designed for convenient fishing.

Big game fishing started as a sport after the invention of the motorized boat. Charles Frederick Holder, a marine biologist and early conservationist, is credited with founding the sport in 1898. Purpose built game fishing boats appeared shortly after. An example is the *Crete*, in use at Cataline Island, California, in 1915, and shipped to Hawaii the following year. According to a newspaper report at that time, the *Crete* had "a deep cockpit, a chair fitted for landing big fish and leather pockets for placing the pole."

It is difficult to estimate how many recreational fishing boats there are, although the number is high. The term is fluid, since most recreational boats are also used for fishing from time to time. Unlike most commercial fishing vessels, recreational fishing boats are often not dedicated just to fishing.

- *Fishing kayaks* have gained popularity in recent years. The kayak has long been a means of accessing fishing grounds.
- *Pontoon boats* have also become popular in recent years. These boats allow one or two fishermen to get into small rivers or lakes that would have difficulty accommodating larger boats. Typically 8-12 ft in length, these inflatable craft can be assembled quickly and easily. Some feature rigid frames derived from the white water rafting industry.
- *Bass boats* are small aluminium or fibreglass boats used in lakes and rivers in the U.S. for fishing bass and other panfish. They have swivel chairs for the anglers, storage bins for fishing tackle, and a tank with recirculating water for caught fish. They are usually fitted with an outboard motor and a trolling motor.
- *Charter boats* are often privately operated, purpose-built fishing boats, and host fishing trips for paying clients. Their size can range widely depending on the type of trips run and the geographical location.
- *Freshwater fishing boats* account for approximately one third of all registered boats in the USA. Most other types of boats end up being used for fishing on occasion.
- *Saltwater fishing boats* vary widely in size and can be specialized for certain species of fish. Flounder boats, for example, have flat bottoms for a shallow draft and are used in protected, shallow waters. Sport fishing boats range from 25 to 80 feet or more, and can be powered by large outboard engines or inboard diesels. Boats used for fishing in cold climates may have space dedicated to a cuddy cabin or enclosed wheelhouse, while boats in warmer climates are more likely to be open.

# Bibliography

Bekker-Nielsen T (2005) *Ancient Fishing and Fish Processing in the Black Sea Region* Vol. 2 of Black Sea Studies, Aarhus University Press.

Bremner HA (2003) *Safety and Quality Issues in Fish Processing* Woodhead Publishing Limited.

Brewer DJ and Friedman RF (1989) *Fish and Fishing in Ancient Egypt* Cairo Press: The American University in Cairo.

Chapelle, Howard L. (1951) *American Small Sailing Craft* WW Norton Company, New York.

Cullis-Suzuki S and Pauly D (2010) "Failing the High Seas: A Global Evaluation of Regional Fisheries Management Organizations" *Marine Policy*, 34(5) pp. 1036-1042.

Cutting CL (1955) *Fish Saving; A History of Fish Processing from Ancient to Modern Times*, L. Hill. Hall GM (1997) *Fish Processing Technology* Springer.

Fagan, Brian (2008) *The Great Warming*. Chapter 10: *Bucking the Trades* Bloomsbury Press.

FAO: *Fisheries Technology: Fishing Vessels Retrieved*, 2 February 2009.

FAO: CWP *Handbook of Fishery Statistical Standards Section L:* Fishery Fleet.

FAO (1999) *Analysis of the Vessels Over 100 Tons in the Global Fishing Fleet* FAO Fisheries Circular C949.

FAO (2007) *The Status of the Fishing Fleet* State of World Fisheries and Aquaculture, Food and Agriculture Organization of the United Nations, Rome.

FAO: Types of Fisheries Hart PJB and Reynolds JD (2002) *Handbook of Fish Biology and Fisheries* Wiley-Blackwell.

Galbraith R.D. and A Rice after E S Strange (2004) *An Introduction to Commercial Fishing Gear and Methods Used in Scotland* Scottish Fisheries Information Pamphlet No. 25.

Gabriel O, Von Brandt A, Lange K, Dahm E and Wendt T (2005) *Fish Catching Methods of the World* Wiley-Blackwell.

Gardner, John (1987) *The Dory Book*. Mystic Seaport Museum, Mystic Connecticut.

Luten JB, Jacobsen C and Bekaert K (2006) *Seafood Research from Fish to Dish: Quality, Safety and Processing of Wild and Farmed Fish* Wageningen Academic Publishers.

McGrail, Sean (2004). *Boats of the World: From the Stone Age to Medieval Times*. USA: Oxford University Press.

NOAA: Fish Watch: Fisheries Gear.

Pearson AM and Dutson TR (1999) *HACCP in Meat, Poultry and Fish Processing*, Volume 10 of *Advances in Meat Research*, Springer.

Prado J and Dremière PY (eds.) (1990) *Fisherman's Workbook* FAO, Rome.

Schultz, Ken (1999). *Fishing Encyclopedia: Worldwide Angling Guide*. John Wiley & Sons.

Shahidi F, Jones Y and Kitts DD (1997) *Seafood Safety, Processing, and Biotechnology*, Technomic.

Stellman JM (ed.) (1998) *Chemical, Industries and Occupations* Vol. 3 of *Encyclopedia of Occupational Health and Safety*, International Labour Organization.

Stewart H (1982) *Indian Fishing: Early Methods on the Northwest Coast* University of Washington Press.

Stewart K.M. (1989) Fishing Sites of North and East Africa in the Late Pleistocene and Holocene. Vol. 34 of Cambridge Monographs in African Archaeology. Stewart KM (1994) "Early Hominid Utilisation of Fish Resources and Implications for Seasonality and Behaviour" *Journal of Human Evolution*, 27: 229-245.

United Nations Development Fund for Women (1993) *Fish Processing* Food Technology Source Book Series (UNIFEM) Series.

Vries, J. de, and Woude, A. van der (1997), *The First Modern Economy. Success, Failure, and Perseverance of the Dutch Economy, 1500-1815*, Cambridge University Press.

Waldman, John (2005) *100 Weird Ways to Catch Fish* Stackpole Books.

# Index